Y0-CLD-305

Ever Westward to the Far East

THE STORY OF CHESTER FRITZ

by

Chester Fritz

and

Dan Rylance

Ever Westward to the Far East:
THE STORY OF CHESTER FRITZ
Chester Fritz and Dan Rylance.
©1982 by the Office of the President
University of North Dakota
Grand Forks, North Dakota 58202
All rights reserved.
No part of this book may be reproduced
in any form or by any means
without permission in writing
from the publishers.
ISBN 0-9608700
Library of Congress Cataloging in Publication Data
Fritz, Chester
    Ever Westward to the Far East.
       Includes index.
       1. Fritz, Chester. 2. Bankers—North Dakota—
Biography. 3. Bankers—China—Biography. I. Rylance,
Dan. II. Title.
HG1552.F74A34   1982   332.1'092'4 [B]   82-10987

Printed in the United States of America
Colwell Book Manufacturers, Minneapolis, Minnesota

Dedication

This book is dedicated to Harold Hochschild, who never locked his front door, and was always gregarious at his home, "Eagle Nest," where he frequently acted as host to many house guests. These were usually Chinese of various ages, down to the third generation; his memory is highly esteemed by a growing circle of Chinese. He made substantial progress in promoting international understanding and had an intimate human feeling for the Chinese people.

He wrote and published a historical documentary on the frontier days in the Adirondacks in his *Township 34*. In his Adirondack Museum he established, so that many could see, a visual history of our frontier days. He was a vigorous horseman who rode daily in the Adirondacks, in all kinds of weather. Swinging from his saddle, he would create his houseguest list for an approaching weekend. As a colonel in the U.S. Army in World War II, his reports from the field were models for fellow officers to copy.

He converted stumbling blocks into stepping stones. He was a fellow traveler in the interior of distant China. He was a general benefactor as evidenced by the several honorary college degrees bestowed on him by leading universities. He created foundations on which others have built their lives, and so raised their heads above the crowd.

From one of the beneficiaries, his grateful pupil,

                                        Chester Fritz
                                        Monte Carlo
                                        April 1982

Harold Hochschild

Biographical Note

Harold K. Hochschild was born in New York City on May 20, 1892, and graduated from Yale University in 1912. Although short and stocky, he was a good collegiate boxer and a tireless swimmer. He swam the half-mile regularly at his home, "Eagle Nest," until he was well into his eighties, and remained an avid horseman.

Mr. Hochschild entered his family's business, the American Metal Company, in 1913 and remained with the firm until 1957, when it became AMAX, Inc. He served as president from 1934 to 1950 and chairman of the board from 1947 to 1957. He visited China immediately after World War I and stayed there for almost two years. Before he left in the summer of 1921, he hired Chester Fritz to represent the American Metal Company in Shanghai. In 1929, Mr. Hochschild allowed Chester Fritz to take the American Metal account to the investment firm of Swan, Culbertson and Fritz. Mr. Hochschild also made frequent trips to company-owned copper mines in Africa and in 1953 announced the lifting of color restrictions and the inauguration of a policy to admit black miners. He also returned to China in 1971 at the invitation of the American government.

Although a successful industrialist, Mr. Hochschild was as well known for his historical and conservation work in the state of New York. Mr. Hochschild considered the Adirondacks and Blue Mountain Lake, the location of the family estate since 1904, to be his permanent home. He was founder of the Adirondack Museum, author of *Township 34*, a history of the central Adirondacks, and was appointed by Governor

Nelson Rockefeller to chair the Study Commission on the Future of the Adirondacks in 1968. In 1977, Chester Fritz donated $50,000 to the Adirondack Museum in honor of Mr. Hochschild.

Mr. Hochschild served in the Army during World War II and spent two years in Europe as commanding officer of a field interrogation detachment, retiring as a lieutenant colonel.

Mr. Hochschild had other interests and was involved in a broad range of humanitarian activities. He served as a trustee of the Institute for Advanced Study at Princeton University and as chairman of the executive committee of the African-American Institute of New York. Mr. Hochschild also took part in the discussion of national policy issues and criticized United States policy toward China in the 1960s. He opposed the continued support of Chiang Kai-shek, whom he considered "discredited."

In 1941, Mr. Hochschild was married to the former Mary Marquand, daughter of Eleanor Marquand and Professor Allen Marquand, founder of the art department at Princeton University. Mrs. Hochschild died in 1974. They had one son, Adam, who is the editor of *Mother Jones* magazine. He lives in San Francisco with his wife and two children.

In April 1980, Dan Rylance interviewed Harold Hochschild in New York City for this biography. The following month, Chester Fritz informed Mr. Hochschild of his intention to dedicate this book to him. In his letter Fritz wrote: "I have always felt that you provided a major stride in my business career because of the prestige and valuable experience I obtained as a representative of the American Metal Company, especially in the later years in the fast-moving Shanghai foreign exchange market."

Mr. Hochschild died in New York City on January 23, 1981, at the age of 88.

Acknowledgements

This book went to press because two people gave their full support to the idea when it initially was proposed in 1979. First, Chester Fritz, who at 87 was eager to participate in extensive oral history interviews and to cooperate in every way possible with the book—a project he labeled a "stout proposal." Second, Thomas J. Clifford, president of the University of North Dakota, who said, "Let's do it." Without the memory of Fritz and the personal support of President Clifford, there would be no book.

Two colleagues, Billie Jo Elliott Rylance, my wife, and James Vivian, professor of history at the University of North Dakota, provided invaluable assistance in all aspects of the oral interviews and in each draft of the manuscript. Their patience, suggestions and personal encouragement made this book stronger and my task so much easier.

A university community is a city of many talents. J. F. S. Smeall, Stacy Thomas, D. Jerome Tweton, Dave Vorland and Robert P. Wilkins read portions or all of the manuscript and made valuable suggestions. Special thanks also to three library colleagues, Janice Bolstad, Audrey Kazmierczak, and Colleen Oihus, who gave freely of their time in what surely must have seemed an endless process. Technical assistance was provided by the University's Office of University Relations, and, in particular, by Jim Penwarden, Stacy Thomas, and Dave Vorland. The book's cover, jacket and other special features were designed by Harvey Jacobson, formerly director of University Relations and now acting vice-president for University Relations at the University of Michigan, and was executed by John Vleck of the Office of University Relations. The map of the 1917 trip to West China was drafted by Karol-lyn Knudson of Grand Forks.

Business associates and friends of Chester Fritz generously shared their thoughts and wide range of experiences with me. Personal interviews with Harold Hochschild, Ralph Stillman and Helen Swart of New York and Charles Culbertson and William Simmons of San Diego were invaluable. Correspondence with Mary Economou in Monte Carlo, Ho Sing Hang in Hong Kong, Sam Judah in San Francisco, Kent Lutey in Delray Beach, Florida, Dr. D. J. Morris in Berne, Luis Ongpin in Manila and Heinz Rothschild of Madrid also provided much assistance. George W. Starcher, president emeritus of the University of North Dakota, now living in Florida, also provided a long personal interview during one of his frequent visits to the University of North Dakota.

Preface

The name Chester Fritz is synonymous with a greater University of North Dakota. Outstanding student scholarships, distinguished professorships, a well-designed library and an elegant auditorium all bear his name. Most alumni are familiar with his stewardship but few, if any, are knowledgeable about his varied business career or his interesting personal life. Although I have been the archivist at Chester Fritz Library since 1966, I shared their ignorance. Chester Fritz remained an enigma to me except for his generosity to the University.

Biographical information about Chester Fritz published by the University publicized his generosity but provided only a few glimpses of his other activities. The brochures repeated basically the same story of an investment banker in the Far East who made a fortune in China before World War II and then retired to a life of leisure in Switzerland. Fundamental questions, however, remained unanswered. Why did Fritz go to China? What exactly was his business in China? What was his life after 1951 really about? And why did he give so much to a school that he attended for only two years?

In 1976 I made a survey of primary material on Chester Fritz at the University. I found most of the material unprocessed and inaccessible, locked in cabinets in the Oriental Room on the fourth floor of the Chester Fritz Library. The most significant materials included letters, diaries, reels of film, and many photographic albums. Later other family albums were located at the Traill County Museum in Hillsboro, North Dakota. Once collected and processed, these items formed the nucleus of a processed manuscript collection on Chester Fritz which was accessioned in 1977 and transferred to the Orin G. Libby Manuscript Collection at the Chester Fritz Libary.

In the meantime, I wrote to both Kathrine Tiffany, Fritz's aunt, and to Fritz himself and requested that they send more material to supplement a rather incomplete manuscript collection. Mrs. Tiffany, shortly before her death in 1978, sent several boxes of correspondence and these items were added to the manuscript collection. Chester Fritz also began to send scattered items but acknowledged he had little written documentation. He added, however, "When one has passed the age of 86 one has much to say!"

The establishment of the Chester Fritz manuscript collection and the hint of Fritz's interest in recording his memories was the genesis of a proposal I made to President Thomas Clifford of the University of North Dakota on November 17, 1978, to conduct a series of oral interviews with Chester Fritz as soon as possible. I expressed my reservations about the success of such a venture to President Clifford.

> This proposal really begins with the assumption that an 86-year-old man would be receptive and mentally able to participate in an extensive oral history of his life for historical purposes. While his receptivity can be secured by letter, his mental ability cannot be ascertained except by personal contact and observation.
>
> I think it is extremely important...to determine his mental state before I invest in weeks of research surrounding his life. It is also extremely important to remember that I have never personally met this man and that he is 86 years old. To suddenly interrupt his life, with an extensive search into his past, with pointed personal questions, is an awesome task. I must meet him and gain his respect on a personal basis to obtain any historical information from him. I also know little or nothing about China, which appears to be his major historical interest.

President Clifford gave his full support and confidence, and I departed for Monte Carlo with many uncertainties and a series of unanswered questions gleaned from the collection of Fritz's manuscripts. There I conducted a series of interviews with Chester Fritz during the first two weeks of December 1979. Following Mr. Fritz's instructions, I lodged at the Mirabeau Hotel adjacent to his apartment in a room he personally selected, overlooking the Mediterranean, at a minimum price he obtained. The interviews were conducted in the room every afternoon.

I met Mr. Fritz the first time in the lobby of the hotel. After we exchanged greetings and gifts, Fritz asked, "Rylance, what should we call our book?" I responded initially with a couple of suggestions, and attempted to explain that writing a book was a long process. He seemed unconcerned. The next day he presented me with a list of people to whom he wanted the book sent as soon as possible. Mr. Fritz also offered twice to assist me financially with my expenses and twice I politely declined. Our relationship improved. The first week of interviews progressed extremely well. Fritz demonstrated a superior memory, keen insights and a marvelous sense of humor.

But at the beginning of my second week, Mr. Fritz began to arrive late for our scheduled interviews, and would excuse himself early. After allowing this to go on for two days, I reluctantly expressed my disappointment with his change of attitude; the interviews were not going well. He replied that he was sorry but that his wife was jealous of the time he was devoting to the interviews. I told him that I understood and that I would not bring up the matter again. From the time of that discussion, however, Mr. Fritz never again appeared late for an interview. In addition, he began to arrive with handwritten notes, on a variety of subjects, written in his bed at all hours of the night.

Unfortunately, the lack of sleep and the continual exercise of his memory began to affect Mr. Fritz. On December 10, 1979, he collapsed from exhaustion outside of his apartment. He called me early the next morning and told me what had happened, that he was under a doctor's care, and that further interviews would have to be cancelled. I expressed my deep regrets at this turn of events and said goodbye. A few minutes later, however, he called again and stated he was sending his valet to my room with three briefcases of correspondence (he had already given me one). I emptied one of the briefcases and returned it with my cassette recorder, several blank tapes and all my unanswered questions. In the months that followed he sent answers to most of my questions, supplied additional information and also expressed his firm desire to complete the book. In June 1980 he confided:

> I keep thinking every so often that I have now reached the bottom of the barrel but strange as it seems in the stillness of the night other thoughts of other places and other days come

into my mind.

I do realize, however, that you have sufficient material now as there has been considerable movement towards you from here and I don't want to learn you have had indigestion!

The exact wording of the title of the book was not determined for some time. Fritz's suggested title, however, of *Ever Westward to the Far East* was perfect and I added a sub-title: *The Biography of Chester Fritz*. I inserted my name as author and mailed it to him for his approval. His response was firm:

> It is my desire that my name appear as co-author of our book. My views are quite decided on this point. I recall that when I gave a speech before the American Club of the French Riviera, I prefaced my remarks by saying, "I would like to come to you on the same basis as was chosen by Herodotus, the father of history, who told his friends and neighbors when he returned from one of his long voyages, 'What I tell you, I saw. It was not told to me. I lived it. It was my life.'" Furthermore, many of the observations of this book will be direct quotations from me and I expect to be quoted often, especially on conclusions I have arrived at as a result of my experiences there and elsewhere.

The strength of Fritz's response was unexpected. I began to experience personally the strength of his power of persuasion, which was an essential ingredient of his business career. We haggled, compromised, and he won. We agreed that he would be co-author of "our book" and that the sub-title would be *The Story of Chester Fritz*.

I completed my interviews with Chester Fritz in April of 1981 in Monte Carlo. Our interview sessions were cordial, relaxed and productive. The gold trade in China after World War II and Fritz's personal life after 1951 occupied most of our time.

Ever Westward to the Far East: The Life of Chester Fritz is the end product of this project. Through the memory of Chester Fritz and my pen, we have attempted to portray dimensions of his long and varied career which are not as widely known as his generosity to the University of North Dakota, but which are equally significant.

                                                    Dan Rylance
                                                    Grand Forks, North Dakota
                                                    February 1, 1982

Contents

I Roots: The North Dakota Years / **1**
II The Transition Years / **23**
III Chester Fritz: A Modern Marco Polo / **41**
IV Mr. Silver / **71**
V Swan, Culbertson and Fritz / **101**
VI Sportsman / **124**
VII Between Two Worlds / **138**
VIII Mr. Gold / **158**
IX The South American Connection / **183**
X To Give With a Warm Hand / **193**
XI Man Man Hang / **213**
Epilogue / **237**
Appendix: Chester Fritz/ Remarks at Dedication of the Chester Fritz Library, Delivered at the University of North Dakota, October 13, 1961 / **239**
Bibliographical Essay / **242**
Index / **244**

I

Roots: The North Dakota Years

Chester Fritz was born March 25, 1892, in Buxton, North Dakota, a small town in Traill County in the northeastern part of the state. Traill County, situated in the broad, level, and fertile Red River Valley, comprised excellent farmland lying between the state's two more populous counties, Grand Forks County to the north and Cass to the south. Years later some of Fritz's business associates in China often referred to Buxton as "a wide place in the road." Perhaps the best anecdote about his birthplace is told by Fritz himself, however:

> There was a young man that went to the University of North Dakota who said to his father one day, "You know father, Chester Fritz, wherever he travels and is asked to fill out passport and registration forms always puts down Buxton, North Dakota, as his home. Isn't that good of him to remember?" I had to!

Charles F. Fritz, Chester's father, was the eldest son of the Reverend Charles T. William Fritz, who was born in Germany in 1840. His first wife died there before the family emigrated to the United States. Charles Fritz, the only son of that first marriage, was born in Berlin on December 20, 1865. Subsequently the Reverend William Fritz remarried and produced a large second family.

The grandfather, Reverend Charles T. William Fritz was affiliated with the Evangelical Kirke whose many congregations in America eventually joined the Methodist Church. Initially he served as circuit pastor for the large expanse between Crookston, Minnesota, and Cavalier, North Dakota. Later in Grand Forks, North Dakota, he helped organize the Evangelical United Brethren Church at the corner of Fourth and Belmont streets and was chosen its first pastor. He returned to the same pulpit on two occasions subsequently in his career. Pastor Fritz died on March 4, 1928; his second wife had died on July 24, 1914. Both are interred in the Memorial Park Cemetery at Grand Forks. Chester Fritz has chosen to lie beside them. "Not so much a question of grandparents," he confided, "as it is close to the University and close to where I started in Buxton, North Dakota. So I complete the circle."

Fritz liked his grandfather, Reverend William Fritz, who was a stern but thoughtful man. One day a big German farmer came to the parsonage to be married. After the brief ceremony, Chester's grandfather turned to his grandson and said, "You know, he is a good man." The inquisitive grandson asked why. His grandfather replied, "He gave me five dollars for the ceremony." Chester, however, was an infrequent guest at the home of his grandfather and his second family; recalling those occasions he later remarked: "I thought I did not belong to that tribe."

Anne Belanger Fritz, Chester's mother, was the eldest daughter of Ferdinand Belanger and Margery Johnston Belanger. Ferdinand Belanger was born in Canada in March 1849, of French-Canadian descent; Fritz remembered him as a "short, hard-working homesteader" who "spoke with a thick French accent." Margery Johnston also was born in Canada in May 1848. She was of Scotch-Irish ancestry and had moved with her family to Neillsville, the seat of Clark County in central Wisconsin. There she met Belanger, whom she married on February 22, 1871. Three daughters were born of this union: Anne, 1872; Kathrine, 1878; and Fernanda, 1881. Chester described the Belanger family in these terms:

> Anne, my mother (the eldest) and Kathrine (an outstanding, noble personality) and the youngest was Ferna. She was a meek, colorless personality. And she practiced on the piano most of the day. Largely, I thought, to keep out of the kitchen. The table was excellent. My grandmother was a

great, great cook.

The Belangers moved west to North Dakota in the early 1880s. In 1884, they purchased a quarter section of land in Morgan Township, Traill County, one of the last parts of the county to be settled. They paid $1,290 for the quarter and in 1889 purchased a second 160 acres in an adjoining section for $1,600. In their later years, being without sons, the Belangers sold the second quarter section in 1898 for $3,560 and the original quarter in 1903 for $4,000. Margery Belanger died in Mayville, North Dakota, in March 1905. Her husband Ferdinand died in Minneapolis four years later in March 1909.

The Belanger farmstead in Morgan Township, which lay only a short distance west of Buxton where his parents rented some land during the first years of their marriage, constituted a second home to Chester Fritz while he was a young boy. Ferdinand Belanger, a warm and loving personality, took a special liking to his first grandchild, and the Belangers were closer to their daughter Anne than the second Fritz family was to Charles. The young grandson particularly enjoyed the Belanger farm in summertime, and the large St. Bernard dog named Don became his first pet. On the last day of his stay each summer, Chester would mount a workhorse amid the cheers of the family, even though he "never went anywhere. It was just a daring exploit."

Charles Fritz and Anne Belanger were married in Morgan Township on December 9, 1890. The groom was a few days short of 25 years; the bride was 18. The couple had met at a social function in the township. Charles was already occupied in farming in the area, while Anne proved an attractive and eligible young woman in the small community. The newly joined couple took up married life in a small wood-frame house on the outskirts of Buxton, where together they farmed a rented parcel east of town. Chester William Fritz, their first child, was born in their home on March 25, 1892. Two more children, a boy and a girl, followed, but both died within a few weeks of birth. Their names and other vital statistics are lost to record. His mother selected the name Chester, which remained unpopular with everyone except her, and his father added William in honor of his paternal grandfather.

The Fritz family moved to Fargo, North Dakota, in the fall of 1898. They had been unable to make a living on rented land and they lacked the opportunity to acquire land. Moreover, Charles, the father, had little formal education. He turned to seasonal harvest work in order to provide for his family. His son described his father during those years as a "ne'er-do-well. He was out of employment frequently. But when threshing season came every fall, he got a job as the separator man. He ran the threshing machine." Charles Fritz found his most regular employers in the Casselton area, twenty miles west of Fargo. When the harvest finished, Fargo offered other varied employment possibilities until the start of the next harvest. By 1900 these odd jobs consisted mainly of selling insurance and working as a driver for the Huffaker and Buritt meat market and grocery on Eighth Street South. In Fargo, the family frequently moved in and out of small apartments before finally finding a more permanent residence in a second-floor apartment at 916 Fourth Avenue South.

Charles Fritz experienced a serious accident during the 1902 harvest season. His son remembered the incident in great detail:

> The threshing machine had a trap door on the top, right over the cylinder, a whirling steel drum, with big hooks in it to thresh the grain, to extract the kernels from the bundles of wheat. Somehow the trap door covering the cylinder was not put back properly by someone else, I was told later, and my father fell into that whirling machine.
>
> The bottoms of his feet were chewed up and they saved one foot. When the news came, I was in school and my mother came to the school house in Fargo and took me on the train out to Casselton to see my father. And I remember going down the hallway, I saw in a jar my father's foot.

The farm accident greatly compounded the struggling Fritz family's problems: it terminated the main source of employment for Charles Fritz and left him with a permanent handicap that dramatically narrowed his alternatives. To offset the disability, Charles Fritz fabricated a special bicycle by tying two bicycles together side by side. The end result enabled him to get about and to return to selling life insurance, but he met with little success. For want of other options, he sold whatever found a market, including lantern slides and a variety of mail-order schemes. His income remained small and irregular, however, so the family lived very frugally thereafter:

> My father never did anything that was constructive. He just drifted along like a wandering minstrel. He liked to go and tell people "how." You see there were no media at that time, and he would ride from one part of Fargo to another and "sound off" like a medieval minstrel. For example, a repre-

sentative from a new life insurance company got hold of my father to hire him to sell life insurance. My father contacted a few people who bought a policy but he never received a cent out of it. Years later, to help him out, I took out a life insurance policy. The company folded up!

Charles Fritz's familiar presence on the streets of Fargo humiliated and embarrassed his young son. There was little compassion during those tender years of youth, only hurt. Young Fritz felt inferior knowing that all his "playmates and companions lived in circumstances far better than our family." He envied young Charlie Pollock, son of Judge Charles Pollock, because "he had a bicycle and delivered the Fargo *Forum*." Fritz had to place pieces of folded newspapers in the soles of his moccasins and was especially concerned "that anyone would see the holes in my moccasins in the schoolroom."

Her husband's misfortune also forced Anne Fritz to seek employment. She worked for a time as a clerk in a stationery store and served as a bookkeeper for two Fargo dentists. Her income remained equally modest, however.

So my mother bought each week what was called a meal ticket in a restaurant which was called Mattson down on Front Street. There the meal was charged to the meal ticket— about 17 cents a meal, and they would punch the meal ticket. So I sat beside my mother and she shared her course with me. The two of us had one meal together once a day.

Fritz attended school in Fargo from 1898 until early 1905, in a school system which prided itself on "aiming all the while for thoroughness rather than to cover a multitude of subjects poorly." When the Central School opened in 1901, one block north of his home, Fritz enjoyed the facilities of a new structure which was situated on a full square block and was one of the most modern edifices of its kind in the state. He also enjoyed playing with his friends and dreamed of things he did not have. For example, he would stretch out on the floor of his modest home with a Montgomery Ward catalog and admire the "Stevens .22-caliber rifle" or "a new bicycle." The telephone fascinated him, as it also did some German friends of the family who were amazed that the instrument "would speak German." He liked the sounds produced by gramophone records that he occasionally heard.

In the summer he and his mother would often return to the Belanger farm, "a happy interval, much more so than my days elsewhere." In

Ever Westward to the Far East: THE STORY OF CHESTER FRITZ

January 1903, the Fargo Carnegie Public Library opened its doors on the former site of the fire-ravaged Columbia Hotel at the corner of Roberts Street and Second Avenue North. Visiting the new library and its contents became a daily habit for Chester Fritz. There he read boys' books of history and war by the British writer G. A. Henty, but found a more personal message in the novels of Horatio Alger, which, according to one assessment, produced a powerful impact upon American culture.

The Alger books are strong medicine....Alger was interested in the struggle, in the ability of young boys of no future, and maybe not even any education to speak of, to pull themselves up by their own bootstraps through courage, honesty, character, and, yes, luck—for the Alger theory maintains that luck comes to those who deserve it.

Horatio Alger stories gave Fritz hope and vision. They also instilled important lessons for success in the future, especially that success comes to those who are assertive and who prefer to bargain. Fritz could not help but contrast the Alger heroes with his father, who above all else was "non-assertive" and, therefore, a sucker for a bad deal. Fritz also discovered that good conduct often produced "luck," and that, in time, virtue was rewarded.

Moreover, Fritz learned that a strong correlation existed between success and education, and that a desire for money was less important than knowing the value of reading and study. The value of a quick wit, the virtue of generosity to those less fortunate, and the importance of a keen alertness to opportunities were among other lessons acquired. Above all, Fritz realized that poverty was no bar to a person's advancement.

"There've been a great many boys begin as low down as you, Dick, that have grown up respectable and honored. But they had to work pretty hard for it." These lines from the Alger novel *Ragged Dick* pointed the proper direction. "I was determined that when I grew to manhood, I would improve my ways of life and raise my head above the crowd and, as the Bible says, 'live a more abundant life,'" Fritz recalled.

The family's seemingly endless series of disappointments left Anne Fritz emotionally drained, perhaps wasted. Unable to cope with the twin burdens of a permanently handicapped husband and the unfulfilled expectations of her sensitive son, she chose a desperate course of action and ran away in February of 1905. After several weeks of worry and no explanation concerning her whereabouts, Kathrine Macdonald, Anne's younger sister, came to Fargo from Lidgerwood. She explained to her 12-year-old nephew that his mother had gone on "a trip out West." According to Fritz, "We never heard from her again. Some people thought a catastrophe had befallen her. After some time, my aunt and others decided that she had died, perhaps in an accident."

Chester Fritz has never talked much about his mother's fate. He has remarked, "No useful purpose can now be served by further research in this regard. As Shakespeare once said, 'What's done is done,' and we should not introduce a Sherlock Holmes review." One person may have known more, Fritz's aunt Kathrine. However, if she did, she carried a family secret with her when she died in 1978.

As for Charles Fritz, he remarried in 1912. Hattie Beikoff, his second wife, was two years younger than his son Chester. The couple lived in Chaffee, North Dakota, where he sold chickens and household products for a living. Four children were born of this union: Morris in 1913; Carl in 1914, who died in 1977; Gladys in 1917; and May in 1924. Charles Fritz died in Chaffee on January 25, 1946, at the age of 80.

The full effect of these two tragic events—the crippling of his father and his mother's disappearance—upon the life of young Chester Fritz will never be known. Yet life continued, despite the family's continuing impoverishment. "I was never hungry," Chester recalled, "but our food was on the meager side."

The disappearance of his mother, however, temporarily shattered Chester's dreams of future success. There was too much hurt, disbelief, and doubt to dream on so soon again. In March 1905, a month after his mother's disappearance, Chester Fritz left Fargo for Lidgerwood, North Dakota, to spend the next three and one-half years with his aunt and uncle, Kathrine and Neil Macdonald. At the age of 12, Fritz was nearly grown. His personality was that of a shy and somewhat withdrawn person who possessed a genuine sense of humility that he never lost. His years in Lidgerwood would provide compensations for the acceptance and affection denied him at home.

No adoption agency could have selected a couple better suited than the Macdonalds to prepare Chester Fritz for adulthood and instill in him the values that engendered his generous sharing of his later-acquired fortune with the people of North Dakota. Both Macdonalds were in the sunrise of their distinguished careers. They formed a professional team firmly committed to making a better education system work in North Dakota. They seem to have been little interested in raising a family of their own. But their devotion to creating equal opportunities for students of rural communities was real and constant. They wanted "a square deal for the country boy."

Neil Carnot Macdonald was born on Manitoulin Island, Ontario, in 1876. The son of Scotch-Canadian pioneers who emigrated to Cavalier County in northeastern Dakota Territory in 1885, Macdonald was raised in a 12-foot-by-16-foot sod shanty that in time housed a family of six brothers and two sisters. According to his mother, Isabel McLeod Macdonald, the family moved from Canada to North Dakota because the "western fever was upon all the people and some of our neighbors were preparing to go west."

Neil Macdonald devoted his life to the betterment of public education in his adopted state. In 1892, at the age of 16, he started teaching near his home. By 1900 he had risen to superintendent of schools for Cavalier County. Between 1903 and 1909 he served as superintendent of schools in Lidgerwood and filled a comparable position in Mandan the following year. During the summer of 1911 he was appointed state inspector of elementary schools, continuing in that capacity until he was elected state superintendent of public instruction in 1916.

Macdonald had graduated from Mayville Normal School in 1896 and completed his bachelor's degree and master's degree training at the University of North Dakota. He obtained a doctoral degree in education from Harvard University in 1921, after having completed the dissertation "Rural Schools and Rural Public Consolidation," based on his twenty-five years of familiarity and experience with public instruction in the state.

Macdonald believed that the most pressing educational problem in North Dakota was "to secure and maintain efficient rural schools." He possessed a genius for compiling and publicizing statistics that told a simple story—namely, that 72 percent of school-age children in the state lived on farms and attended one-room schools and that 60 percent of teachers in those schools had failed to complete a single high-school-level course. Even more striking was the fact that just 33 percent of the 80,000 farm children in North Dakota finished the eighth grade and only 5 percent graduated from high school. These statistics stood in stark contrast to their urban counterparts, where fully 81 percent completed the eighth grade and 30 percent obtained a high school diploma.

The Macdonalds' crusade to implement their rural school consolidation program was frustrated by those who opposed change or were compromised by their political involvement. In 1916 Neil Macdonald

Roots: The North Dakota Years

joined the burgeoning Nonpartisan League and won election as state superintendent of public instruction. His plans, however, for a progressive education system soon became linked to radical causes and ideals in the League platform. He suffered a humiliating defeat in the fall 1918 election at the hands of Minnie J. Nielson, superintendent of schools for Barnes County. Republican conservatives accused Macdonald of socialism and with "corrupting the state's children with socialist books." According to Louis Geiger in his *University of the Northern Plains: A History of the University of North Dakota, 1883-1958,* Macdonald's plans for reform were "twisted into a sinister move to subvert the schools and to wreck the colleges, especially the university." Macdonald's defeat was more than a political disappointment. According to Elwyn Robinson in his *History of North Dakota:*

> The state had replaced a dynamic leader and nationally recognized authority on rural education with a county superintendent who was not even a college graduate and hence could not qualify for the state's highest teacher's certificate. It was a misfortune for both the rural schools and the farm boys, whose welfare was so close to Macdonald's heart.

Neil Macdonald died prematurely at Glasgow, Montana, on September 8, 1923, of uremic poisoning. At the time, he was enroute to Seattle Pacific College, where he had accepted a deanship. Still bitter over his political battles and defeat, he earlier declared his reasons for forsaking the state:

> Left North Dakota, 9-1-1921, for Spokane or Seattle to seek my fortune in the Far West, to begin anew as a schoolman after being despoiled by the crooked politicians in North Dakota. It means for the present, at least, setting sail from the port of blasted hopes and political crooks upon an uncharted sea for the port of missing men.

Thirty years later his widow, Kathrine Macdonald Tiffany, wrote his finest epitaph: "He burned himself out for the North Dakota schools, night and day, so the country boy could have his chance. He was 20 years ahead of his time. Has North Dakota caught up with him yet?"

Kathrine Belanger Macdonald Tiffany was born in 1878, just five years before the founding of the University of North Dakota. At the time of her marriage to Neil Macdonald in 1904 she was already a highly motivated teacher and an outstanding innovator in public education in North

Ever Westward to the Far East: THE STORY OF CHESTER FRITZ

Dakota. Her attainments compared favorably to those of her husband. Having first attended Mayville Normal School, she was graduated from the University of North Dakota with a bachelor's degree in English and in 1908 received a master's degree in the same discipline. She had already taught in a variety of schools, ranging from a one-room school house in Morgan Township to a larger institution in Hatton. In 1903 she served as both teacher and principal of Lidgerwood High School, where she was teaching at the time she was married.

Following the premature death of her husband in 1923, Kathrine Macdonald continued her profession, teaching English in the state of Washington at Seattle Pacific College and at Whitworth College in Spokane. She also taught at Wheaton College in Illinois. She remarried later in life to Dr. Orrin Tiffany, president of Seattle Pacific College and later a member of the Wheaton College faculty, and outlived him by many years. She died on April 18, 1978, a few months short of her 100th birthday, having won acclaim as the oldest alumna of the University of North Dakota. Kathrine Macdonald's influence upon Chester Fritz was fundamental to his maturation and subsequent success.

Lidgerwood is located in Richland County, in the southeastern corner of North Dakota. In 1905 it was a prosperous town of 750 people. Wiley Avenue, the town's principal street, presented a solid two blocks of business establishments lining both sides of the thoroughfare. It possessed a large merchant hotel, a huge general store, a hospital, mill, and a new brick public school building. Both the Soo and Great Northern railways connected Lidgerwood to the outside world; this enabled the leading bank to advertise, "Just received, a block of $10,000.00 eastern money, for first mortgage real estate loans." A large settlement of Bohemians constituted a significant percentage of the community's population. The Bohemians built their own wooden Catholic church instead of attending the earlier established, brick St. Boniface Catholic Church. Lidgerwood's local pride centered on its large opera house, complete with stage and oil footlights. All in all, it seemed a typical American community, a main street in the Middle Border, which, as the perceptive eye noted, contained gradations of economic standing, ethnic diversity, religious rivalry, and cultural competition.

Chester Fritz easily adjusted to a routine in Lidgerwood that would occupy his next three and one-half years. The Macdonalds, having no time for housekeeping, rented a second-floor apartment across the

Roots: The North Dakota Years

street from the high school. Fritz controlled the modest space above them.

I got a semi-attic room. In that room was a big iron pump that connected to the cistern. It was not a very friendly pump because every now and then I would bump into it. There were no electric lights. There was no plumbing. We had a telephone booth out in back where the Sears and Roebuck catalog was very useful. So I stayed in that attic room. I had a cot. It was comfortable.

The Macdonalds and Fritz took their meals at the big boarding house a block away operated by the prominent Movius family. Here, every day at regularly scheduled times, young Fritz would join the 20 adults, many of them teachers, who patronized the establishment. His payment was prorated accordingly, $8 per month. To earn his board, Fritz worked a variety of odd jobs, including gardening and chores at the boarding house. He paid nothing for his sleeping accommodations.

During summers, Fritz traveled north to live with his father in Chaffee near Casselton. Soon, however, he hired out to the Pagel farm, two miles west of Chaffee, where he worked as a farm laborer.

There I worked for a dollar a day. As the summer wore on I was shifted from one job to another. At the start, I was cultivating corn. Later I had to plow a huge clover field which was a mile away from the farmhouse. So four miles a day were occupied going to work and then back to the farm buildings, and this delayed the completion of our work. I recall Mr. Pagel's second wife was rather unpleasant because I heard her say to Mr. Pagel, "When are they going to finish plowing that clover field over there?" Well, she didn't take into consideration that I had to walk four miles every day before I started plowing. Back at lunchtime, and then return to the field, four miles which could have been spent plowing!

Every two weeks we walked to the village of Chaffee. The Pagel boys played pool and I sat around and waited for them. I longed to have a Hershey bar, which cost five cents. But I denied that pleasure as I wanted to save my money to go to school in the autumn. I have been self-supporting since I was 12 years old.

The Macdonalds believed that daily hard work and good study habits produced winners. In high school, competition among peers formed an

11

integral part of that formula. They believed strongly that if competition started early in the high school experience with proper nourishment through community acclaim, such conditions would ultimately result in a successful adult. For young Chester Fritz, the emphasis on study and competition became the central theme of his supervision by the Macdonalds. The ambitious couple, professionally committed as they were to their educational theories, was far too busy to provide a daily dose of parental affection and attention to their nephew. Their style accommodated little pampering, and both believed that the misfortune of "the Fargo years" could never be corrected. Realistically, the future seemed more important than the past. They indicated approval and support when Chester worked hard and kept his nose to the grindstone, because they were able to provide the unique intellectual and educational opportunities. Probably no other home in North Dakota could rival the Macdonalds' wide range of interests or the lofty level of their discussions. As Fritz recalled:

> We would sit in the front room around a kerosene lamp. We would huddle up around that fringe of light. The conversation was always very interesting. Neil Macdonald was a great man....Kathrine Macdonald was a stern disciplinarian and she insisted on me spending long hours on studying. I was right under the books there. Yes, I was on the firing line. There was no chance to escape.

Although still shy, Fritz thrilled at the Macdonalds' intellectual range and marveled at their devotion to structured education. He gained confidence and maturity under their caring eyes, and he dated the beginnings of his keen competitive spirit from this time.

The monthly high school program, an event usually held at the Opera House, ranked high among the innovations the Macdonalds introduced at Lidgerwood. Advertised widely, these monthly assemblies progressed from grade school skits and singing to secondary school plays and lively declamation contests. All of the town's graduating seniors had participated in a variety of forensic and theatrical experiences as spring commencement approached.

Chester Fritz was no exception. From the spring of 1905 until his graduation in June of 1908 his name regularly appeared in the local press, which credited him altogether with four recitations, two humorous stories, two declamations ("The Skeleton in Arms" and "The Chariot

Roots: The North Dakota Years

Race"), a play (the trial scene in Shakespeare's "Merchant of Venice"), and a debate (Resolved: That women should have the right of suffrage in the United States).

The titles of speeches delivered and the choice of topics debated generally indicated an atmosphere of intellectual stimulation, educational relevancy, and timely issues. The high rate of participation, not to mention the force of personal exposure, served to challenge the students, as is indicated by some of the topics debated: the abolition of capital punishment; the probabilities of honestly acquiring a million dollars; the enfranchisement of blacks; whites' treatment of American Indians; Lincoln being a better president than Washington.

Hoyt Lynch, a classmate, was Fritz's best friend in these years. Both were members of the Lidgerwood football team, which played an irregular schedule of games with nearby schools, and both enjoyed the usual after-school activities common to boys of that era. There are memories of retreats to the Lynch family store, where both snacked on free peanuts and visited at length with a Czech employee. Fritz also welcomed his uncle's companionship whenever possible. He particularly admired Macdonald's public style and sense of humor. Almost without exception, Macdonald would greet his student body with a characteristic inquiry, "How goes the battle?" When a particular individual indicated an impetuous nature, Macdonald would turn to his nephew and mutter, "They don't know what they don't know." The uncle, although he carried about 225 pounds on a normal 5-9 frame, once challenged Fritz to a 60-yard dash and beat him. "It took me down a few pegs," Fritz admitted.

Chester Fritz approached adulthood by the end of his senior year. The young tree, bent by familial tragedies and straightened under the careful nurturing and pruning of his foster parents, bore fruit upon its maturation. The success Fritz achieved in the spring declamation contest, together with his high academic standing, was due to hard work. The fifth annual Lidgerwood High School Declamatory Contest was held in the Opera House on May 6, 1908. His recitation of "The Chariot Race" won first prize in a field of eight competitors and automatically qualified him to represent Lidgerwood in the statewide contest, which was to be held at the University of North Dakota on May 14. Both the local contest and the state competition formed part of the Macdonalds' college preparatory program. That year Lidgerwood also entered its best athletes in the state track meet for high school boys at Grand Forks during the same weekend. The opportunity to perform and the free trip to the University marked a memorable occasion for the town's outstanding students.

Nineteen contestants vied for distinction in the declamation competition that year, with girls and boys divided into separate categories. The rules required that only four contestants could qualify for the finals in each category, which meant that all four boys automatically moved to the final round. The fifteen girls first endured an elimination round. First and second place winners in each category received awards of $12 and $8.

All finals were held in the evening at the Baptist Church. In the boys' competition, Frank King of Hankinson won first place and Fritz second place, as determined by cumulative scores. King received a total score of 256 points from the three judges, Fritz 253. It later was discovered, however, possibly the next day, that the criteria for the boys' competition incorrectly had been decided "on the basis of the percentage given the speakers by the judges, instead of on the basis of their selective rank." A recount was requested according to the correct criteria, and the University awarded Fritz first place and Roland Young of Cavalier second place. But, to complicate the judging further, both students had tied in rank scoring with 5 points each. That is, Fritz received five points for his two second places and one first place, while Young got five points for two first places and one third. It was decided, therefore, to utilize the cumulative score applied the previous evening in order to break the tie. Fritz took first place, because his cumulative score of 253 topped Young's score by two points.

University officials announced the results on the morning of May 16, and the following day the *Grand Forks Herald* ran the headline: "Fritz first, Young second." According to the *Herald's* account, "President Merrifield yesterday adjusted the matter and sent the boys home happy with their prizes." This was certainly true of Fritz. Merrifield's insistence of fairness impressed him. He was elated with the $12 in prize money; but just as important, it confirmed his belief that virtue would be rewarded. Roland Young was pleased, too. On the other hand, Frank King, the dethroned contestant, finished third, for which there was no monetary prize.

On June 5, 1908, Chester Fritz was graduated from Lidgerwood High School, successfully completing a four-year program in just three and one-half years with sixteen and one-half earned credits. His courses, all taught by college-trained teachers, included three years of English, two of Latin, basic and advanced algebra, plane and solid geometry, general and advanced history, physical geography, geology, physics, public speaking, business law, bookkeeping, music, and drawing. With a combined grade point average of 93.83, he ranked first in a class of ten.

Although he did not deliver the traditional address at commencement exercises, Fritz nevertheless was named valedictorian of the class of 1908. Neil Macdonald's younger brother, Alexander, and William Parizek, Fritz's roommate at the University the following year, graduated second and third among the graduates. They, too, completed the requirements in three and one-half years. Two of the ten graduates were not natives of the community—Alexander Macdonald and Chester Fritz. Both boys had been invited to Lidgerwood by their sponsors in order to take advantage of an opportunity to receive better education. Naturally, the Macdonalds took pride in the result. Later Kathrine Macdonald frequently recalled those years as being vital to Fritz's development:

> In Lidgerwood High School he was a diligent and quickly understanding student...when there was available time aside from studying his regular textbooks he liked to read articles and books on travel and wondered if he would ever have money enough to take a tour through Yellowstone National Park.

Fritz returned to the Pagel farm near Casselton upon graduation to work on a threshing machine not unlike the one that had disabled his father some years past:

> I got the job during the threshing season, where I got extra pay, a dollar a day extra, to be the fireman on the power edge of the steam engine. I would get up in the morning at 4:00 a.m. when it was pitch dark and walk some distance out in the field to where the engine and separator were located. I would immediately take a long iron rod to clean out the ashes in the flues of the engine, then build a straw fire to start heating the water. I wanted the heat to start immediately so as not to delay the bundle wagons arriving with bundles of wheat shocks. It was a race against time!
>
> In the evening, at the end of the day, it was my job to run beside the belt with a pitchfork, and we used the handle or my hand to pull the belt, the drive belt, between the separator and the engine, off the flywheel of the engine. One evening, I did not get the belt off in time. So I came up with my hand

Ever Westward to the Far East: THE STORY OF CHESTER FRITZ

wedged between the huge drive belt and the flywheel of the engine. And here I was, in a fraction of a second, facing against the big traction wheel, which was very huge, and my hand was wedged under the belt of the flywheel, which gave the power to the separator. I was about to be hoisted up and have a catastrophic accident which could have severely damaged my shoulder and my face. At that moment, a fraction of a second, that wheel stopped! I had a feeling that He, the Lord, had intervened and saved me.

Ultimately, the Macdonalds decided that Fritz should attend the University of North Dakota. Chester's aunt afterward explained the process in broad phrases:

As for Chester Fritz himself, he was brought up to admire and respect the University of North Dakota. His mother had attended it; others of his relatives attended it; and he was taught to love and respect it somewhat as a child comes to love and respect his grandparents, though yet unseen. When he went to high school, the city superintendent, the high school principal, and the leading teachers were alumni of the University of North Dakota. In that high school when young people graduated, if they were of college caliber at all, and could afford it, the only popular thing to do was to attend the University of North Dakota. It was very unpopular to mention going anywhere else. An occasional son of a plutocrat would risk public opinion and perhaps think he was gaining a little prestige for himself by going to an eastern college, but he soon found out that he was properly ostracized by his comrades in that high school community. It was treason to the University. It was treason to the state.

To Fritz, the question weighed less than heavily on his mind in 1908. He viewed it as an opportunity "to get out of the province" or "just to go to the University." The Macdonalds, Fritz said, were "very insistent" that he attend the institution and acted as "real recruiters." In Fritz's mind, Grand Forks and the University represented two giant steps from his Fargo years and one long step beyond his high school experience. No one consulted his father in Chaffee. Father and son had grown farther apart, and at this point Fritz had come to rely on the counsel of his foster parents. It seems simply to have been a case of opposing interest; and whatever else, Fritz could not conceive of taking up permanent residence in a sleeping room in the back of a rural North Dakota bank.

Roots: The North Dakota Years

Neither harbored any resentment; it amounted to a mutual recognition of separate roads. "He was up in the clouds, the wrong clouds," Fritz said of his father.

The university that welcomed Fritz in the autumn of 1908 consisted of a compact campus lying on the prairie two miles west of Grand Forks. Institutional bulletins advertised it as a community of eleven buildings, all heated by steam and "lighted by electricity." Room and board for the entire academic year did not exceed $152. For $3.75 per week, students received a furnished room, use of a bath and laundry, and regular meals. Total enrollment for the 1908 instructional year numbered 906 students, 418 men and 488 women. Only three of those counted as graduate students; the Model High School, with 200 students, attracted the largest number of students. Enrollment in the College of Liberal Arts, including Fritz, was 129 students, 93 men and 36 women.

Classes began on September 22, 1908. Much of the first week, however, was occupied with the already-traditional rivalries between the freshmen and sophomores. The 1908 confrontation seemed "fiercer and more bitterly contested than for years past," according to the student newspaper. Webster Merrifield, president of the University, believed the incident that year was "the most disgraceful fight in the history of the institution." Although there is no direct evidence that Fritz took part, it seems doubtful that he could have avoided it, considering the small compass of his new world. Too, the freshmen of 1908 made it quite plain that they would resist the hazing and abuse visited upon them by the sophomores.

Academically, Fritz was well prepared to pursue college studies. The Lidgerwood preparatory program facilitated his transition and placed him on a competitive plane with his peers, whether from comparable environments or the more populous cities in the state. Perhaps Fritz exaggerated somewhat when he remarked, "I doubt any other high school had to work as hard as we did," but after all he lived under the watchful eye of the superintendent and the principal. Alexander Macdonald also entered the University that same year.

Literary societies were the most important student organizations in those years. Fritz, as the winner of the annual state declamation contest, became an attractive candidate. In October, both Fritz and Maxwell Anderson were initiated into Ad Altiora ("to greater heights") in a brief ceremony convened in the old stockroom on the second floor of Main building. The next January, at the annual banquet at the downtown

Ever Westward to the Far East: THE STORY OF CHESTER FRITZ

Northern Hotel, Fritz was elected the society's secretary. That spring he was chosen to represent the membership in the Main Declamation Contest, an annual speaking event held in conjunction with commencement exercises. The fact that he did not win did not prevent the student newspaper from commending his "splendid reading of 'Regulus to the Carthaginians.' Mr. Fritz has a fine voice, and his gestures were perfect. He seems perfectly at ease on the platform."

Fritz roomed with Bill Parizek of Lidgerwood in Budge Hall during his freshman year. In spring he tried out for the track team as a hurdler but met with little success. Herbert Movius, also of Lidgerwood, invited Fritz to pledge at the Varsity Bachelor Club during his sophomore year. Comparable to the Blue Key today, "The Bachelor Club became a society of student leaders that enjoyed special favors from the faculty." In 1910, their house, the first fraternity on the University campus, was completed on the banks of the English Coulee, with Fritz one of its twenty residents. The Bachelor Club inclined toward exclusiveness, both academically and socially. Dances held there were described as lasting "from seven thirty to eleven thirty, a red rose for the 'favordance,' subdued red lights, grey suede and gold programs, and supper by candle light." Fritz escorted Blondie Holt, an attractive coed from Northwood, North Dakota, to such a dance on at least one occasion.

Of course, there was more to student life than social gaiety. Fritz worked at a variety of odd jobs in order to help defray part of his room and board bill. His chief employment was at the State Public Health Laboratory, which the Legislature established on campus in 1907. Located in Science Hall, the laboratory received bacteriological samples for testing from everywhere in the state and, as well, conducted examinations on pathological tissues. After the Great Northern train dropped them off every evening, Fritz picked up the containers at the University station for delivery to the lab:

> I had to take them up to the top floor of Science Hall and put them in a huge, heated cupboard for examination the next day. And I had to go up these stairs, and right opposite near the top floor, the cadavers were stored and the room was pitch dark. I had to climb up those stairs every night after 9 p.m.

Fritz found most of his classes interesting and enjoyable. He took freshman English from Ella Fulton, the first dean of women; German from Samuel Pease; and mathematics from Elwyn Chandler, who he

Paternal grandfather Rev. William Fritz, front row left, and family. Chester's father Charles, standing third from left.

Maternal grandfather Ferdinand Belanger and family. Chester's mother Anne, standing right; Kathrine Belanger standing left.

Charles and Anne Fritz, Chester's parents.

Baptism picture of Chester Fritz, May 14, 1892.

Chester on Valentine's Day, 1895.

Chester Fritz as a young boy in Fargo.

Morgan Township School in Traill County, where Chester received his earliest education.

Neil C. and Kathrine Belanger Macdonald in 1905.

Lidgerwood High School class of 1908, with valedictorian Chester Fritz in front row, left.

The University of North Dakota campus, circa 1910.

Budge Hall, Chester's UND dormitory home in 1908-1909.

Cast of the "Twelfth Night," performed at UND in May 1910, with Chester Fritz, third from right in front row.

Chester Fritz, second from right, part of a student work crew during "Campus Day," 1913, at the University of Washington.

Chester Fritz, age 21, at the University of Washington, 1913.

Henry Boyd and Chester Fritz (right) on the steps of the Delta Tau Delta fraternity house, University of Washington, 1914.

Fisher Flouring Mills, Seattle.

Flour salesman in the Far East, 1915. Fritz on right.

Fritz (with bow tie) and Charles Richardson (seated behind Fritz) in Singapore, 1916.

A journey across China: Chester Fritz visits a Buddhist temple in Yunnan province during his six-month 1917 trip.

The journey: Fritz in a four-man chair on the Fourth of July, 1917; hence the U.S. flag.

The journey: Mr. Wang, the magistrate of Kweiyang, greets the traveler.

The journey: Fritz (center) with Chinese gentry who entertained him at dinner in Kiatingfu.

The journey: The view from Fritz's chartered boat on the upper Yangtze.

The Bund, Shanghai, 1920s, a fertile ground for an energetic businessman.

Nanking Road, the main shopping street in Shanghai.

Above: Chester Fritz supervising the unloading of silver bars at the customs jetty, Shanghai, in the 1920s.

Left: Learning to play polo, 1920s in Shanghai.

Below: Chester Fritz, left in front row, and his friend Ezra Shamoon (third from left in front row) at a party in Shanghai.

Above: A world traveler: Fritz (rear of car) sightseeing in Czechoslovakia in 1923 while on home leave.

Right: Chester and Bernardine Szold Fritz in Darien, Manchuria, the day after their marriage, June 19, 1929.

Below: Fritz home in Shanghai, where Chester and Bernardine lived from 1929-1936.

Left to right: the partners: Joseph Swan, Charles D. Culbertson, and Chester Fritz.

Swan, Culbertson and Fritz advertisement, 1931.

The partners at the paper hunts in the early 1930s. Fritz, second from left, Swan with pipe, Culbertson on right.

The firm's annual staff dinner, April 11, 1934, in Shanghai.

Chester Fritz and Taoist priest in Hangchow China, 1933.

Six members of the firm of Swan, Culbertson and Fritz in 1934 (Fritz third from left, Swan to his left, Culbertson on far right). All were entitled to wear the red coat as expert horsemen.

Roots: The North Dakota Years

described as "a fluttering bird going around the classroom." One class in particular presented difficulties, as recounted in the following dialogue:

Rylance: What class did you do the poorest in?
Fritz: Now you are getting warm! (chuckle) You know something you are not telling me! (laughter)
Rylance: We'll get to it!
Fritz: Okay....I cannot remember that professor's name. I thought he was the most ineffective teacher. He did not look at anybody when he was talking. And I had the misfortune of talking outside his classroom, it was downstairs in the library building, and I was walking outside with some friends, and I was talking too much and I didn't give any compliments to this professor. And he flunked me!
Rylance: What class was this—history?
Fritz: No! No! Political science! He flunked me!
Rylance: I really did not know that.
Fritz: Oh, the secret is out!

During the summer of 1909, between his freshman and sophomore years, Fritz jumped a freight train to Billings, Montana, for his first trip west of North Dakota. There he took a job at the Grant Hotel in exchange for his board. Billings radiated a western atmosphere quite unlike the settled, agrarian culture of the Red River Valley. He thought the mountains even more beautiful than he had imagined. Here he soon discovered that through personal assertiveness and a "good line," one could successfully make sales and actually earn money. His sideline, in addition to working at the Grant Hotel, was selling Wyoming-bound tourists tickets on which he received a commission.

That Montana summer instilled confidence in Fritz and activated his bigger dreams. It whetted his appetite for more travel and renewed his growing eagerness to quit the prairies of North Dakota. Financially, he easily exceeded the $1 per day he had earned in other summers on the Pagel farm. He also discarded the uniform of his former trade, the black shirt and bib overalls; living in the Grant Hotel offered a richly satisfying alternative to his father's humble accommodations in the backroom of the Chaffee bank.

19

Fritz returned to North Dakota at the close of summer determined to spend but one more year there. Lack of an immediate alternative, as well as a sense of loyalty to the University and his background, kept him at his college studies where he had started. Yet the experience of the mountains in central Montana, his encounters with new and different people, and the opportunity to do something other than farm work convinced him of a need to plan for a permanent change of course and direction.

Professor Frederick Koch returned to the University of North Dakota in the fall of 1909 to resume teaching English and public speaking. He completed his master's degree at Harvard the previous June and during the summer toured Europe, where he became engaged to an 18-year-old American woman in Athens. Back in Grand Forks, Koch found the administration of President Frank McVey imaginative and "hospitable to the maturing of his own half-formed dream of developing a school of regional drama." He also met two exceptional members of the sophomore class, both keenly interested in drama, Margaret Haskell and Maxwell Anderson. In late December 1909, at the Sigma Chi fraternity house, the "Sock and Buskin Club" was born. Koch was chosen director, and Anderson his assistant.

The student newspaper called the development "very intellectual," while subsequent meetings of the newly organized group at the president's home further contributed to its elite reputation. The club had as its purpose "the study of literature as drama" and the "invitation of a movement to establish as soon as practicable, a university theater" on the campus.

Frederick Koch soon became Fritz's favorite instructor; "I thought he was quite impressive," he said. Under Koch's guidance, Fritz enhanced his skills in dramatic reading and received added encouragement to cultivate what Koch already had identified as an "excellent speaking voice." Privately, Fritz had less time for his classmates Anderson and Haskell. He thought Anderson "a dour fellow" and referred to Haskell somewhat caustically as "supposedly the most literary minded at that time." Fritz's involvement with the drama club and its development dated from the spring semester of 1910.

With important institutional support from President McVey, who thought such a theater would be good public relations for the University, the creation of a University theater proved to be no difficult process. In February, the club started considering an outdoor theater, fixing its gaze on the banked English Coulee to the south and west of Main building.

The east side of the coulee banked high, providing an ideal vantage to the audience watching the action unfold on the low, gradually sloping opposite bank.

The Sock and Buskin Club shortly announced it had chosen to produce the Shakespearean comedy "Twelfth Night" on June 13, 1910, on a stage straddling the waters of the English Coulee. In late May and early June, newspaper coverage and broadsides commenced promoting the production and its cast, which was said to comprise "the best talent at the University." Although Anderson did not win a role in the club's first performance, Fritz played three parts: Roberto, the sea captain; Fabian, the servant; and the priest.

More than 400 people witnessed the premier performance of the University's theater group on June 13, the first open-air production ever staged in North Dakota. The *Grand Forks Herald* published its review the following day.

> For over two hours of a perfect summer night, one of such as occurs but rarely in North Dakota during June...supporters and friends were transported in spirit back to the seventeenth century and the days of the bards of Avon.

The *Herald* characterized the play as "light and airy" and "full of amusing situations." The paper editorialized that the outdoor ambience had attracted many converts and predicted this mode of production might well become a regular feature of dramatics on the campus.

As one of the cast, Fritz vividly recalled his own opening line, "This is a lyria." The unexpected and hilarious incident that broke up the house, however, prompted greater detail:

> When I played in "Twelfth Night" at the University of North Dakota, I was on the stage with Lawrence Fisher, a very good actor at the University, who played the part of Sir Toby Belch, which was a Falstaff-type character. We had costumes which were sent to us from Minneapolis. He had a pillow in his costume, as he was supposed to have a large belly. Suddenly, when I was looking at the audience and he was standing behind me out of my vision, I heard a great roar go up. It seems that the suspenders holding up Sir Toby's tummy with the pillow had broken and here he was having a miscarriage on the stage. He nearly broke up the show!

Fritz's days as a student at the University of North Dakota ended hectically. In addition to his roles in "Twelfth Night," he needed to practice his presentation of Ben Hur for the Main Declamation Contest. He managed to safeguard the reputation of the literary society he represented, but failed, in two attempts, to capture first prize. The reviews spoke of his "very strong and forceful" delivery and cited his interpretation as giving "new meaning and significance" to the material.

Meanwhile, he also prepared for a permanent departure from North Dakota at month's end. The decision stemmed from a mixture of reasons. His yen to travel to the mountains and beyond had not lessened. Also, he had tired of the level North Dakota prairie that he had come to know so well, which he remembers as being "flat as a floor." Of course, a college education remained important, but the commitment could not override his desire for a different landscape and topography. In his own mind, as well, he had paid "his dues" to the Macdonalds; he had attended "their University" for two years, so that it was now his opportunity, if he so decided, to go elsewhere. Certainly farming would never be his life's interest, and living with his father promised no future. His experience in North Dakota had not been without its disappointments; he wished physically to separate himself from those financially lean and emotionally wrenching years. It is best described in his own words: "You see, I wanted to get away from North Dakota. I wasn't very happy there."

The main line of the Northern Pacific railway, linking St. Paul and Seattle, offered a means of escape. It enabled him to act on both his desires and expectations and ultimately provided a huge step toward fulfillment of "Ever Westward to the Far East." Chester Fritz was now on course!

II

The Transition Years 1910-1917

The years between 1910 and 1917 were ones of transition for Chester Fritz. They began and ended in uncertainty and unemployment, laced intermittently with moments of unsought adventure. During this period Fritz moved permanently from North Dakota to the state of Washington, then to the British colony at Hong Kong. He completed a college degree, served as an apprentice in a major west coast industry, and obtained his first job in the Orient. He broadened his rural North Dakota experiences with urban and cosmopolitan contacts in Seattle and the Far East. And he fulfilled his desire for travel abroad. Indeed, Fritz matured both in mind and spirit through the decade, finally making a personal decision as to where he wished to spend a large portion of his adult life. In China, Fritz found a career.

A regularly scheduled westbound run of the Northern Pacific Railroad departed from St. Paul, Minnesota, on the evening of July 2, 1910. Seattle, its destination, would be reached on the morning of July 4. Chester Fritz boarded the train as its "third cook," according to the exaggerated but clever entry added to the employees' list, which gained him temporary employment and provided a free ride to a point of no special significance. Fritz recalled that he journeyed to Seattle "simply because it was the end of the line, and I liked the scenery and there were great mountains nearby."

His trip west provided other vivid memories of the experience:

> I went down to St. Paul...and got a job in the dining car, which carried a crew of three. The job saved me the railroad fare. I got on the train about 10:00 p.m. The railroad officials did not become aware of my shortcomings until the following morning, when the two colored waiters appeared at the pantry and called to me, "Two hot dinners." Well, I never learned those words in my vocabulary at the University.
>
> Fortunately for me there was a feud in progress between the chef and the second cook. And each was siding with me and overlooking my shortcomings. My main job was to bake potatoes. In fact, the Northern Pacific advertised itself as the line of the "big baked potato!" The potatoes were from Idaho, of huge size, and when baked I would slit them open and squeeze them so the mouth would open and I would drop in a big square of butter and a dash of paprika for color. After two days, the fat chef said to me, "Young fella, if you stay with me two years, I will make a good cook out of you." I replied, "Thank you very much; I will think about it." I am still thinking!
>
> On the train it was very hot and I recall, as we passed through Montana, the heat was intense, particularly in the dining car. At night we slept on the floor...on the soiled linen. I perspired so heavily in the car that the two $10.00 traveler's checks I had in a chamois around my neck became blurred from the perspiration. I feared I would not be able to cash them but, fortunately, I realized the cash.

As he alighted the train in Seattle, Fritz surely was filled with high, youthful hopes. But he had only a small bag of personal linen strung over his shoulder and $20 in his pocket. He rented a small room in an old house by the waterfront and, the next day, embarked on what turned out to be a futile search for employment. But in looking for work, the young, transplanted North Dakotan soon realized that not much importance was given "to how much you know" but rather to "who do you know"—and "I knew nobody."

The Transition Years

Hard times characterized Fritz's first year on the West Coast. The excitement of communing with the many moods of a seemingly endless ocean or basking in the shadows of the majestic mountains on the near horizon early gave way to the desperation of economic survival. Jobs of practically any description were few and precious. After weeks of relentless hunting, Fritz happily received an offer of work as a timekeeper in a lumber camp, the only position he found that was "suitable for my qualifications or lack thereof." Yet, because taking it would require leaving Seattle and thus eliminate the opportunity of attending the University of Washington that autumn, Fritz reluctantly declined the offer.

The hope to stay in Seattle at all costs did not materialize. Job prospects, however, became worse. Employment became a day-to-day, week-by-week struggle. Night desk clerk jobs at hotels and part-time labor positions during the day provided the only means of employment. As fall approached, Fritz was forced to abandon his plans to enroll at the university. He simply could not afford it. He spent the greater part of the next year in Vancouver, British Columbia, working in the order department of Robertson, Godson and Company, a wholesale plumbing, heating, and hardware firm, where he took phone calls and handled the correspondence connected with filling incoming orders. He was forced to choose between this steady employment or trusting to a series of temporary options.

For Fritz, his first year away from North Dakota must be judged a failure. Little of it progressed in the way he had planned. Independence and distance proved an unexpected handicap. Although the environment remained more colorful than the monotonous wheat fields of the Red River Valley, it lacked the assurance of small-town life and the cohesion of a rural community. A sense of insecurity haunted his new existence, and there was only Horatio Alger's prescription to lean on. Fritz remembered that year, the hardest of the five years he spent on the Washington coast: "Apparently there was a drive within me to succeed regardless of the odds. I had an abundance of raw courage and it carried me through the first year."

The second year proved better than the first year. Chester Fritz returned to Seattle during the summer of 1911, his 19th year. He obtained a thirty-six-hour per week job at the Owl Drug Company store located at the corner of Third Avenue and Pike Street, where he operated the cigar counter on the swing shift six nights a week. Bruce MacDougal, a former employee at the store, recommended Fritz for the job. Later MacDougal became Fritz's first roommate at the University of Washington, once Fritz felt sufficiently confident to enroll that same fall. An unvarying routine marked the course of the ensuing three years: Fritz attended classes in the forenoon hours; he studied with MacDougal at the Alpha Tau Omega fraternity house during the afternoon; and he worked at the drugstore in the evenings. The city trolley line provided transportation between the campus and the store, and a self-service dairy lunch booth near the drugstore supplied the evening meal consisting of "a fried egg sandwich in a round bun and a mug of milk for ten cents."

The first decade of the twentieth century comprised "the golden years of growth" for the University of Washington. Seattle's population increased nearly three-fold between 1900 and 1910 from 80,671 to 237,194. The university grew with the city rather than the state. University enrollment increased from 630 in 1902 to almost 2,300 in 1912. The faculty, which totaled 177 members in 1912, included many "highly trained, young scholars from the best graduate schools in the United States." Even so, the university's startling growth clearly had strained the facilities to accommodate it: the campus consisted of just nine major buildings, and only the chemistry department had qualified as a Ph.D.-granting discipline.

Academically, the University of Washington found itself attempting to accomplish the transformation between a regional college and a recognized university. Curriculum reform stressed the broad program of liberal arts, cautioned against "premature specialization," and proclaimed a balance between "required and elective courses." Charles Gates, author of the commemorative work, *The First Century at the University of Washington, 1861-1961*, viewed the institution at the time Chester Fritz attended it as one of "intimacy and informality" and as possessing "a mood of spontaneity the more pronounced because the University was yet strong."

Campus Day, annually observed on May 1, perhaps best illustrated these intimate and informal features. On that day, the most popular of all university-sponsored celebrations, "work parties organized along class lines" to grade lawns, improve footpaths and walkways, build benches, and recover gardens from their winter doldrums. In 1913, nearly 700 students or 59 percent of the total enrollment participated in this annual ritual.

For Fritz, his transfer from the University of North Dakota to the

University of Washington involved more continuity than change. Both institutions were enjoying comparable stages of evolution, despite the contrast in founding years. Both radiated optimism toward their futures, and both actively courted status and prestige among their peers. Student life at both institutions inclined toward clubbiness, strong class identification, hazing, and organized inter-class competitions. At the same time, however, important differences existed, owing largely to contrasting population densities, dissimilar geographic conditions, and uneven economic opportunities. The University of Washington could capitalize on broader and more varied urban resources, and because of it, benefited directly from the growth of a supportive city and state eager to keep the institution competitive with other Pacific Coast universities.

Fritz attended the University of Washington from the fall of 1911 through the spring of 1914, when he was graduated with a bachelor's degree in economics. He also entered the law school at the start of his senior year and continued a year of law courses, but then "realized I wasn't a lawyer," according to his own assessment. His extracurricular activities necessarily were limited to a nominal membership in the university's dramatic club. "As I worked six days a week I had no time for social activities," he later recalled. "Perhaps the work did me no harm, but at the same time I lost many of the advantages of college life."

Fritz did, however, take up fraternity life at the university. He joined the Delta Tau Delta fraternity in his second year at the campus and lived in its house. The fraternity, he remembered...

> ...had a dormitory on the third floor. So after work I crawled into my bunk, which was the upper bunk on a double-decker. Most of the members were already asleep and snoring, so one had to exercise caution in climbing into bed. If you didn't, you'd hear about it in the morning.

The friendships he developed through the fraternity included at least two of long-standing duration, those with Harry Boyd and Malcolm Douglas. Douglas, who later became senior judge of the Washington Supreme Court, later reminisced:

> We found time to play some tennis, go canoeing occasionally, and do some reading. In those days there was quite a craze for Kipling. To me, a lover, almost a worshiper of Rudyard Kipling, *Kim* had always held a peculiarly seductive charm. Chester was intrigued, too, by the story of the old, red lama adopting the irrepressible Kim, "little friend of all the

world," as his chelah and the entrancing tale of the two of them wandering down the Grand Trunk Road across India in search of the River of Healing. Chester was later to follow in their footsteps.

After graduation in 1914, we roomed together at the Knickerbocker Hotel at 7th and Madison for approximately a year. We were both as poor as church mice. I was trying to get a start in the law practice with meager success. He was selling cigars at the Owl Drug Store. We allowed ourselves a budget item of ten cents for breakfast. On Friday nights we celebrated by going to the New York Cafe at 2nd and Cherry where we could get a rib steak for 30 cents.

The growing importance of Seattle as a center of international trade seemed clear. Major contacts with China, Japan, and beyond were generally encouraged and promoted. And the university, sensing presciently an opportunity to identify with regional interests, followed suit. It separately sought to realize in cultural and educational spheres what the city and its environs were well toward establishing in commercial relations. The university created a department of Oriental history in 1919. Campus attractions and extracurricular activities indicated heightened awareness and contact with Asia. In 1913, Meiji University in Tokyo invited the university to send its baseball team to Japan for a special game. The University of Washington's English club sponsored a series of Chinese plays in 1913. In 1914, the political adviser to the Chinese consul-general in San Francisco addressed the student body on the complexities of the Chinese republican revolution.

Few persons either living in the city or connected to the university could long remain ignorant of things Asian. Certainly not Chester Fritz, whose own keen interests led him aggressively to search out and question people who had Asian experiences to recount. When time permitted, too, he liked to browse the Seattle Public Library for travel books, often with a focus on Asia. He was captivated particularly by one of Harry Franck's books, *A Vagabond Journey Around the World* (1910), wherein the author asked rhetorically,

> What would befall the man who set out to girdle the globe as the farmer's boy sets out to seek his fortune in the neighboring city; on the alert for every opportunity, yet scornful of the fact that every foot of the way has not been paved before him?

The Transition Years

Franck rejected the notion that travel was the prerogative of the wealthy. Rather, he insisted that any man "with a bit of energy and good health could start without money and make a journey around the globe."

Fritz wanted to agree with Franck, and eventually he personally would demonstrate the validity of the point. Yet, for the moment, Fritz knew too well the frustrations of anticipating the future in an unfamiliar setting. Physical proximity alone would not suffice; survival and success depended also on being able to respond to opportunities created in personal contacts. So that, while travel to the Far East loomed as a distinct possibility, timing and readiness remained beyond his immediate control.

Opportunity knocked unexpectedly for Chester Fritz during a chance meeting with a seasoned export agent who operated in the Far East. There are two versions of what followed. One version comes from Edith Allen (Mrs. Kirby Holmes), daughter of Stanley Allen, a Briton by birth, who had spent many years in Hong Kong representing the Sperry Flour Company of Oakland, California. Allen resigned in 1910 and joined the Fisher Flouring Mills of Seattle, starting as head of its overseas trading department, but ending as the manager of the company's export division. Mrs. Holmes recalled,

> Well, my father knew Chester Fritz; how he met him I'm not sure, but I think through a Mr. Richardson, who was the connection for Fisher Flour in Hong Kong. Mr. Richardson used to come to Seattle many times. I do remember him because he was an old friend of both my father, and his wife was a friend of my mother. And the story is that he met Mr. Fritz when he was a bellboy at the hotel Mr. Richardson stayed in while Mr. Fritz was working his way through the university.
>
> ...Mr. Richardson was very taken with this young Mr. Fritz, and I guess told my father about him because when Mr. Fritz graduated he was offered the job of going out to work for Fisher Flour in Hong Kong. My father was the export manager, and so he must have something to do with his going. I am quite sure.

The second version was told by Malcolm Douglas:

> Then one night Chester encountered Destiny, in the form of a customer at his cigar counter named Richardson. Richardson was an old China hand, a prosperous businessman

engaged in importing and exporting, a polished gentleman, and a gourmet. He was attracted by Chester's keen mind and winning personality. He arranged for Chester to have a year's training in the flour business at Fisher's and after that to enter business with him in China.

Charles Edward Richardson was born in San Francisco on September 4, 1871. A large man, weighing over 300 pounds and typically attired in white tropical suits, Richardson looked and acted the part of a successful foreign trader. By 1914, he was an eighteen-year veteran of Far Eastern trading, mostly in Hong Kong and mainly in the flour business. Richardson discerned in Fritz a likely business assistant who possessed a flair for meeting people; Fritz recognized in Richardson a prospective mentor whose experience lay in the lands of his reveries. Thus, Richardson offered not only the opportunity Fritz sought, but also employment with a reputable firm willing to transport him to Hong Kong in May 1915. Although Fritz's relationship with Richardson ultimately ended in doubt and discord, the association lasted six years, until 1921, and completed Fritz's formative years.

When the Fisher Flouring Mills hired Fritz in June 1914, he joined one of the leading commercial enterprises of the Pacific Coast and came under the spell of two of the outstanding entrepreneurial talents in American business, O. W. Fisher and his son O. D. Fisher. The commercial and financial success of the Fisher interests rested firmly on adhering to these three cardinal rules: never divest of business property once acquired; keep risks to a minimum by investing only in basic commodities; and take a minority position in any enterprise only when it includes a strategic advantage in deciding operational policy. Fisher's lumbering interests started in the Ozarks in 1889, expanded to Louisiana in 1899 and, in 1906, to Washington, where operations eventually merged with the Weyerhaeuser Timber Company. Meantime, branch interests developed in banking and real estate which, in the mid-1920s, led to insurance and radio broadcasting, and to television after World War II.

Fisher once confided that he turned to lumbering because he failed to get a job in a grist mill. In 1903 Fisher bought the Gallatin Milling Company of Montana, which, despite its name, mostly bought and merchandised wheat. Its 31 country elevators supplied the bulk of wheat that fed Fisher Flouring Mills in Seattle when it commenced operations in June 1911. The mill's initial daily capacity of 2,000 barrels doubled in 1917 and doubled again in 1924. In 1943, the mill announced "Zoom Is

The Transition Years

Coming." Soon Zoom became a popular American breakfast cereal. The mill had a new product and the Fisher family another winner. By 1947 the mill was acknowledged the fifth largest in the United States. Operations long concentrated on producing flour for household consumption, and exports accounted for less than 15 percent of the whole until after World War I. However, the export trade grew importantly in the 1920s but declined sharply during the Depression. It recovered profitably after World War II.

The Fishers built their mill on Harbor Island, a new industrial area of Seattle. Fritz found the huge mill, situated beside part of the dock where ships used to come up and load flour directly under the chutes, a "fascinating sight, indeed."

Fritz started working for the Fisher Flouring Mills immediately upon his graduation from the University of Washington in June 1914. He first worked in the testing laboratory alongside Perry Wing, measuring the gluten content of flour by baking "expansion loaves" of bread. The baking also served to meet another need: "We ate those loaves with peanut butter for lunch," Fritz recalled. "We were down in that laboratory for all of the day."

Fritz transferred to the main office after several months in the laboratory. There he came under the influence of the head of exporting operations, Stanley Allen, who seems to have treated Fritz as something of a "fair-haired boy." Apprentice Fritz worked under Allen with the mutual understanding and support of Richardson. When Allen decided to locate a Fisher employee in Hong Kong, according to Fritz, "I would be the one."

Of course, privately there was more to the Allen-Fritz relationship than merely Richardson's personally stated recommendation. Fritz exhibited to Allen the same enthusiasm for the Orient that he had to Richardson earlier and as a result evoked the story-telling proclivities of his boss. Allen, a self-described "Manxman born in Liverpool, married in San Francisco, and with two children born in Hong Kong and Seattle," told Fritz that he went by the name "Little Fish" in the Far East because of his five-foot-three stature. Fritz had fond memories of Allen. "I loved to talk with him about Hong Kong and he had a great influence on my life. His tales of Hong Kong life fascinated me and I hoped I could do likewise one day."

To Hoyt Lynch, his high school friend in Lidgerwood, Fritz related his progress to date and expectations for the future in a letter of January

1915. He allowed that the world had "used me fair since leaving that grand, old commonwealth of North Dakota, which is noted for its beautiful women and fast horses (translate literally)." He spoke of his graduation and observed that "since last summer I have been with the Fisher Flouring Mills, working in the testing laboratory, and so by this time I have received a splendid technical training in the flour milling business." Fritz then indicated his ambition to become an "export man" because that was "the department where the money is made"; he also explained that of all of Fisher's overseas markets, China took in "the largest share."

An opening developed in Hong Kong during the spring of 1915. The circumstances of Fritz's departure from Seattle contrasted strikingly with the circumstances of his arrival five years before.

> I was full of enthusiasm at the prospect of this voyage and I recall that when I departed from Seattle on the train, I felt honored that Mr. O. D. Fisher, head of Fisher Mills Company, and Mr. Stanley Allen, as well as my college roommate Malcolm Douglas, accompanied me to the railroad station.

En route Fritz spent a few diverting days in San Francisco, including a trip to the Panama-Pacific Exposition, before boarding the Pacific Mail Line's steamship *Korea*. His cabin mate in one of the two upper-deck accommodations was a traveling auditor for the Standard Oil Company of New York, Sam Noxon, who "coached me as to the life of a foreigner living in the Orient" from his repertoire of wide experiences.

An unexpected letter from Neil C. Macdonald also caught up with him in San Francisco:

> We hope you will always keep yourself clean in body and mind, and that you will always prize honesty and integrity and lofty ideals of conduct dearer than life itself. Good health and good character in connection with great capacity and a desire for service are the most valuable assets any young man can possess. These you possess in no small degree; and that you do, you cannot fail—and will not fail. Whether or not your fortune is at the end of the rainbow, resting so far away, makes little difference, so long as you earn a good living in an honest manner, and *spend* it in a *wise way*.

In 1958, forty-three years later, Chester Fritz returned the letter, badly worn and yellowed, to Kathrine Macdonald Tiffany. He attached a personal note: "This letter I have always treasured and have reread it countless times. Use it at your discretion."

The *Korea* docked in Hong Kong following an uneventful voyage across the broad Pacific. For Chester Fritz, his adventure of "Ever Westward to the Far East" truly had begun.

> I found life in Hong Kong fascinating, especially the movement of the ships in the large harbor, which was constantly occupied by majestic ocean-going liners. Smaller coastal steamships and great fleets of Kwantung junks also filled the harbor with their brown sails. These junks sailed to faraway places in the islands and colonies of Southeast Asia. It was said that Marco Polo traveled on these junks in the 13th and 14th centuries when he returned to his hometown of Venice.

Hong Kong translated literally from the Chinese means "Good Harbor" or "Fragrant Streams." Hong Kong is not the name of a city but a small island of 29 square miles upon which is located the city of Victoria. The island is situated off the southeast coast of China at the mouth of the Canton River and opposite the Chinese province of Kwangtung. It is separated from the mainland by a narrow channel and possesses two capacious natural harbors—Deep Water Bay and Tytam Bay. The island's topography is mountainous with little tillable land. The climate is subtropical with temperature seldom dropping below 40 degrees. The wet season begins in May and continues with little relief until August. On average, the island receives about 90 inches of rain per year.

Hong Kong is an important British possession. It was ceded to England in 1841 by China and confirmed by the treaty of Nanking in 1842, which terminated the Opium War. The treaty dealt an effective blow against the long-term Chinese policy of exclusion. It opened four additional ports, including Shanghai, and forced China to pay Britain an indemnity of $21,000,000 to cover the cost of confiscated opium. It also abolished the cohong system and allowed British traders the right to do business with any Chinese at the open ports. In 1866, the Peking treaty added the peninsula of Kowloon (about 5 miles in area) to Hong Kong. Hong Kong is a free port. The colony is administered by a governor, executive council, and legislative council.

Obviously, Fritz was much better prepared to succeed in Hong Kong than he had been on reaching Seattle. Armed with letters of recommendation from Stanley Allen and a list of important persons to contact, Fritz early applied for membership in the fashionable British "Hong Kong Club." Only later did he learn that eligibility was largely confined to those associated with banking and shipping. His membership, once formally voted, amounted to a minor triumph of an American, and his room assignment there, "Dai Bat O Fong" (large number eight room), indicated as much. Situated at one corner of the second floor, the view to one side overlooked the famous harbor and, to the other, the large plaza fronting the Law Courts and the Hong Kong and Shanghai Banking Corporation, "destined to become one of the world's great banking institutions."

The process of adjusting began almost immediately. For example, "the Chinese servant who waited on my dining table at the club was addressed as 'Boy,' although he was about 65 years old!" More importantly, the city's living costs were "very low" and the club's dues "very reasonable." The combination of favorable exchange rates and the Chinese dollar, denominated according to a silver standard, valued at about 50 cents American, yielded a measure of unfamiliar affluence. Yet, rather than spending his $125-per-month salary, Fritz lived frugally by taking his meals at the Hong Kong Club, where "the menu was repeated every week. If you looked down at the soup and saw it was Mulligatawny, you knew it was Friday!"

British customs governed the active social life available to foreigners in the colony. Black ties prevailed at formal dinner parties during the winter months; white mess jackets styled after British naval officers' uniforms were favorites for summer. Calling cards, dropped in special residential boxes with panels marked "In" and "Out," functioned as a preliminary gauge of one's respectability. Failure to be contacted within two or three weeks after having left behind one's card sufficed to indicate that no invitation would be forthcoming. Everyone, too, conceded that "the Peak," where no Chinese were permitted to live, qualified as the most prestigious residential area. Although cooler, living on "the Peak" remained as elsewhere a struggle with dampness, so that homes typically included a drying room, according to Fritz, to safeguard shoes from becoming as mildewed "as your disposition."

Several months elapsed before Fritz received an invitation to dine at "the Peak" in the home of a distinguished British family. He remembers the evening as having begun in this manner:

> As other guests arrived, I overheard my host say to one of
> the other guests, pointing his finger modestly in my direction,

The Transition Years

"You know that chap over there is an American but he is really very nice." I knew then I had a chance of passing quarantine.

Under Richardson's tutelage, Fritz went on assignments to all parts of Southeast Asia. In French Indochina he found exorbitant tariff rates imposed on all items not of French origin. In the Chinese district outside Saigon known as "Cholen City," he learned from cutthroat Chinese merchants "that one of the Chinese ships was selling flour at prices that were far too low." But he was told that the captain "got a certain kind of satisfaction in causing his competition to also lose money. A strange psychology!" In Bangkok, capital of Siam (Thailand), he took time to view native festivals and learned after the fact that it was common practice for the Siamese to douse a stranger with a bucket of water. In Java, he visited the sprawling Dutch plantations and dined in their mansions. On one occasion he was very impressed by a huge Dutch clock but felt compelled to inquire of his host how he determined the correct time. The Dutchman replied, "Oh, it is very simple. When it is three o'clock, it strikes seven. Then I know it is eleven-thirty."

Still, on all of these trips and many others, business tended to follow the same established patterns.

> In all of these localities the merchants or the traders were Chinese whose trading instincts were superior to those of the natives. The Chinese were the people who possessed the wealth. It was said that in the Philippines 85 percent of the retail trade was in the hands of Chinese merchants. I made these visits in 1915 and 1916.

In late 1915, while selling flour in Singapore, Fritz became quite ill. Every second day at about mid-evening he would take to his bed, unable to function because of a sustained fit of shivering. The physician diagnosed intermittent malaria, which he treated with a generous prescription of quinine.

In Singapore, Fritz stayed at "the leading hotel...a medieval type of hotel called the Raffles owned and run by the Sarkies brothers, Armenians. The room I had was very primitive. In fact, in back of the room was a small additional room where there was a galvanized washtub from which you dipped out your bathwater and douched it over your bare body with a tin dipper. Overhead was a huge wooden-bladed fan, and you slept under a huge mosquito net. Beside you, which was called in the lingo of those days 'a Dutch window,' was a hard roll, pillow-like substance, long and round. It looked something like a cigar and you put it between your knees and slept on your side in order to keep free of perspiration. In my days there were great numbers of mosquitos in Singapore."

At times selling flour produced extraordinary results. Fritz, in Singapore, once routinely telegraphed Hong Kong to forward a shipment of "3,000 Big Gun to Macaser," Big Gun being a brand of popularly traded flour. Since, however, the British prohibited privately coded cable, he correctly sent the message in plain English. Fritz was ignorant, of course, that coincidentally the British had received information that German-made guns were being shipped from the southern Philippine Islands to Macaser, in the Dutch East Indies. Within a day or two, a British official came knocking at his room in the Raffles to inquire about the meaning of the telegram.

Official: Did you send this cablegram?
Fritz: I did.
Official: What is Big Gun?
Fritz: Flour! (Fritz thereupon produced an empty flour sack carrying the "Big Gun" brand.)
Official: (dumfounded expression) Oh!

The story, however, did not end there. Paul Carroll, a San Francisco businessman, met Fritz in Singapore shortly after the incident. Carroll's version, as printed in a West Coast newspaper, was "pretty badly mutilated." It read, in part:

> An odd story comes by indirect routing from Batavia, on the Island of Java, about Chester Fritz...who is selling flour in the Orient for the Fisher Flouring Mills of Seattle. It relates how Fritz got himself into a British jail in the course of a very simple business transaction, and almost had to change the brand of the flour he was selling in order to get out.
>
> It was all because the big local mills turn out a special flour known as the "Big Gun" brand. Fritz, who had already found that the German twang to his name was not unduly popular in some British colonies, landed a big order at Batavia and hastened to the cable office, where he wired, "Rush one thousand Big Guns to Batavia," and signed it "Fritz." The British authorities went straight up in the air over

this, and the Seattle salesman was under arrest before he had got two blocks away from the cable office. The message was so clearly warlike that he had to argue for two days before they would even let him offer any defense. Then he succeeded in finding a merchant with a few sacks of "Big Gun Flour" on hand, which were offered in evidence. Finally they let him send his cablegram, changing the term Big Guns to simply read "sacks of flour."

After almost a year of field experience behind him, Fritz began to promote his business and himself through various West Coast publications, including *The Washington Alumnus* of February 1916. An article entitled "A Trade Missionary" touted Fritz as a world traveler who had seen "more of the world in less time than has any other graduate of the University of Washington in years." The article also commended Fritz's business acumen, praising him for successfully having applied the "scientific method" to the selling of flour. It ended with an admixture of travel and adventure tales derived from Fritz's own letters to Malcolm Douglas, the author of the piece.

Flour and Grain, a Seattle trade journal, continued in March where the *Washington Alumnus* story left off, noting that the first story had caused a stampede among university men who desired to emulate Fritz's success. They flocked to the flour mills seeking employment that promised "rapid promotion toward the Orient." As for Fritz himself, according to the author, the name may "sound Dutch," but he was "born in Dakota."

Fritz forwarded his own effort to the *Flour and Grain Critic*, where it appeared in August 1916. In "Hong Kong, the Threshold of South China," Fritz provided a concise historical understanding of the city's importance in international commerce, followed by a description of the flour trade at that time with special reference to Southeast Asia:

> Each year the Chinese consume more and more flour, which is known in the Cantonese dialect as "min fan." One of the most popular uses to which flour is put, is the making of "min," a kind of noodles and vermicelli and also the making of steamcakes and roastcakes. Small pastries, biscuits and bread are also made.
>
> Since the advent of American flour in the Orient, some forty years ago, Hong Kong established itself as the flour entrepot. California was the pioneer in exporting to China, and later Oregon and Washington became the leading exporters. In

1892 Oregon and Washington supplied about 20 per cent and today these same two states supply 99 per cent of the American flour to the Orient. However, we must not overlook the fact that there are several active competitors for this tremendous trade. Flour milled in Japan, Manchuria, Shanghai, Canada and Australia have, at various times, been strong factors in the subsidiary markets, which Hong Kong serves. The writer has even seen quantities of Indian flour, milled in Bombay and Calcutta, offered in the markets of the Straits Settlements, which Australian and American flour ordinarily control.

American millers operate in the Orient by selling to the few large flour merchants of Hong Kong, who act as entrepot merchants. The burden of market fluctuations involved from the time of the purchase of the flour until its arrival and subsequent sale and also the fluctuations of exchange must be carried by the Hong Kong merchants. They in turn sell and distribute through their own commercial connections with their countrymen in the markets of the interior, along the China Coast and in Indo-China, Siam, Straits Settlements, Federated Malay States, Sumatra, Java, Celebes and the Moluccas. For in all the various markets of the colonies and countries of Eastern Asia, the Chinese are the distributors, both wholesale and retail, and no native can compete with this shrewd man of commerce.

It is through such methods of handling that a sack of American flour eventually reaches the consumer. From this it must be apparent at once how difficult it has become for new brands to force an entry in the flour markets of the Orient. The Hong Kong dealers, naturally, will only buy those brands which are readily sold and for which they are having repeat orders from the out-lying ports. No dealer will take the chance of stocking an unknown brand or "chop." The brands which receive the bulk of the Hong Kong support are those which have been on the market for many years, early suiting the needs and maintaining their quality. The Chinese flour importer in Hong Kong has but little opportunity of making new brands popular in the subsidiary markets, and the local Hong Kong market is of very little importance.

Assume that a Chinese merchant in an out-port wishes a quantity of flour. He communicates his order to his agent or representative in Hong Kong, who in turn notifies a Chinese flour broker. The broker goes out upon the market calling upon the various flour merchants, until he has secured satisfactory prices and terms. The broker receiving a brokerage of from a half to one cent per sack; the Hong Kong representative or correspondent of the out-port merchant attending to the shipping arrangements.

Chinese business, with its various ramifications, is indeed a complicated process and seems to be only understood by the Oriental mind. It is often astonishing to realize the annual turnover of the large flour hongs of Hong Kong.

World events, not local ones, ruined the flour trade in China. General F. S. Heintzleman, reporting from an American consulate in Manchuria in June 1915, observed that World War I had "diverted the flour trade of the United States...to Europe to fill the ever-increasing demands there." Thomas Sammons, at the Shanghai consulate, stated in September 1916 that "Shanghai flour continues to replace foreign imports," even at a premium of $2 in gold per barrel. F. D. Chesshire in Canton seconded the report, noting in addition that too many American agents depended on consular officers to distribute their trade catalogues.

If, however, the future of the flour trade turned bleak, the future for precious metals practically glittered. Sammons observed from Shanghai early in 1917 that speculators "in Chinese gold bars and telegraphic transfers were much in evidence throughout the year." Since silver, China's ancient medium, was being used to cover gold purchases, Sammons doubted that the amount of the gray metal "left in China must...barely suffice for trade requirements," so that the country would inevitably again become a competitor in the world's silver markets. Scarcities continued throughout the year, with silver prices attaining values not known for the previous twenty years.

Meantime, when the United States government decided to prohibit flour sales to China because of wartime demands elsewhere, Chester Fritz, so recently congratulated for his salesmanship, suddenly discovered that "I was virtually out of a job." The *Flour and Grain Critic* of February 1917 announced that Fritz had undertaken a four-month tour of the interior of China. In a disapproving tone, the journal suggested that the disagreeable odors of the "heathen Chinese" lifestyle likely would cancel whatever "educational" benefits might result and concluded that such a trip would contribute nothing to the promotion of American business interests. China itself could be no more interesting than "any other dead thing"; besides, American "problems are water not land" so far as China was concerned.

It might appear that Fritz in 1917 was near to duplicating his experiences of 1910. After all, unemployment is the same whether in Seattle or Hong Kong. The two situations, however, were notably different because much had changed in the interim. Fritz had earned a college education, acquired the foundations of a trade, traveled to a number of unusual places, and won a measure of acceptance in a foreign culture. Moreover, he had taken a liking to living in the Far East and believed other opportunities lay before him. Fritz had no intention of retracing his steps eastward. In fact, this unexpected turn of affairs might prove a blessing in disguise—an opportunity to realize yet another dream.

III

Chester Fritz:
A Modern Marco Polo

Marco Polo, a Venetian, visited China in 1275 and stayed for seventeen years. Chester Fritz, a North Dakotan, visited China in 1915 and stayed for thirty-six years. Marco Polo's life and career in China is well known. Chester Fritz's life and career in China is unknown. Marco Polo in 1295 wrote a classic account of his experiences in China, *Travels of Marco Polo*. Chester Fritz wrote an unpublished account of his 1917 trip to western China.* Although Marco Polo and Chester Fritz lived over 600 years apart in time, their careers share many similarities. Both men traveled in and wrote about China. Both men demonstrated courage and zest for adventure. Both men filled their rice bowls in China. In many ways, Chester Fritz was a modern-day Marco Polo.

*The original journal consists of a penciled log written on seven small tape-bound notebooks. Their provenance is quite simple. The notebooks remained in his personal possession until the completion of the Chester Fritz Library at the University of North Dakota in the fall of 1961. Between 1961 and 1964, his aunt, Kathrine Macdonald Tiffany, collected the original notebooks and, according to her nephew, "edited them and

Ever Westward to the Far East: THE STORY OF CHESTER FRITZ

The six-month journey of Chester Fritz began on February 14 and ended on August 7, 1917. It started and ended in Hong Kong. In between Fritz traveled over 7,500 miles on a journey that lasted 174 days. He traveled by ocean steamer, river raft, pack horses, sedan chair, and foot. The trip cost approximately $1,200 American, financed almost entirely from Fritz's savings from his two previous years of employment in China.

The desire to see the interior of China began soon after Chester Fritz arrived in Hong Kong in 1915.

polished them up." Mrs. Tiffany effected grammatical changes, altered the written quality of the account, compiled a map, inserted an introductory statement, and prepared a typewritten copy of her efforts. Several copies of her version were produced under the appropriate title of "Chester Fritz's Six Month Diary Through Inland China to Tibet" and distributed to personal friends. Both the original notebooks and available copies of Mrs. Tiffany's edited rendition are now preserved in the Orin G. Libby Manuscript Collection in the Chester Fritz Library.

The addition of an introduction remains the most doubtful feature of Mrs. Tiffany's work. Although Fritz intended the diary to be entirely personal, merely to satisfy the divers needs of a 25-year-old traveler, his aunt supplied a second, deliberate purpose: "After his fact-finding excursion he was also instrumental in having shipped from China to the United States quantities of tungsten, then much needed in the production of high-speed steel."

The statement is erroneous on two counts. Chester Fritz had not been engaged in a "fact-finding excursion," especially in the sense of a premeditated assignment; and neither did he discover nor ship tungsten to the United States as a result of time spent in the interior of western China. It is true that upon completing the trip, Fritz investigated the area north of Canton, where he verified the presence of tungsten ore and shortly became involved in the first shipment of the metal to the United States. Yet none of this stemmed from his six-month journey and, indeed, cannot rightly be considered as having been any part of it. Fritz himself provided the clarifying explanation during oral interviews conducted in 1979:

> She wrote in the introduction [that] she was afraid people would say—well, Chester Fritz was in China getting away from the war. I planned the trip long before the war. I started the trip and was en route two months before America entered the war. So the introduction to the diary is not correct. She was trying to save me from being criticized. I did not go on that trip to look for tungsten.

Moreover, the entry dated August 7, 1917, is of Kathrine Tiffany's composition and not to be found in the original notebooks:

> In Hong Kong again. The long journey completed, three ambitions achieved: really seeing those places; getting to know firsthand how those people live; and discovering new production fields of tungsten, now needed by the United States.

North Dakota Quarterly 49 (Spring 1981), 7-8.

The Hong Kong Club had a wonderful library particularly strong on books about China. And I occupied room number eight and the library was down on the floor below. I spent many evenings sitting under a wooden fan in comfortable leather chairs reading their books on China. Fantastic! The British are great readers you know.

In particular, I was impressed by a book written by Edwin J. Dingle entitled *Across China on Foot*. The Dingle book had a great effect on me and I decided definitely when the time came or it was possible, I would like to make a safari through western China, and reading that book is what started me on the trip.

Forty years later I heard a news story about Edwin J. Dingle, then, I think, a member of the British Parliament. It was during World War II and I said to myself, little does Mr. Dingle know how he influenced my life!

Across China on Foot: Life in the Interior and the Reform Movement (1911) by Edwin Dingle told the story of the author's trip across China from the Yangtse River to British Burma. Although Dingle used a 1,600-mile stretch of the Yangtse River to begin his journey, he completed the rest of the journey on foot. The purpose of the trip was personal adventure—to see China from the inside. He boasted: "So far as I know, I am the only traveler apart from members of the missionary community, who has ever resided far away in the interior of the Celestial Empire for so long a time." Dingle's assertion both fascinated and challenged Chester Fritz. He made up his mind that when the opportunity presented itself, he would make a similar journey. Edwin J. Dingle would not be the only foreign traveler to reside in western China.

The opportunity for such a journey came unexpectedly in 1917, after the United States government's prohibition of flour sales to China. In discussing his future with Charles Richardson, Fritz confided, "I am not interested in going back to Seattle to work in the mill. I want to stay in China." Although Richardson and Fritz discussed possible joint ventures in establishing an export business, no commitments were made. Finally, Fritz told Richardson he had decided to go to the interior of China."

Preparations for the trip began immediately. There was no reluctance to use all of his "slender savings"; it was a "chance of a lifetime." Fritz hoped to find a companion to make the journey with him. "I wanted

Ever Westward to the Far East: THE STORY OF CHESTER FRITZ

someone to go with me but no one was interested." As one American employee stated, "There was nobody as crazy as Chester Fritz to go on a trip with him like this." Although Fritz had started to learn Chinese, both northern Mandarin and Cantonese, he was not fluent in the language. Dingle had not been either. The Dingle book provided many other helpful suggestions. But two important differences should be noted. Fritz would end his journey on the Yangtse River rather than begin it there. Second, Fritz would not just walk; he would also ride in a four-man sedan chair: "It was very important, at least, I thought so, because it gives you a status. It shows you're a man of substance and means. You rarely ever see a four-man chair. So it's a bit of a sensation."

St. Valentine's Day 1917 marked the inauguration of Chester Fritz's six-month journey through inland China. With the hoisting of the anchor at noon in the port of Hong Kong, the trip proffered an auspicious beginning. Fritz had purchased supplies and all were loaded; the steamer, the *Sunkiang*, proved comfortable. In addition to Suen, Fritz's "Manchu boy" who served as a personal valet and translator, and the crew, a Mr. Tong was the only other passenger.

Traveling on the South China Sea, the *Sunkiang* passed through the Kiungchow Straits. On the third day the steamer stopped at the port of Pakhoi (Peihai). As early as this first port stop Fritz demonstrated his constant interest in both people and their means of making a living. He commented in his diary that a "Sampson woman and her little six-year-old boy rowed us to shore. She said she had bought him for $4; he was an Annamite; his father was a soldier serving in France." Fritz spent the day visiting various businesses and noting the large amounts of manganese ore piled on the shore awaiting shipment.

Steaming westward across the Gulf of Tonkin, the *Sunkiang* docked at the port of Haiphong. For Fritz, the city exuded a distinct French aura. In spite of the mobilization of a great many Frenchmen for World War I, the bureaucracy in Haiphong remained large and unwieldy. The French government demanded many concessions from its territorial subjects. Through identity passes, taxes were levied on each individual and also on each village. Heavy import duties were exacted from goods not of French origin. Even foreign flags were prohibited from flying on ships in the harbor on all but special holidays.

On February 21, Fritz traveled by rail to Hanoi where he arranged for his tour through Yunnan Province. The following morning on a meter-gauge track, the French railroad twisted through low-lying hills to the

Red River. Crossing the river, the train left behind French Indochina, crossed the southern border of China, and entered the province of Yunnan. The topography changed quickly from hills and valleys to canyons and gorges. As Fritz recalled later, "It had fifty-nine bridges on the second day through the mountains. My God, what a railway!" At Mongtsze-Pi-tche-chai, Fritz took a side trip on an overland route with a carrier-coolie and two chairs. He stopped at Mongtsze for a good meal at the Kalos Hotel, visited a French bank, and noted the mineral importance of the area: "Mongtsze is the great tin market and furnishes 90 percent of China's tin. The large caravans came in from Kochin, some eight hours distant."

Chester Fritz spent several days in Yunnan-fu, the capital city of Yunnan Province. There he stayed with Howard Page, a friend who helped him procure a "four-horse caravan for $40 Chinese (about $20) for the trip to Kweiyang and arranged with a chair hong for a four-bearer chair at $11 to Chu-China-Fu (five days)." Fritz also arranged with the foreign secretary for a soldier escort:

> When I crossed China, I was always accompanied by two armed soldiers. At the start of their escort you gave them your card and at the end of the journey they would bring the card back. And you were supposed to give them coppers, as I did. One happened to be a small boy about 15. He had no gun but in the back of his girdle was a brush cutter, a sickle-knife. I asked him, "What would you do if pirates or robbers came?" He looked surprised and said, "Well, I would run away." It was very good to know what your allies were like!

In Yunnan-fu, Fritz met many Chinese and a few foreign businessmen and officials. He also found time to visit a few of the firms dealing in Tung-Chwan copper and zinc and inspected an antimony firm. But he enjoyed most spending a day on horseback, visiting temples in the surrounding country; "among them were the Black Dragon, the Flower Temple and the Copper Temple."

Later a report reached Fritz that robbers had attacked a large caravan on the Kweiyang Road and escaped with many valuables—"Not exactly encouraging," reads the diary entry. But fortunately, the departure of the journey was delayed when the horses Fritz hired were still not unloaded from their previous trip. The postponement offered the small Fritz entourage an opportunity to travel with a large caravan of 45 horses, thus enhancing their protection from a possible attack by robbers.

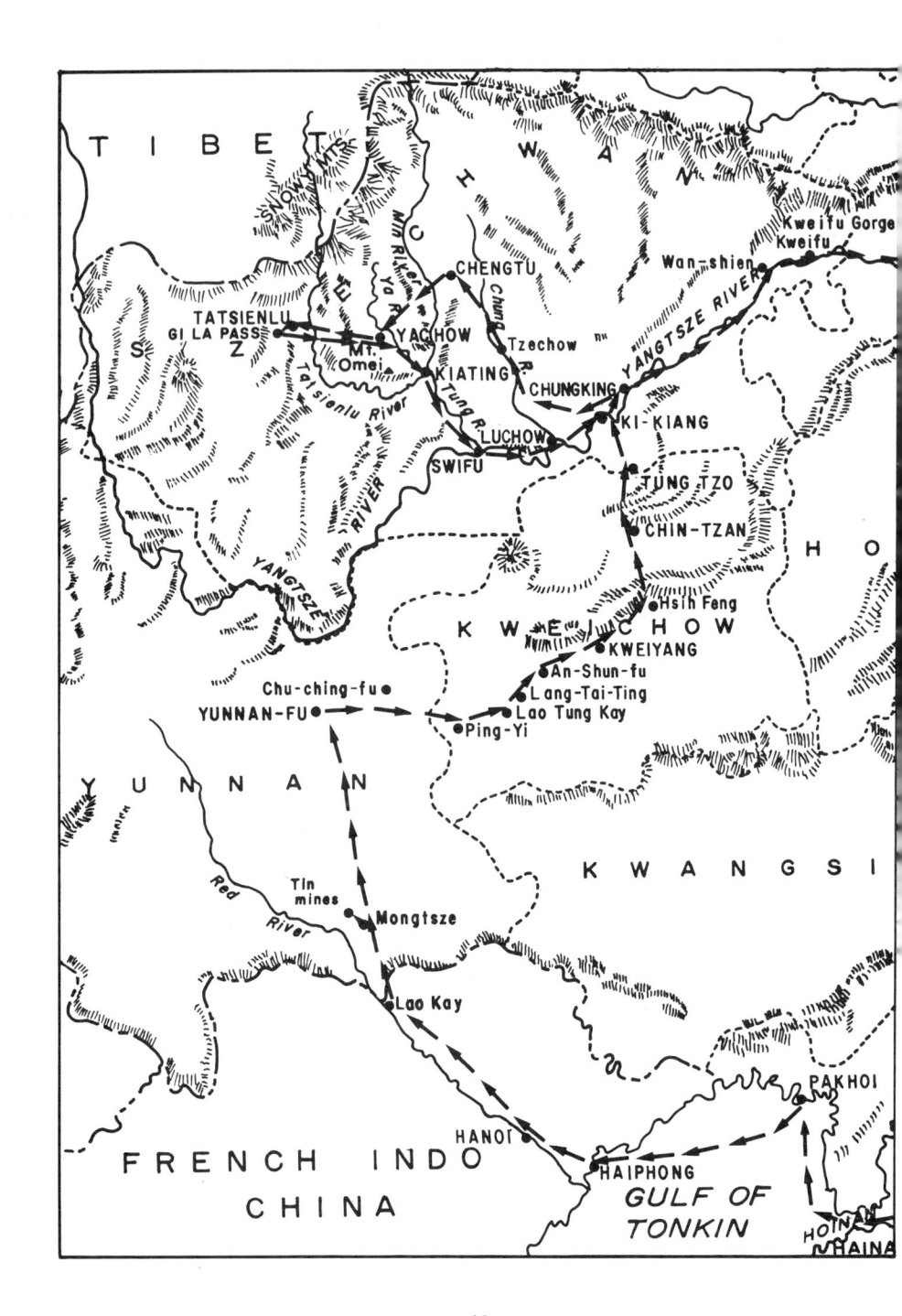

Ever Westward to the Far East: THE STORY OF CHESTER FRITZ

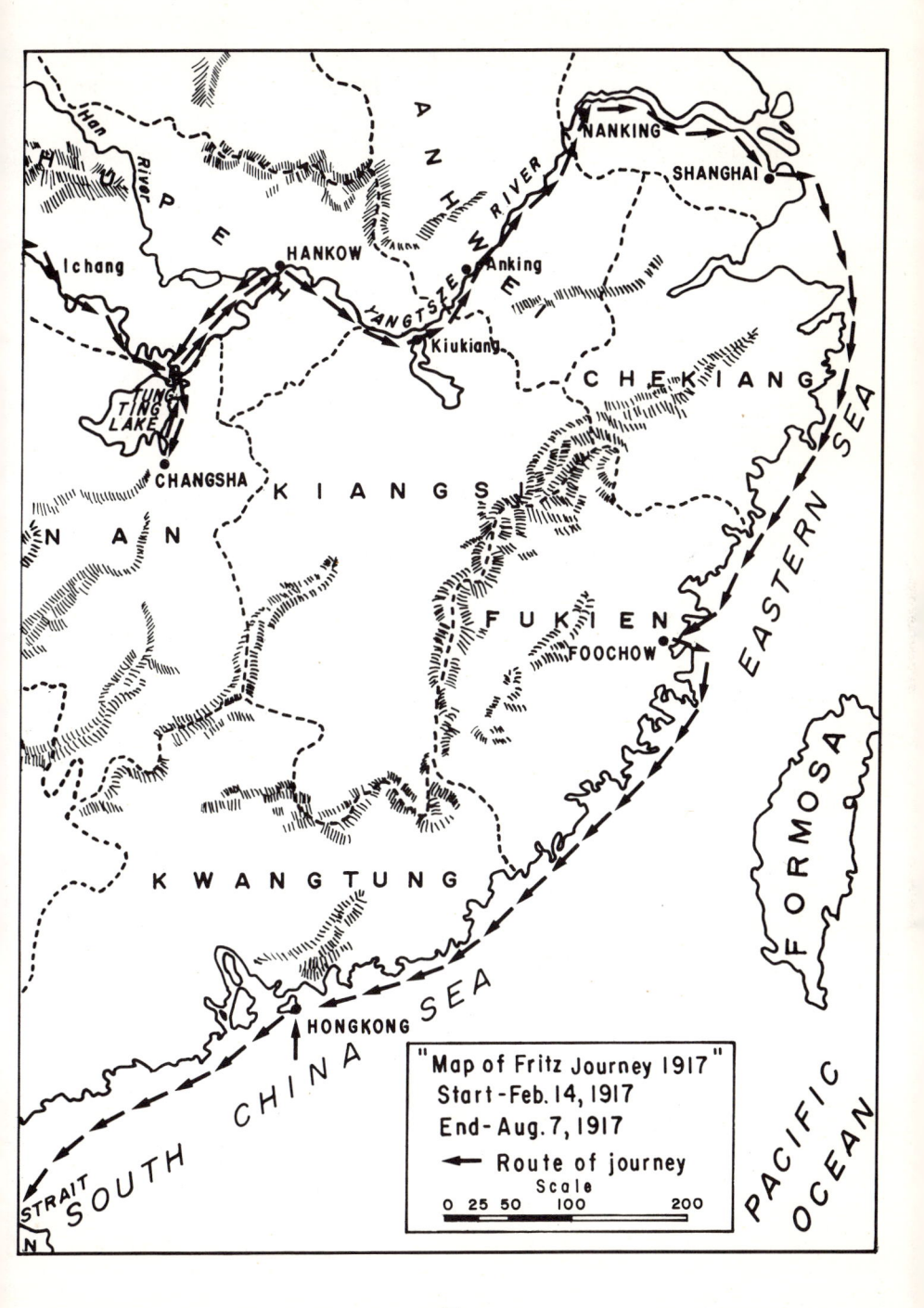

Chester Fritz: A Modern Marco Polo

"Map of Fritz Journey 1917"
Start - Feb. 14, 1917
End - Aug. 7, 1917
← Route of journey
Scale
0 25 50 100 200

Ever Westward to the Far East: THE STORY OF CHESTER FRITZ

On Thursday, March 8, Chester Fritz and his four chair coolies, two soldier escorts, two mafoos, four horses, and Suen departed with the large caravan from Yunnan-fu. It was a beautiful day. They met many Chinese coolies traveling in the opposite direction with baskets, eggs, chickens, charcoal, and short logs to sell in the provincial capital. Several minstrels and performing monkeys also were seen along the journey. The caravan traveled about 75 li or 25 miles per day. To ensure safe conduct through the surrounding territory, the escort soldiers would run ahead to present an introductory letter to the magistrate or governing official of each village.

Reminiscent of Dingle's commentary, Fritz recorded his impression of the people. "The number of blind people, idiots, and deformed people is appalling; and over half the people have goiter, and badly." Progressing further into Yunnan Province, the situation worsened. "The villages look more forlorn than those of previous days. Filth and squalor everywhere. One old man had two strings tied around his waist and chest to keep the wind from blowing the tatters too much." Tea rest houses, serving rice cakes and tea, were the usual resting place for the chair bearers. There, grass sandals could be bought for the coolies for 1 or 2 cents per pair. In the evening Fritz and his attendants usually tried to stop at an inn for the night. The layout of inns varied but usually contained separate courtyards; "a person has to pass through the first two to get to the third....Each inn has its loud-barking dogs, its grunting and squealing pigs, and the poor chickens find it a task to pick up a living." Another regular comment by Fritz centered on inn odors and the best place to escape them. "I find I prefer the top room in front, for it is more free from prying eyes and noises of the court and adjacent stoves, and also from the smells which are legion!"

Early arrival at an inn was a virtual necessity to find a room. Arriving late on one occasion, Fritz and his company lodged in the entrance hall. All spent a restless night as people constantly walked through while yelping dogs, pigs, and horses added to the general melee. In some locations Fritz acquired good accommodations, while of others, he could only write, "the last word in filth and lack of comfort." Accommodations were sometimes nonexistent; on one occasion Fritz spent the night in a "filthy hunt, very crowded quarters—and, oh, the smells!"

When possible, Fritz stopped frequently at the various China Inland Mission stations scattered throughout western China. The missionaries were often the only foreign people he saw between days of difficult travel. He enjoyed their company and listened to their travel advice. They were often his sole source of information of news outside China. The chance to enjoy "home-cooked" meals, be invited to tiffin, and converse in English made the China Inland Missions a welcome sight.

In the prefectural city of Chu Ching-fu, Fritz called at the Fatien Bank for cash, $50 in Yunnan half-dollars. Recalling the procedure, Fritz explained:

> The Chinese postal office was quite well organized under very difficult transport circumstances. I got the silver dollars from them, mostly in half dollars, and those I carried in a canvas belt around my waist. And with the silver dollars, I periodically bought what the Chinese call cash. It's a round brass coin with a square hole in the center. And the rate was generally around 1,800 cash to one silver dollar, although the exact rate varied in every town as China had no fixed rate. I often had drafts from Shanghai; the big merchants or officials liked to have them because they had to make remittances to Shanghai to buy imports. You see, there was no proper bank system in rural China.

In Chu Ching-fu, the travelers again were delayed. On the morning designated to renew the journey to Peh Shui, Fritz's mafoos failed to show up. The chair coolies relayed the message that the mafoos had taken "a French leave" because Chu Ching-fu was their native district. At this unexpected delay, Fritz toured the city and chronicled his experiences. He noted that the magistrate forbade women to visit the temple of the Goddess of Mercy, yet observed that many women, in their best garb, faithfully burned joss sticks to the goddess in hope of bearing a male child. Near the city wall Fritz observed, "I saw a small, newly born baby, recently thrown there; this seems to be a common practice." In another entry Fritz noted another interesting Chinese scene:

> A visiting Chinese and his small son called on the China Inland Mission and were much frightened by the "foreign dog" that ran out barking to greet them. The child was badly scared; so the father started patting the ground and then the child's head to bid the spirit return again to the son.

The mafoos returned the following morning. The weather turned cool under a driving mist and raw wind when the Fritz party pushed its way across the Chunching plains and began the ascent of the mountains. Villages were scarce and the path steep and treacherous. By midday,

Ever Westward to the Far East: THE STORY OF CHESTER FRITZ

March 16, the travelers crossed the border between Yunnan and Kweichow provinces. At the border, Fritz photographed the four carved lions on high bases, two facing Yunnan and two facing Kweichow.

Based on earlier readings, Kweichow Province aptly was referred to as "the Switzerland of China." The mountains and valleys gave a wilder appearance, with the trail continually ascending and descending. It "is a labyrinth of hills and valleys—hundreds of small hills, an ocean of them, of every shape, but most are shaped either like a pyramid or a sugar loaf." The constant ascent was exhausting for the coolies, and in retrospect Fritz regarded this stage of the journey as one of the most difficult. It was also one of the most rewarding; Fritz was surrounded by mountains.

The aboriginal Miaotze people intrigued Fritz above all others he saw on the trip. They originally had inhabited the Kweichow Province, farming the valleys and bottoms since Biblical days. In time, however, the Chinese usurped the most arable land and pushed the Miao further and further up the mountain slopes. Their lives by 1917 were characterized as being "a poor beggarly existence":

> The Miao's crude house usually has three rooms: one for the farm implements (such as they are, perhaps including a fanning mill); one for the cattle, pigs, and chickens; and one for the family. This room is likely to have a shelf, a bench, a few straw mats and rags in a corner for a bed, and in the middle of the room a hole in the ground for the fire and for a two-stone grinder. Many Miao's are too poor to eat rice, so eat a boiled roughly ground corn.

Fritz described the Miaos as "a cross between a Japanese and Chinese" and took many photographs of them. He also thought they were much cleaner than the Chinese. The women's feet were unbound, and they walked in a free-swinging stride. While the Miao men looked more like Chinese in their dress, the women wore "skirts with ample folds and a sort of pleated apron both fore and aft with puttees wrapped around their ankles. They wear silver ear rings, large in circumference, in each ear."

In more detail than anywhere else in his diary, Fritz continued his elaboration of Miao culture:

> The Miao love litigation, and it is encouraged by the yamen (public officials) underlings. Their moral level is below that of the Chinese—heavy drinkers. Among the ta-hua Miaos

around Weining there are no decent women, some being married to several men at the same time. They have no written language. They have no idols, nor temples, nor priests, and worship no gods. They practice certain rites with reference to the dead and to demons; this is to appease the evil spirits. They have music festivals twice a year to insure a good harvest. Their musical instruments of bamboo have reeds from 3 to 15 feet long; the sounds are monotonous. Their dancing is like taking steps or pacing; it is a sober activity; neither men or women smile while dancing. The predicted buffalo fights usually do not materialize. They have soothsayers and sorcerers. Miao young people, unlike the Chinese, do their courting quite openly. When there is a wedding feast it is held at the bridegroom's home; and the guests bring presents. Legends of the tribe are chanted. Sometimes one singer or chanter will lead in the story part, and the others will come in the chorus. Sometimes guests will sing the virtue of their host, praising the kindly way in which he received them and the rich food provided for their enjoyment. He replies belittling himself and grieving over the contemptible style in which the guests have been treated. The bride returns to her parents' home—another festive occasion—where she remains until she is sent for by her husband's family.

The Miao courtship itself begins in a special area designated as the courting yard. The Miao man looking for a wife...

...dons his best sport suit and a parasol and goes to a village and to its courting yard and begins to give a low-toned, long whistle. After some time the young female eligibles appear in their best dresses; and if he fancies one of them he makes friendly advances, and the two lovers then chant each other's praises back and forth in turn. Later he sends his friends to her home to inquire what presents the girl's father would like to have or would require, in pigs, casks of wine, bags of rice, and similar commodities. Then follows a big feast and she moves to his village. After the first son is born, she returns to her village, for the son is to reside there. In the event that a village has two courting grounds, a girl who exchanges her field or lot [goes to a courting yard to which she has not been assigned] is liable to a severe beating.

Few white men, however, traveled the Chinese interior, with the notable exception of missionaries. On several occasions, Fritz was automatically assumed to be a new pastor. Fritz experienced irritations similar to those Dingle had experienced a few years previously: "The curiosity of the crowds is annoying and discomforting. One finds no privacy. Every gesture, every moment is followed with marked attention." At the same time, Fritz was judiciously fair about this daily experience as he recalled the 1917 trip:

> It's understandable. China lived in isolation for centuries and they had no contact with foreigners until a few traders came to the treaty ports. So they were intensely curious to see a foreigner in central China which was unheard of. They saw only an occasional itinerant missionary and those missionaries wore Chinese clothing.

In the city of Lang-Tai ting, an auctioneer was selling baskets of coal, and Fritz's appearance caused the crowd to lose interest in the auction and stare at the "white man." He noted, "I moved on, and it must have been a relief to the auctioneer." Every evening, when they arrived at an inn, crowds of men and children would gather to watch Fritz eat. In one instance, Fritz's enthusiasm to take photographs of a Chinese Punch and Judy show "attracted a bigger crowd than the show."

As the journey continued, the paucity of white men in China also contributed to another phenomenon: camaraderie among the foreigners. Chester Fritz made every effort to visit the missionaries and the few white businessmen on his journey. They in turn invited him to dine, or for lunch. Often they relayed messages and in all cases tried to advise Fritz or help him arrange the next segment of his sojourn. During one stage, Fritz made the comment, "(Mr. A.) Hayman accompanied me some 5 li outside the city wall—really regretted saying goodbye to him—I was the first Caucasian he had seen in some nine weeks." Near Kweiyang it was reported that except for missionaries only one foreigner per year passed through the area.

Chinese market days were loud and raucous as people weighed goods and haggled over their value. "Pei pangs" (outdoor memorials to the dead) and beggars abounded. Fritz claimed that begging in China was "a profession like any other calling." Market day demanded a full retinue of beggars stopping at each shop. And the Chinese traders fascinated Fritz, with each trader carrying his Chinese scale in a wooden case thrust through his girdle like a sword; and thus goes forth to haggle and perhaps buy. It seems that to haggle and to argue over a price is one of the joys and sports of the Asiatic, and especially the Chinese. They also quarrel over the accuracy of each other's scales and also over the quality of the silver chunks.

The walls of Kweiyang, the capital of Kweichow Province, rose between the mountains and contained eight million inhabitants. Far inland and with no river transportation, foreign visitors were few. Soldiers halted Fritz at the city gates and issued him identification necessary to enter the city. The Fritz party found an inn situated on the "shoe and hat street," but moved the next day because of rats. He toured the local pei pangs and temples. Fritz also purchased several local Miao silver pieces and took photographs of the city.

The next morning, March 31, Mr. Wang, the magistrate of Kweiyang, called on Fritz. They ate a Chinese lunch. Mr. Wang "boasted that he had never taken a bath, yet handed me a cookie!" Fritz afterward took photographs of Mr. Wang and had someone else take a picture of the two of them together. On the way out Mr. Wang accompanied Fritz to the farthest door, "a high honor"; but later in the day when the two men met on the street, "We passed Mr. Wang on the street but could not look at him or recognize him; for if we did, it would have been necessary for him to stop and get out of his chair and bow and speak. So in the summertime, they shield their faces behind their fans, to avoid having to get out of their chairs."

Another interesting experience in Kweiyang involved a visit to a local Chinese barber:

> I went into a Chinese barbershop to have my hair cut and I had a barbershop experience that I'll never forget. After cutting my hair, he cleaned my ears, having some eleven different knives, scrapers, tweezers, hooks, and brushes. He would have shaved the inside of my nose, the top of my eyelids and my forehead, had I not headed him off. The most novel and startling of all was his massaging of the body; it was more like being man handled! He swung my arms vigorously, jerked my body, and pummeled my back. I'll always remember that Kweiyang barber; he also had the distinction of attending the provincial governor. I paid him 20 cents for all he did for me, that being twice the fee charged at

the other shops.

On April 3, with a gift of the New Testament from a member of the China Inland Mission, Chester Fritz set out on the next stage of his journey. He still retained one of the original Yunnan-fu coolies and had added another in Chu-shing. Two new coolies hired in Kweiyang completed the four-man sedan crew. Suen mounted and, very proud of his position, rode beside his employer. Pack horses and soldiers finished the party.

Larger mountains greeted the party as they moved north through Kweichow Province. "These mountains are a different type from those in western Kweichou being of greater mass and not so many small ones." Fritz also noted in this region that many of the mountains had "stone walls built on the peak." These walls formed a fortress into which villagers fled from robbers and "marauding bands." The area contained salt mines, and the travelers passed many coolies carrying salt.

In Sung Kan, a city near the border between Kweichow and Szechwan provinces, a Chinese official approached Fritz. He asked the young American to carry his valuables to Chungking because he felt that robbers would be less likely to attack a foreigner. Szechwan Province was notorious for its "robber zone." Fritz agreed to the request to transport the mandarin's goods, but the official also traveled very close to the Fritz party.

On the morning of April 13, the Fritz entourage crossed the border into Szechwan Province, where the Chinese seemed better dressed and more prosperous. The road was good, but the weather was drizzly and foggy. On the 18th, the party ferried across the Yangtse River, landing in Chungking. The stop was midway on Chester Fritz's journey.

The next day in Chungking, Fritz learned for the first time that the United States had entered World War I. He spent a considerable portion of his time in Chungking observing the local businesses and found Szechwan Province blessed with many rivers which were utilized for commerce. Fritz described some of the exports:

> Chinese medicines largely of the Chinese materia medica. They ran all the way from tigers' bones to bat dung, and similar substances....But the main exports are hides, casings, feathers, bristles, wax, and vegetable tallow. Musk and wool from Tibet are also large items.

Vegetable tallow, a product achieved by steaming and sieving the seeds of a large tree, was marketed in both Europe and America. The sieving process produced three by-products: fat ("Pi-yu"); oil ("Ting-yu"); and seeds. All three were used in making candles and soap. Another product in Chungking was "gall-nuts." One type was used for tanning and dying; "Chi pei tzu" was used in Chinese medicine. Fritz also noted:

> The Chinese also have soap-trees which yield a pod-like fruit and when this is soaked, it gives a good lather. A varnish product is made from the fruit of the persimmon tree. The Chinese pound the pulp and decompose it in water, and after 30 days the pulp is removed and a nearly colorless varnish is the result. This is used largely for domestic trade, in gluing and water-proofing native umbrellas.

After taking ill and feeling homesick for his family in Hong Kong, Suen left Chester Fritz in Chungking and prepared to go home. Fortunately, with the aid of a foreigner, Fritz procured a new English-speaking boy and the change proved advantageous:

> The way the "boy" (Chang) arranged everything was marvelous! I never before on this trip experienced such speed and dispatch. This is a great blessing to have a "boy" who is resourceful and experienced and possessing executive ability. I do not have to look after every little detail and so many things for myself that I formerly did.

The party set forth en route to Chengtu, the next major stop on the trip. The flagstone roads were in "much better condition than the roads of Kweichow." On this segment, Fritz received information that he would need to have six escort soldiers since there were many robber bands in the area. The inns were in a better state of repair. Grazing cattle and productive fields lined the road. Chicken and other food stores were easier to procure and of a higher quality. And in the villages and towns along the way, people appeared well dressed and prosperous.

Along the road the vegetation was prolific. Tung oil, lacquer, wood-oil, varnish, and paper-making products all originated from the lush landscape. Near Tzu-lin-Ching great salt wells dotted the horizon. In the area around Pi Hsien and Wen-Chiang Hsien huge quantities of hemp were grown for cordage, rope, and cheap fabric. Tobacco and sugar production also played an important economic part in the area. Fritz explained the processing of each of these products in his diary and took great interest in the Chinese methods of extraction. He also recorded his estimate of the probable profit of each product.

Szechwan Province suffered not only from maurading robber bands but also from a civil war. Kweichou provincial soldiers numbering "about 3,000," with the aid of additional Yunnanese troops, controlled the civil and military governor of Szechwan. The Szechwan military attempted to protect their province and gathered forces "to oust the Kweichou," but feared the Yunnan troops would "return to assist the Kweichou faction." As Fritz indicated, "trouble may break out at any hour." After a tenuous peace was arranged, Yunnanese soldiers and their followers marched southward to their native province. For peace, however, the Szechwan people had paid dearly:

> In the afternoon we met many horses and coolies carrying weighty boxes of silver. The silver in taels 10 chunks. This money is being paid to the Yunnanese troops and officials by the Szechwan troops to leave the province peaceably. We met money box after money box.

Traveling northward the next morning, Yunnanese soldiers tried to commandeer his coolies into carrying their equipment. The coolies' hands had been bound, and only with difficulty was Chang able to free them.

During the next few days, Fritz reported regularly on the exodus of people in the war zone of Szechwan Province. "All day long we met straggling groups of soldiers in threes and fours; then came a long string double-file. They were a hard looking lot." Two days later, Fritz identified others retreating:

> On the road between the hours of 7:00 and 11:00, I counted over 90 chairs, mostly three-man chairs, with the great number of passengers being ladies and a few children, and sweethearts of the returning Yunnanese and military people.... There was also the usual long line of carrying coolies.

Fritz soon found out, however, that the returning soldiers carried not only their silver but compelled women to accompany them:

> This forenoon we met a young Chinese lady, sitting in a chair and wearing a white turban of mourning; she was weeping. Her story was that she had just buried her father, a man of means, and was in her chair resting at an inn, while en route home, when she was compelled by a Yunnanese officer to go with him; so she was now en route to Yunnan. I have been told that there are many cases of Yunnanese officers taking

young women and forcing them to go to Yunnan with the returning troops.

The next morning Fritz again met with another tragic family situation precipitated by the civil war:

> On the roadside we met a fairly well-dressed lady, weeping as I have never before seen a Chinese weep. Her story ran thus: She and her daughter lived a few days north of Chengtu; a Yunnanese soldier or petty officer, having promised to marry her 15 year old daughter, was taking the latter and her mother in chairs with him to Yunnan; but here he had cruelly told the mother that he did not want her and had shoved her out on the roadside, alone and friendless, and with little money. The loss of her daughter and her own plight were extremely hard to bear. The daughter was powerless and had to take this rude separation.

Proceeding en route to Chengtu, the travelers passed through the magnificent Chengtu plains, a densely populated area about 85 miles long and 60 miles wide. The farmers had made this area "fertile and productive with irrigation." The local crops consisted of groves of bamboo and fields of barley and mustard. The road was excellent with much traffic.

Chester Fritz celebrated his arrival in the city of Chengtu with a bath and pedicure at the local bath house. He spent time visiting the many missions, including the China Inland Mission, the Canadian Methodist Mission, and the American Methodist Mission. The Union University of West China, sponsored by the various foreign missions, impressed Fritz with its faculty, curriculum, and lovely campus. Here Fritz shopped for Tibetan items, his choice purchase being a unique "brass Buddha for $5.00—the best I have yet seen." He also purchased curios, crepe ties, Chengtu scarves, a large drapery embroidery, four strings of beads, and a charm box.

Fritz planned to leave the city of Chengtu on the morning of May 16 but again some of his coolies failed to arrive. In desperation, he hired city coolies at $10 cash per man for the difficult journey ahead. The road out of Chengtu was busy with travelers. Rumors of strife, rebellion, and armed bands confronted the group at each stop. Indeed, the British consul general, upon hearing of the intended journey to Tachienlu, had warned Fritz that he would "never get through." Making good time, however, the group ended its journey through the Chengtu plains on

May 18 and began a slow ascent through rolling hills. By the next day the terrain became quite mountainous and late in the afternoon the tired travelers arrived at the city of Yachou.

In Yachou, Fritz stayed with Mr. and Mrs. Bailey of the American Baptist Mission. Here, too, he met Dr. Parry of the China Inland Mission, who would accompany him for the rest of the journey to Tachienlu. Dr. Parry was a veteran of 33 years of missionary work in China. In preparation for the next stage of the journey, Fritz paid the two coolies he had hired in Chengtu and arranged to hire two replacements. With more mountains ahead, Fritz left many of his newly acquired purchases at the mission to be picked up on his return.

The area around Yachou was most noted for its great tea production. The best tea was consumed locally; the twigs and sweepings were sent to Tibet. After processing, the tea was pressed into bricks weighing about six pounds each. Four bricks were then bound together to form a "pao." With the eye of a potential exporter, Fritz noted the transportation process of the tea once it became a pao.

> This weighs about 25 pounds and measures about four feet long. Sometimes a small packet is inserted in the end of the "pao" as a cumshaw to the re-packers and muleteers of Tachienlu. These paos are carried on the backs of coolies, the average load being eight "paos." Loads of twelve and thirteen pao are common; and once I saw a coolie carrying sixteen, weighing 400 pounds.

The road out of Yachou was very wide with deep gorges to either side. The mountains, however, were smaller than those in Kweichou but better covered by trees. Indeed, the farmers had a difficult time growing enough to live on.

The continuous ascent and descent proved hard on the coolies. During this stage of the journey, Fritz experienced more difficulty with them. They frequently complained about the weight of their loads and tired quickly, although their loads were lighter than the amount they had contracted for. When the weather drizzled, the coolies objected strenuously to continuing. Fritz attributed their complaints and dissatisfaction to opium: "Four are opium smokers. This accounts for the poor service they are giving."

At this point, the travelers passed long lines of coolies, each accompanied with a relief coolie. With much inquisitiveness, Fritz learned of their unusual cargo—gall's eggs.

The gall [egg] is about the size of a small cranberry. These eggs are packed in paper or in coarsely woven hemp sacks and carried in airy crates, with all possible speed to farmers nearing Keating and around Hungya. Hundreds of coolies are engaged in this transportation. The little larva hatch quickly, and if the weather is hot, the coolies frequently travel at night with lanterns. The 200 miles over exceedingly difficult roads is covered in six days! Aided by relays they make 30 to 40 miles a day.

These little "galls" are tied up in a big leaf and suspended to the branches of the tree. The larva quickly hatch and ascend to the leaves and stay there for 14 days—as the Chinese say "until their mouths and limbs are strong." During this time they are said to moult. The insect then descends and attaches himself to the underside of the branch and begins secreting wax. In the early stages, wind and rain are greatly feared; for they might injure the insects. The wax deposit looks like snow or hoar-frost.

This unique wax and its unusual mode of transportation greatly interested Fritz, and he asked more questions about its substance and use. He found that the wax was colorless, odorless, tasteless, and brittle. It melted at 180 degrees Fahrenheit (ordinary wax melts at 100 degrees Fahrenheit) and largely was used in coating candles. This unique wax also was sought by stationers to give a gloss to high-grade paper, by pharmacists for coating pills, by jewellers to give polish to jade, and by weavers to give luster to cloth. Approximately 100,000 pounds were produced annually in this region and shipped to all parts of China.

Climbing steadily, often through a driving rain, Fritz began to notice Tibetan architecture. The houses "have a hole about one-foot deep and three-feet square in which they build a fire and over which a large linked chain, hung from a cross beam, supports a heavy hot-water bottle. Around this fire the family squat on little benches arranged in a square." The houses, built of stone, usually were two or three stories with a flat roof. People lived on the second story while the main floor was reserved for livestock.

Fritz claimed that Tibetans rarely if ever washed themselves. With a dark tan and a life long accumulation of dirt, they appeared almost black. The men wore long, heavy skin coats throughout the year. The women wore much jewelry: large earrings, necklaces, and rings.

Ever Westward to the Far East: THE STORY OF CHESTER FRITZ

Buddhist influence demonstrated itself in the daily lives of the Tibetans:

> Prayer-wheels are many and are constantly sending out these six mystic syllables. "Om, mani padme hum" meaning "Hail Jewel (Buddha) in the lotus. Amen." They believe a constant repetition, a piling up of great quantities of these salutations, insures them of a certain and safe arrival into a paradise. Each Tibetan has his prayer-wheel, which he is constantly turning, and he has his rosary of 108 beads and the three strings of counters. Fluttering prayer-flags and water-propelled prayer-wheels are everywhere, sending up their messages to Buddha; thus great merit is being accumulated.

On May 31, the Fritz entourage traveled through a pass called Gi-La (in Tibetan) or Cheta (in Chinese). To the north was Mt. Jara, 25,584 feet high ("Some Mountain!"). Below, to the other side, stretched a "high-table land" with fine grasslands for the yak caravans. Fritz was enthralled by the scenic view: "The picture made by these great mountains, Himalayan in character, with their snow crests, against a delightful clear blue sky was indeed marvelous! Its like I shall not see again!"

The following day the party arrived in Tachienlu, a city Fritz called the "Gateway to Tibet." The city, favorably positioned on the great highway between Peking and Lhasa, was well established both economically and commercially. Especially intriguing to Fritz was the cosmopolitan collection of Asiatic people gathered in the city: "Tibetan muleteers, lamas, Tibetan traders, Chinese, and Tibetan-Chinese half-castes—all this variety of people."

Fritz made a very advantageous acquaintance in Tachiénlu. He sent his calling card to the king of Chiala to see if he would receive him. Later the same afternoon, the king invited Fritz for cakes and a Tibetan form of tea. The tea was thick and brown, with butter added and drunk down only to one-third cup. To the remaining tea was added a mixture of ground roasted barley flour and more butter. The combination was then kneaded into a dough and eaten. Fritz considered this dish (tsamba) "not half bad."

In an interview in 1979, Fritz explained the importance of the king of Chiala and the unusual presents he gave the king:

> I went to call on the king of Chiala, right on the border between China and Tibet. The Chinese had whittled down his power so he was largely a figurehead. And I sent word that I

Chester Fritz: A Modern Marco Polo

wanted to call. I sent my boy Chang with four presents and he carried them over, preceding me by a half-hour. Each present was wrapped in red Chinese paper. When I left Hong Kong, I had no idea of calling on royalty so I didn't have much in the way of presents but I did select four items: a two-pound tin of Jacobs cream crackers in a red wrapper, a scroll in bright colors, really an ad for Williams Pink Pills for Pale People; a thermometer which I had never used; and a tin of sardines.

In return, Fritz asked the king to watch for items which he wanted to purchase, and through his influence, Fritz was granted permission to visit a local lamasery.

The Dumb Festival was in progress at the time of Fritz's visit. According to religious tradition, on alternating days for sixteen days people must not speak to one another. Inside the lamasery in the front altar room toward the back, stood five statues of Buddha. People in the altar room used their left hands to count their rosary beads while mumbling "the mystic prayer." Fritz noted other impressions in his diary:

On the altar railing was a pyramid-shaped rack on which were placed many butter lamps. On the side walls were great Buddhistic paintings. Three red lamas were lighting the lamps of the room. On the floor along the walls were mats on which lamas were sitting, having with them their drums, bells, thunder bolts, prayer-wheels, and incense pots. The King's daughter and party were there, dressed in fancy, bright clothes. They threw rice at the Gods and then did several Kow tows; but between these, each person with the palms of his hands together touched his forehead, his mouth, and his chest, somewhat like crossing themselves.

During his stay, Fritz purchased four Tibetan pictures for $12, which he considered a very good buy. He traded the king one medicine chest for a "fine brass Tibetan teapot." Fritz purchased another fine teapot of Deye make, a prayer-wheel, four pairs of "massive silver Tibetan ear rings," and three finger rings. Fritz took pride in his purchases: "I came away with $55.00 worth of Tibetan curios—quite a swag—but I regret that I had insufficient silver to buy a rug. But that can come later by post."

On June 5, Fritz set out for his return to Yachou and by the following day had reached the east bank of the Tungho River. He continued to follow the river south and again the sheer beauty of the scene impressed the North Dakota traveler:

Ever Westward to the Far East: THE STORY OF CHESTER FRITZ

The road from Lu-ting chiao followed along the east bank of the Tungho, a steep bank from 500 to 700 feet above the river—thus according a beautiful panorama that changed with each bend of a swift moving river—upon whose current no boat can live. In breaks between the steep mountains bordering the river the beautiful Snow Mountains can be seen. The mountains average an altitude of from 18,000 to 20,000 feet—and are Himalayan in contour. Their snow-clad peaks, with the sun flashing upon them against the Tibetan sky, afford a picture that will live very long in my memory.

No one in western China was responsible for the roads or their condition. Often the roads were quickly built for military and commercial use and forgotten. Roads through rice fields narrowed each year as farmers needed the ground for larger crops.

Due to the physical state of the roads, Chester Fritz considered that "horseback or by sedan chair is the only means of traveling over these roads with any degree of comfort." Perhaps more important than the comfort of the chair was its status: "It is an objective and visible sign of respectability and its presence insures respect. In out-of-the-way places it is of greater service than a passport."

At Yachou, on the morning of June 13, the travelers started downriver through rapids on a raft 80 feet long and 10 feet wide and equipped with Chinese-style beds. Fritz immensely enjoyed the raft journey. Although dangerous, it was a welcome change after so many days of slow overland travel. By mid-morning of the following day, the party reached Kiating.

Fritz spent only one day in Kiating at the junction of the Min and the Ya rivers. In this city, noted for its high-grade silk, the young adventurer purchased some silk cloth to be made into shirts. He visited both the China Inland Mission and the American Baptist Mission. That evening he dined on excellent food in the presence of the Kiating gentry. Leaving the city of Kiating, Fritz set out on the first stage of his return trip to Chungking. During this segment, he traveled with a Mr. Reib, an employee of Standard Oil Company in Chengtu. Each of the men had a four-man chair and a "boy" in attendance. After ferrying across the Ya River, they stopped at Omei-hsien for the night. The town contained a great temple that boasted "a large Goddess of Mercy," a massive figure of 48 arms and eighteen pounds of gold leaf per arm. They were approached by the abbot but declined to make a suggested donation to the temple.

The next morning Fritz accomplished about 41 li, stopping at the foot of one of the five sacred mountains of China. Mt. Omei, the only sacred mountain in western China, rises to an altitude of 11,000 feet. The sacred mountain contained 3,000 small and 24 large Buddhas. But more important: "The tooth of Buddha is kept here—a large mastodon tooth, yellow with age." The old monk did "chin chin joss" before opening the box containing the tooth. The tooth measured 14 inches long. Fritz and Reib also toured the Elephants' Bath Temple, which was one-third of the way up Mt. Omei and contained the statue of an Indian saint astride "brass elephants with three tusks on each side."

The next day, the two Americans planned to follow the Buddhist pilgrimage to the summit of Mt. Omei with their coolies and chairs. The price, however, for the coolies was exorbitant so the men set out with only one attendant. They climbed "uneven stone stairs for about 30 li" to the temple where they "witnessed a Buddhistic ceremony," ate a light supper, and obtained acceptable quarters for the night.

The following day, they reached the "Golden Summit" or "China Ding" about noon. Here they saw three temples perched on the edge of a cliff with a drop of more than a mile straight down. There fences were built on the edge of the cliff, as occasionally pilgrims fell over the edge after being overcome by "Buddha's Glory (a peculiar natural phenomenon) which occurs when the sun casts over one's shadow a border with a halo upon the clouds far down below."

At Kiating, Fritz entered one of the most dangerous stages of his journey. He planned to take a boat to Chungking; but because the river was noted as "no-man's land" and was beset by fierce and dangerous robber bands, the local magistrate only would arrange for an escort to the point at Ma ling Cha where the robber zone began.

Fritz arranged for a boat, nine oarsmen, and four soldier escorts at a cost of $40. To his surprise, however, twelve more soldiers, a friend of one of Fritz's escorts, a coolie boy, the owner of the boat, and her two children, Dr. Parry, and a Mr. Cunningham also wished to join the trip. With the passenger list greatly enlarged and a free ride guaranteed, Fritz recorded the journey and its unexpected results:

> At 9:30 o'clock we started; we crossed the Min River towards the Great Buddha figure, where the water of the Min races around the steep cliff, making a right angle turn just as it is joined by the main current of the Ya and the Tun rivers. This made a tremendous current. We were swept toward the

cliff, and the stern of our boat missed the rock by inches. We thought the danger was past; but the next moment, the left side of our boat crashed into a great rock, forming part of the bank.

The crash threw one man and some cargo overboard. Even worse, the rock rent great leaks in the boat. The crew was forced to beach the boat and spent several hours repairing the damage. The uninvited guests, "having had too bad a scare," left the boat, now preferring to walk, and warned Fritz not to reboard because the pilot was incompetent.

Fritz nevertheless continued his journey by boat and tied up at the town of Chen-Wei Hsien. The local magistrate refused to grant Fritz any escort and advised him not to continue. Fritz decided, however, to go 60 li farther and seek an interview with the head man there, who he hoped would pass word to the robbers to allow safe passage for the boat. Unfortunately, the head man turned out to be incompetent and nothing was accomplished as planned. Fritz ordered the boat on without an escort only to be stopped by the first of many robber bands about 21 li downstream. Fritz met the leader of the band on shore and described the incident: "He was young, clean-cut, well dressed, and unarmed, carrying only a fan. He was polite and courteous, and said he was satisfied when he saw we were foreigners, and added: 'Please don't take it to heart!'"

The next group of robbers were poorly disciplined, lacked leadership, and looked dangerous, as Fritz recalled in great detail after meeting with them:

> Now, for instance, on the upper Yantsze pirates got hold of our boat. We had to pull in to the shore because they started shooting from the bank. I thought it was a signal from the wall city not to go any further, because this was Yo Bo, the start of the robber zone. The robber zone was a no-man's land between the Suchnan army and the Yunnan army. The river was in flood, in spate, as the British say, and we pulled in. It took awhile to get to the shore. And I saw these two robbers, young lads about 12 years old, holding a gun and bobbing up and down while they pointed it at the boat and me. When we landed nothing happened so we waited for a while. Finally a very well-dressed, slim, young Chinese appeared in silk. He bowed, I bowed and I invited him on the boat. We served him tea and we talked about everything except what was on our

minds. Finally, I said, "Don't you see that we are flying a foreign flag [American]. We're immune, we should not have any interference." He replied, "It doesn't mean anything. Anybody can make a foreign flag." He continued, "We are an old and honorable society (robbers). We don't rob foreigners." Then he said, "By the way, do you have any silver or guns?" I replied, "No, we are poor people." In principle, as I have told others, I did not carry a gun on this trip. There is nothing secret in China and if you have a gun that means you have something of value and that you are prepared to fight for it. What hope do you have if you start shooting? You are in a vast sea of Chinese far away from any protection. As we pulled away from the shore, one of my boatmen turned to another and said, "Those pirates are just like us. They have two eyes and two ears." So naive!

Seven times that afternoon robbers and Yunnanese soldiers fired at the boat. By evening the boat had safely arrived at Swifu. But the next day's journey seemed even worse; Fritz had been told that the river between Swifu and Luckow contained no fewer than twelve locations controlled by bands of robbers. The crew, evidencing its fear...

...sacrificed a rooster, cutting the throat and letting the blood drip upon the blessed end boards of the bow (the Dragon Head) which had been moistened with rice wine; sacrificial paper money was placed on the bow. Feathers were placed on the sticky blood, and chin-chin and Kowtows were performed. Two lighted candles were kept burning all evening. This was to please Wang Fa Yeh, the Chinese River Neptune. At the "Horse Door," the entrance during the day to our compartment, the young swimmer placed a few joss sticks and chin-chinned.

On the morning of June 27, the crew refused to continue further until they could travel with some Japanese boats that were awaiting a large military escort. Fritz chafed at the delay and by the following day became irritated: "Still inactivity—getting on my nerves—lying here in a small boat—waiting, waiting." On the third day he was furious: "Am fed up with this waiting." Finally on June 30, Fritz, his crew, twenty soldiers, and their commanding officer set out. His boat led the procession, flying the American and the Yunnanese soldiers' flag. The rest of the journey to Luchow was accomplished with only minor delays and difficulties.

Traveling north from Luchow, Fritz passed through areas rich in salt, fruit, and sugar. At (Chung) Pai Sha wine and linen were the major commodities. Vegetables and mandarin oranges also contributed to the prosperity of the area.

On July 4, Chester Fritz and Bruce Smith, manager of Standard Oil Company in Chungking, put on a boxing match.

> I had just arrived the night before in Chungking from this long trip coming out of Tibet. The Americans were having a picnic and they invited the British and other nationalists, chiefly missionaries. They planned to have a program and they asked me if I would box. Well, I said, "I'm not a boxer." But I was so happy to see foreigners again, I agreed to anything. So we boxed. Bruce Smith inquired of me, "How are we going to end this?" I said, "This is not my line of activity!" Undecided, we agreed to give the event a humorous turn and we turned on the referee, gave him a few punches and walked off. Later I sang "My Little Gray Home in the West." I'm not a singer but I agreed to anything!

Chester Fritz received his first mail in five months at Chungking. He enjoyed dining with the new American consul, visiting with members of the China Inland Mission, and chatting among the various foreigners posted in Chungking. Fritz was lonely for company, and the days spent in Chungking raised his spirits as he prepared to finish his long trip. He was tired but pleased that the most difficult part of the expedition was now over. Fritz arranged for the final segment of his journey down the Yangtze River aboard a Standard Oil freighter *Mei Tan* on its maiden voyage.

The freighter, built like a destroyer, had a 1,500-horsepower engine, larger than other boats on the Yangtze. On the first day out the boat averaged 22 knots sailing from Chungking to Ichang. "When we hit rapids, her deck would be awash. When we hit big whirlpools—which have tremendous force—the bow would swing, and then the boat would roll." On the evening of July 10, the *Mei Tan* tied up earlier, "three hours past the usual tying up place, having made record time."

The following day the freighter coursed through one of the most treacherous passages of the river, the Yangtze gorges:

> At day break, we were off with a bang, tearing down through that dark and gloomy Kweifu Gorge—whose walls rise straight up for hundreds of feet. Paths chiseled out of the

Chester Fritz: A Modern Marco Polo

solid rock walls are used by the trackers in groups; sometimes there are as many as from 150-200 trackers for one large junk. If the junk hits a heavy swirl and jerks back before the trackers can untie their lead rope, they are pulled off the high cliff and killed on the rocks, or drowned in the whirlpools. Each year the toll of deaths in the gorges runs into the thousands—some say about 20,000 annually. Frequently, the bamboo towing rope breaks; then away goes the helpless junk, caught in the whirlpools and perhaps thrown against the dangerous rocks—which are numerous. This is the great danger. It is said that about 20 percent of the junks are wrecked. But at this season, the flood current season of the year, the percent may be as high as 80 percent. We saw few junks going up river. Coming down river no small boats, for it is too dangerous for them. Small boats run the additional risk of being caught in the vortex of a large whirlpool and then being sucked under.

Gorge after gorge we raced through at what appeared mad speed. Captain Lyons said if we would ever hit a rock, at our speed, there would be an explosion and all would be over.

It was like a ride on a wild horse, racing over obstacles. It was an experience I shall not soon forget. The scenery, the gorges, the canyons, the rapids, the whirlpools—all terrible and yet wonderful.

The *Mei Tan* brought its crew and passengers safely into port at Ichang. The next day, July 12, Fritz boarded the Standard Oil Company's best river steamer, the S.S. *Mei Foo*. With the river calmer and the steamer more comfortable, Chester Fritz relaxed in the privacy of at last having a cabin all to himself, which made the journey to Hankow a peaceful interlude.

Chester Fritz spent three days in Hankow, a prosperous city with a wide promenade two miles long, well kept and safe, featuring English, Russian, French, German, and Japanese concessions—a prosperity based, in part, on its flour mills, black tea, iron works, sesame seeds, and buffalo and cattle industries. The influence of the Japanese on the city was prominent. According to Fritz, they exercised "a powerful hold on the trade and the shipping," controlled the "great iron works at Hanyang," and positioned "15,000 soldiers in barracks." After a tour of the city and some visiting, Fritz spent a relaxing evening devouring six bowls of ice cream.

The next stop for the returning American was the city of Changsha. Fritz believed that after Chengtu, Changsha was perhaps the finest city in all China. He was quite impressed with its wide streets, prosperity, absence of beggars, and above all else, its cleanliness. He was tired of filth.

The remainder of the trip was enjoyable and picturesque but relatively uneventful. Fritz arrived in Shanghai, the leading commercial city in China, on July 27. Little did he then know that Shanghai would later become his home for many years, the place in the sun where he "filled his rice bowl." On August 7, 1917, Chester Fritz arrived in Hong Kong, the port from where he had started six months earlier. His journal ended with this simple entry: "The long journey completed."

The immediate benefit of the trip was a sense of pride and a feeling of accomplishment. Chester Fritz completed a journey through western China that few foreigners before or after him would ever make. He took the road least traveled. Moreover, if he never experienced another day in China, Fritz had seen more and would remember more about this trip than the total experience of the majority of his foreign acquaintances, who seldom, if ever, ventured out of the treaty ports of China. In this regard, Chester Fritz set himself apart from the great majority of foreign tourists.

This sense of accomplishment, however, was little publicized. In fact, most foreign contemporaries and associates of Fritz in China knew little about the 1917 trip until many years later. Fritz privately, however, savored a deep sense of personal satisfaction—particularly when talk centered on "the real China" and came from the mouths of foreign travelers, who after spending a few weeks in a treaty port suddenly became an immediate expert on everything Chinese. During these moments, Chester Fritz would say to himself, with both humility and pride: "They don't know what they don't know."

In terms of personal growth, the trip was the beginning of a deeper understanding of the diversity and continuity of Chinese culture—an understanding that would continue to expand over the next 34 years. It would continue despite the philosophical, economic, or political changes that would overwhelm China between 1917 and 1951. Fritz would apply this understanding to other countries in wider travels, to Japan, India, and parts of the Third World.

In personal relationships and business ventures, he always carefully listened to people and to their ideas before making decisions. He also ceased to judge people, conditions, or opportunities merely because of the political banner flying at any given moment. The experience of 1917 made Chester Fritz a citizen of the world.

The tour also yielded an important lesson for doing business in China. It confirmed to him the one essential ingredient for financial success in China: "I tell you, they argue with you all the time. If you do not haggle in China, you do not survive!" Chester Fritz also believed the 1917 trip was instrumental in his being offered in 1921 the position of representative of the American Metal Company in China. "Now because of that experience in China, I acquired a certain status and it impressed the American Metal Company. That's how I got the job and Harold Hochschild saw that and he was impressed by my trip."

Finally, for Chester Fritz in the autumn of his life and walking that last mile, the 1917 trip through western China today remains a favorite topic of discussion, the foremost example of courage and personal accomplishment of his younger days. At age 88, when most people suffer from faded memories, Chester Fritz described in simple but beautiful words his recollections of that unique journey some 63 years before:

> The Lord of Fortune or fate brought me to China and carried me on my safari in west China, which was a unique experience. And brought me much valuable experience and a certain amount of prestige.
>
> I had long held an irrepressible desire to make a trip into the interior of China. But when I started, I never had any idea of extending it into a six-month journey. But the lure of an open road and a fascinating civilization, and at times the beautiful scenery, it lured me on. And I saw many strange people, aboriginal tribes people, who were in China long before the Chinese came. I felt I was in Biblical days, where they lived in simplicity....Most things to me then were in reverse. White, for example, was a sign of mourning and red was a sign of joy. It seemed to be a never-never land where everything seemed to be true and yet false. Where nothing is wasted.
>
> The Chinese lived in a most frugal way. And they didn't seem to have much happiness—at least, that was my observation. While their faces in the aged were heavily wrinkled, they were the wrinkles of anxiety and worry and not the

wrinkles of smiles or laughter.

At age 25, Chester Fritz had come a long way from the prairies of North Dakota to the interior of China. Without permanent employment to match the maturity of his Chinese experiences, Fritz rejoined Richardson in Hong Kong. Having decided to stay in China, it was his best option for continued employment until something more challenging came along. By 1918 Chester Fritz had shown himself to be a person of spiritual faith, personal confidence and resolve, and studious temperament. These attributes shortly would stand him in good stead and eventually would carry him far.

IV

Mr. Silver

Chester Fritz laid the foundation for a long, richly varied, and highly successful career during the years between 1917 and 1929. A combination of perseverance, affability, and happy coincidence aided and abetted his good fortune, while his own keen sense of self-interest fixed his eye on the more promising opportunities. The gentlemanly decorum of British Hong Kong, the business trips to the exotic ports of Southeast Asia, and the private adventure of a six-month journey deep into western China strengthened his desire to remain in the Far East, especially China. Yet, the absence of a permanent career and the challenges inherent in trying to decide his future course occasioned moments of uncertainty, even anxiety. His dependence on Richardson for employment added to his unease. From August 1917 until spring 1921, Fritz continued as Richardson's junior partner and assistant. Frustrated except for one exhilarating year-long venture in the marketing of a newly appreciated strategic metal, Fritz cast a longing glance toward other opportunities he hoped would be more rewarding.

The year 1921 proved the most pivotal. In his 30th year, Fritz terminated his business relationship with Richardson, accepted an assignment with the New York-based firm of American Metal Company, and shortly made Shanghai his residence. By the close of the year, he had become the company's sole representative and agent in China and was personally responsible for the importation of large consignments of silver into the country. In this capacity, Fritz routinely was exposed to the subtleties of the precious metals markets, the intricacies of dealing with local and foreign exchanges, and the sophistication of arbitrage brokering. As a result, he increased both his self-esteem and his mastery of recently acquired skills. Fritz became an experienced, reliable trader and earned the nickname "Mr. Silver." Personally these years numbered among the most satisfying of his long life. Moreover, the experience gained during these years later yielded still larger dividends. Fritz had established a career. He had found the means, as the Chinese commonly put it, to "fill his rice bowl," and then some.

Although Fritz reestablished a working relationship with Richardson upon his return to Hong Kong in August 1917, he never rejoined Fisher Flouring Mills because the American flour trade in Asia virtually had collapsed. He simply functioned as Richardson's agent for any conceivable business arrangement that might develop. Thus, while their relationship showed signs of strain, it endured for the lack of viable alternatives. Indeed, Fritz grew skeptical of Richardson's business ethics or, rather, the lack thereof. Richardson, ever watchful for a new scheme, no matter how dubious, had few inclinations toward keeping adequate records. According to Fritz, Richardson at times practiced "a strange brand of business ethics. He would be quite flexible or as the Chinese might say, 'he bent with the wind.'"

The only successful business venture between Richardson and Fritz began in August 1917. It ended abruptly in the waning days of World War I. During this short period, however, Fritz acquired and lost his first fortune—in the unlikely business of strip mining and marketing tungsten.

The mineral tungsten was first identified as a distinct element in Mexico in 1791. Yet, nearly a century passed before it found application in the manufacture of incandescent lamps, where tungsten filaments combined longevity and low energy consumption. Because tungsten also possesses the highest melting point of any metal, it can be alloyed to produce high-speed cutting tools, precision instruments, and armaments. Wolframite, the chief ore from which tungsten is extracted, is usually found in placer deposits because of its insolubility and high specific gravity.

A German priest first discovered tungsten in China in the late nineteenth century in southwest Kiangsi Province. However, Chan Ku-li, founder of the Kong Kwan Mining Company, claims credit for being the first to locate large commercial placers of wolframite. Even so, there is little evidence of serious tungsten mining prior to 1914. Conditions changed dramatically in 1917 when extensive alluvial deposits were uncovered in Kwangtung Province. By the end of the year approximately 1,200 tons of high-grade tungsten concentrates had been exported from China, mainly to the United States. As of September 1917, tungsten ore was being sold in China for about 800 Hankow taels per long ton, a 600 percent increase in price since the previous spring. By 1918, wolframite production in China totaled 9,000 metric tons. More than 5,000 tons of the ore, valued at $4.8 million, found its way to the United States, where domestic tungsten production remained low, largely because of cheaper foreign sources. In fact, China established a virtual world-wide monopoly in the production of tungsten for the next decade.

Increased importation of tungsten into the United States coincided with a resurgence of economic nationalism. In 1918, Republican Congressman Charles B. Timberlake of Colorado introduced a bill in the House of Representatives to place a duty of $10 per unit on all foreign concentrates of the metal. The bill passed in September 1919, but failed in the Senate in early 1920, where the Committee on Finance insisted on limiting the effect of the provisions to three years. However, Midwestern agrarian congressmen, worried over rapidly declining farm prices, passed the Fordney-McCumber tariff act which President Warren G. Harding approved on September 19, 1922. Although originally designed to raise duties on farm commodities, the measure attracted over 2,000 amendments by April 1922. These included an amendment to fix a duty on tungsten at 4.5 cents per pound, or $7.14 per short ton. Although nearly $3 less than the tariff contemplated by the Timberlake bill, the bill remained protective of American tungsten producers.

In the fall of 1917 several Chinese miners, with experience working in the tin mines of the Federated Malay States around Kuala Lumpur, had approached Richardson and Fritz with ore samples taken from the area north of Canton. The miners wanted their samples identified. In Hong Kong, a government analyst confirmed the mineral as "Hock Tai," or high-grade wolframite. The significance of the discovery, according to

Fritz, lay in the fact that "there was no production then. It was not known to the outside world that China was a producer of tungsten."

The two transplanted Americans reacted quickly. Richardson and Fritz privately established a partnership on the basis of 75-25 percent. Next, they engaged the services of two American mining engineers, Percy Kincaid and Philip O'Neal, who worked in the Philippine Islands. Third, they secured a letter of credit from the American Express Company in New York. A division of labor followed, with Fritz taking over the purchasing, packing, and transportation of the ore in Canton, while Richardson managed affairs in Hong Kong.

The actual mining of the ore was simply accomplished. Chinese farmers raked the rich alluvial deposits from the surface ground and coolies carried the collected ore to a warehouse in Canton. Fritz made periodic boat trips up the West River to purchase the ore, which he stored in the rented basement of a large building situated in the foreign concession called Shameen, a sand bank in the Pearl River. The upstairs contained a small office, from which he hired local coolies to sack the ore and bind it with bamboo sticks for shipment across the Pacific to the United States.

Shipping the ore to the United States proved more complex and risky. British wartime measures included a prohibition against exporting strategic commodities from any of its ports, in this instance Hong Kong, unless first destined for Great Britain. To circumvent the policy, Fritz chartered a Chinese ship in Swatow, another treaty port just north of Hong Kong. The ship, a small and older vessel, the *Kit-Ann*, listed visibly to one side as the first cargo of 105 tons, packed in bags of 100 pounds each, filled the hold. "Dear God," Fritz exclaimed, "I hope it arrives in Swatow." In Swatow, the cargo was transferred to a second coastal vessel that conveyed it to Shanghai, where it again was reloaded on a trans-Pacific steamer headed for San Francisco. A "silk train" then rushed the shipment to its final destination, the Atlas Crucible Steel Company in Buffalo, New York.

Richardson and Fritz seemed to be shouldering the entire burden of financial risk. Crucible Steel refused to commit itself to an unfamiliar source of supply for an untested quality until the ore safely had reached the United States. In fact, however, the capital outlay was small because the partners' letter of credit, although but a fraction of the selling price, met over 70 percent of their investment.

Back in Hong Kong, both men waited anxiously for a telegraph

Mr. Silver

message from America. After some days, Bob Buchan, manager of the American Express branch, ran to their office proclaiming, "This is it!" Fritz well recalled the "news of joy. This was our whole livelihood. I cannot remember the exact price but it was a big profit."

The news of the first successful shipment encouraged others. Operations expanded rapidly, supported by Chinese farmers' increased strip mining and the steel company's calls for more ore. The first and easiest task involved increasing the number of shipments without waiting for confirmation of sale before dispatching another. This meant having to spend more time in Canton preparing the ore for shipment and arranging transportation. Of course, there was risk in having several shipments en route without the protection of yet being able to sell the product forward, but it seemed a minor one, particularly when compared to the second risk.

At Richardson's urging, Fritz negotiated the purchase of tungsten from other areas, including a shipment from Weichow on the the East River. "Then we were in real trouble," because local army officers greedily prevented the shipment from leaving until prices rose. For weeks Fritz tried in vain to win release of the shipment. Meantime, he found some diversion in the West Lake area, famous for its assortment of pretty temples and pagodas.

> I stayed there for ten days on a beautiful lake where I rented a comfortable flower boat. I gave dinner parties to Chinese merchants and secured the services of a Chinese cook. He was a dream! I can still see him sitting on his haunches with eight or ten charcoal burning braziers in front of him with a different dish in each one.

At year's end, 1917, Richardson and Fritz had significantly increased the number of tungsten shipments to the United States, accounting for 700 of the 1,200 tons exported from China. If 1917 had been a good year, 1918 promised even better returns. The simultaneous consignment of four large shipments suggested their optimism. At that point, however, the market suddenly disappeared.

> With the collapse of Bulgaria in World War I, the metal market closed tightly and we could not sell any of the four ore shipments. So we lost all our profits and most of our capital.

It should be explained that Germany controlled 90 percent of the world's tungsten supply before World War I. Passage of the Timberlake bill, under pressure from Colorado and California producers, promised to raise tungsten prices to $7 per pound. With the collapse of Bulgaria and the end of international hostilities, Germany attempted to regain control of the market, advertising in her distressed condition to sell tungsten for as little as 25 cents per pound. This effectively undercut competition worldwide and destroyed the China trade lately established by Richardson and Fritz.

In 1919, in a mixed effort to salvage something from the tungsten venture, Fritz returned to the United States for the first time since departing in 1915. He located the four most recent shipments and arranged for their long-term storage. He visited several New York bankers to request an extension of credit. He paid a courtesy call on Harold Hochschild, vice president of the American Metal Company, Ltd., of New York, a major producer and refiner of non-ferrous minerals. Fritz also journeyed to the nation's capital where committee hearings on the Timberlake bill were in progress in the Senate. He talked privately with Congressman Timberlake and strongly urged passage of the measure "in order to put the market price up." But the Fritz mission failed. "The measure which concerns us so much in Washington," he wrote Aunt Kathrine despairingly, "is marking time and no decision has been reached. Our affairs are still in suspension and the uncertainty of it all is not to my liking."

What had developed so quickly ended abruptly. The tungsten metal market closed "like a steel trap." Despite the addictive excitement inherent in the metals trade, Fritz's first experience ended in bankruptcy. The many variables involved ensured that the trade would always be fraught with uncertainty. Yet the rapidity of realizing an initial profit with so little operating capital made a deep impression. He filed away mental notes on transporting schemes, on establishing lines of credit, on how to deal with foreign exchanges, and on the unpredictability of international relations. Clearly, selling forward and a sense of timing were essential to any success.

While Fritz was supervising a shipment of tungsten from Swatow to Shanghai in 1918, an earthquake rocked Swatow, destroying a number of buildings and killing many people. "The sound of the earthquake was like a heavy iron cross being dragged across iron rails," he recalled. "It was a peculiar sensation to feel the earth rocking under you." For days after the earthquake, Fritz also noted a peculiar scene on the country roads leading out of Swatow. The Chinese peasants searched through

Mr. Silver

holes left in the road by the earthquake looking for "the hairs of the dragon" who, they believed, caused the disaster by shaking its body.

On another tungsten assignment, Fritz traveled a long distance up the West River from Canton. He passed a Chinese customs point, called a "likin station," which was difficult for river craft to reach due to the low level of the river. Yet he had to stop at the station because it levied mandatory transportation taxes on all manner of cargo using the waterway.

Fritz's boat was detained; and because he was identified as a foreigner, he had to produce his passport. Unfortunately, he had packed it in his luggage. Yet, desiring to avoid further delay, he remembered a ruse he had learned of while visiting the interior of China the year before. He cut one side of an Eastman Kodak film package and had it sent to the customs office. In a short time, he was given clearance, either because the officials could not read English or because the color was "imperial yellow."

While Fritz was in Canton, Chinese merchants expressed curiosity regarding one of his personal effects, a native paper umbrella. The Chinese thought it amusing that a man of his means carried such a commonplace item. When finally asked to explain it, Fritz reminded them that it was both inexpensive and in keeping with local styles, and that one was several times more likely to lose an expensive umbrella than a cheap one. The Chinese seemed impressed.

Chinese cuisine never wanted for surprising innovations; on one occasion, Fritz recalled,

"I was chewing on something like shoe leather. I asked my host, 'What is it?'"

"He replied, 'Duck's feet.'"

"Duck's feet!"

"Years later I repeated the story to a lady in Monte Carlo who had lived in China. She replied, 'Duck's feet is very good if you put celery salt on it.'

"Well, I don't carry a flask of celery salt around with me!"

In Canton, Fritz particularly became intrigued by the unusual behavior of the Cantonese boat women. These women operated passenger boats between points in the city, and some spent most of their lives on these craft. He described their fascinating manner in some detail:

> When I was there the boat women would frequently engage in arguments which were fantastic! They would shout

and scream at each other for long periods of time but they never physically touched their opponent. As the shouting became more conspicuous many people would gather around to view this strange street performance. Finally, exhausted, the two women would walk away from each other and then suddenly turn around and shout again at their opponent, each trying to surprise the other and get in the last word. After several observations I learned it also was considered a very fine act or deed for a bystander to make peace between the two contenders. But often the attempt failed and the peacemaker found himself in a precarious situation.

Meanwhile, Richardson had conceived his most grandiose scheme, which involved the establishment of a smelting plant in southern China. He hoped to construct a smelter to refine lead ore and offered Fritz another partnership on the standard 75-25 percent formula. Richardson had also begun extending personal loans—possibly bribes—to local Chinese officials. Fritz thought the whole scheme impractical and the dealings with local officials "very precarious." He demanded an accounting of their tungsten partnership, but Richardson could not produce any profit/loss statement and, worse, refused payment of outstanding salaries. Therewith, Fritz began looking for other employment among the various contacts he had established in Hong Kong.

At this time I got a job with the Dunbar Flour Company in Hong Kong. Mr. Lambert Dunbar, who had inherited the business from his father, had the idea that I should go up to Harbin in Manchuria. Northern Manchuria was hard wheat country and Dunbar wanted me to see if it was practical to bring flour from Harbin to the Hong Kong markets. But the freight rates were prohibitive and it was not feasible commercially in 1920. I also had a brief assignment in Eastern Siberia.

Fritz also received an offer from a large American firm but declined it because "the position would take me away from China, in which I had so much confidence with regard to future developments."

His relationship with Richardson remained troublesome. When Fritz returned to the British Crown Colony in early 1920, Richardson had already put into effect other ventures. One of these involved securing a contract to ship foreign bar silver to Hong Kong to the Canton mint, the single largest consumer of silver in the world. The Los Angeles Steam

Navigation Company hired Richardson and Fritz as its trans-Pacific agents to supervise the loading and unloading of its fleet in Hong Kong. But Fritz acknowledged that "the joys of being a steamship agent have no fascination for me, although the present experience will always stand me in good stead." He also admitted that he knew little of shipping. We employed "a very nice Dane, who looked after it for us."

Fritz broke with Richardson in a temperate, almost apologetic letter dated February 12, 1921. He reminded his senior partner of past conversations "concerning the money due me under the arrangement agreed upon," and indicated he had "been forced to seek for a settlement thru other channels." Yet, he concluded, "I am not unmindful of your numerous kindnesses to me in the past."

Still, Fritz never collected his rightful share of the partnership before Richardson died of dropsy in Swatow in October 1924. Penniless, Richardson spent his last two years misrepresenting himself as an agent of the Fisher Flouring Mills, signing contracts in its name for $23,000. A few years later, Fritz gave Richardson's widow $2,000 and occasionally looked after her few Asian interests when she returned to the West Coast.

Fritz looked more to the future than the past in communicating the break with Richardson to his aunt and uncle:

> There are so many different factors which entered into my decision that I will not bore you with details, which I prefer to label, "A Forgotten Chapter." I have no regrets and am looking forward with real eagerness to the immediate future and trust that the wheel of fortune will be as just to me as it has been in the past.

His comments on United States domestic and international affairs, though brief, were pointed.

> Now that the States have prohibition and the Republicans are in the saddle, I hope they are content. We have made a sorry mess of our relations with Europe and the League [of Nations]. As diplomats, we are raw recruits, when compared to the experienced and trained minds of Europe.

Ironically, Richardson's scheme for acting as a conduit in the sale of large quantities of silver to the Canton mint eventually launched Fritz on his first successful career. Although Fritz knew of the plan and, indeed, called on the American Metal Company's offices in New York in 1919 partly to discuss the scheme he did not figure as a principal at that stage. Thus, Fritz claimed no responsibility for the debt incurred by the mint to the company soon after Richardson took charge of managing the contract. In fact, Fritz returned to China in early 1920 to find the contract already in force without his direct participation.

Even so, Fritz became an employee of the American Metal Company in the summer of 1921. The company was yet a small, family-owned enterprise whose existence dated from 1887. The history of the company began almost 200 years earlier in the German feudal kingdom of Hannover. There, in about 1700, the private banking firm of Liebmann and Cohen was nominated fiscal agent to the court and financed several mining ventures in the Harz Mountains. The bank prospered and in 1824 established a branch office in the free city of Frankfurt, which became the sales representative for minerals mined from the Hannover-Braunschweig districts. In 1860, the bank established another branch, the Henry R. Merton Company in London. Twenty-one years later, under the leadership of Leo Elligner and Zacharais Hochschild, the Frankfurt branch reorganized as Metallgesellschaft (Metal Company). Together the Frankfurt and London companies attained great influence in the international non-ferrous markets.

With the discovery of rich copper deposits in North America and the growing appreciation of American smelting and refining technology, New York became the third principal center of the company's operations. Between 1887 and 1914 the American branch likewise prospered and expanded. It entered into a smelting agreement with the International Nickel Company, acquired ownership of the Balback Smelting and Refining Company in New Jersey, and developed extensive silver mining interests in Mexico. Yet, even in 1914, the total number of stockholders were fewer than forty and all three branches "retained what was virtually a family relationship."

The crisis of World War I forced important changes upon the company. Internally, the New York branch achieved independence when "the old relationship between the Frankfurt, London, and New York branches was dissolved for all times." Externally, the American office began seeking new markets in 1919. Harold Hochschild, vice-president and son of a founder, described the atmosphere:

> World War I was followed by a short-lived boom in this country especially in foreign trade. In fact, it was the spurt in foreign trade that was the real impetus. The European countries were recovering from the war and it took them a year or two to re-establish their connections with Latin America, the

Far East and other regions. American companies rushed in to fill that gap without knowing very much about the conditions of trade in those countries, particularly in the Far East. This included the big banks and our company among others. We were selling our silver in New York to the well known brokerage firm of Handy and Harman. And we heard that much higher prices were being paid in China. We were anxious to establish direct connections with China. As I recall it, we asked the National City Bank to recommend an agent to us. And they recommended a man by the name of Charles E. Richardson who was a flour broker in Hong Kong. His assistant was Chester Fritz.

The contract signed between the American Metal Company and the Canton mint called for delivery of two million ounces of silver per month. The price of each delivery depended on the silver price quoted by Handy and Harman brokers in New York on any stipulated day. Company vice-president Hochschild was crossing the Pacific even as the post-World War I boom in the United States turned into rapid deflation. Prices in all commodities, including silver, plummeted. Silver dropped from $1.25 per ounce to about 60 cents within weeks. Hochschild explained the situation in China in 1920:

> When I got to Hong Kong I found that several million ounces of silver had accumulated there at much higher prices than 60 cents an ounce because the director of the mint could not pay for them.
>
> I discovered that the director of the mint was a small up country political figure who knew nothing about silver or finance....To pay us American dollars for the silver that we shipped the director had to buy these dollars in the foreign exchange market in Hong Kong. The Hong Kong dollar like Chinese currency was based on silver. At that time, money in China was pure silver, i.e., so much weight of silver went into each unit of the currency. Thus, the value of the American dollar in terms of the Hong Kong currency fluctuated with the price of silver. When the price of silver went up, the Hong Kong dollar went up and the American dollar went down. When the price of silver went down, the Hong Kong dollar went down and the American dollar went up. If the director had covered his foreign exchange at the same time that the

price of silver we were selling him was being fixed by the New York quotation, he would have run no risk and this is what we understood he was doing. But I found when I arrived there that he had been speculating on silver going higher so that he could clear a profit over and above his minting (lending) profit by speculating on the foreign exchange. I believe he was doing this for his own account, not for the government's account. Anyway, it had disastrous results because speculation frittered away the money, most of the money, that was needed to pay us. I should add that I do not recall that Chester had anything to do with this. The mint business was handled exclusively by Richardson.

Hochschild extended his stay in China, and he and Fritz became good friends. Fritz secured a temporary membership for Hochschild at the Hong Kong Club, where they often dined together at the same table. Of comparable ages, similar temperament, the same broad inquisitiveness, and little interest in such diversions as golf or bridge, the two young Americans talked at length about China. Hochschild's interest in China's history and culture grew, and he learned of Fritz's unusual travels in western China.

I think hearing about his trip stimulated my trip interest to see something of China, getting to see something of China itself, and the countryside. Most of the American and British businessmen out there had no interest in learning anything about China. Chester was a rare exception in that respect.

Hochschild recalled the mutual playfulness that the two shared:

There was a table in the Hong Kong Club where several Americans lunched together and Chester was a member of that group and I often went there with him. Another member was a man named Wylie who was shipping manager of Standard Oil of New York in Hong Kong. Another member was a man named Geare who was the manager of the Vacuum Oil Company in Hong Kong.

There was a Standard Oil ship in port for repairs called the S.S. *Astro*. The captain of the ship was a tall, lanky Scandinavian-American named Anderson. The captain expected Mr. Wylie to entertain him because he had nothing to do while his ship was being repaired. Wylie could not get rid of the captain as he just followed him around.

Mr. Silver

When the ship finally sailed someone thought it would be a very good idea to send Wylie a fake wireless from the captain of the S.S. *Astro* saying the ship had broken down and was returning to port. Geare, the manager of Standard Oil's competitor, agreed to handle this and place a fake wireless on Wylie's desk. But when Geare got back to his office he sent a telegram to the Manila office of Vacuum Oil and requested they cable Wylie with the message and sign it with the captain's name. But the office in Manila sent it to the Standard Oil office in Manila instead and they in turn put it in their own code and sent it to Hong Kong and began to cancel cargo orders for other shipments after the ship left Manila.

When the manager of Standard Oil in Hong Kong, who had known about the joke on his shipping manager saw the message in the private code of Standard Oil he said, "How the hell did Vacuum Oil get ahold of our private code?" So the fat was in the fire. Fortunately the thing was stopped before the charter was cancelled. But there were a lot of messages going back and forth. The upshot was that a bill for wireless and cables for about $350 had to be shared by the perpetrators.

Chester and I were among them. Everyone was worried on both sides because the director of Standard Oil Company from New York was due in Hong Kong in a few days and no one wanted him to find out about this and think that all the two companies were doing out here was playing practical jokes on each other.

Three consequences flowed directly from Hochschild's nearly two-year sojourn in China. He concluded that the risks were too great to engage in silver business with provincial institutions, such as the Canton mint, which did not enjoy the support of the Peking government nor possess any experience in the silver bullion trade. Hochschild suspected, however, that a profitable connection might be developed with Chinese bankers in Shanghai: "That was the main lesson we learned," he observed. So, he offered Chester Fritz the job of representing the American Metal Company in China. Fritz accepted at a salary of $900 per month. Hochschild explained that...

...Richardson treated Fritz badly. As I recall it, he cheated Chester and tried to cheat our company and others he did

> business with and Chester did not want to stay with Richardson. So before I left China in 1921, I offered Chester the job of representing our company out there and he accepted. I think for awhile he stayed in Hong Kong to collect two or three payments that were still due us and he did collect some of them before the mint was unable to pay anymore. Then Chester went to Shanghai and opened an office for us there and we began doing business through him with modern style Chinese, Japanese, and British banks—in fact, with all the foreign banks there.

Fritz recalled the first assignment from his employer: pursue efforts to collect the debt owed by the Canton mint.

> I had interviews with the commissioner of finance of Kwangtung Province. He arranged for me to meet Dr. Sun Yat-sen. They met me near the Bund in Shanghai with two soldiers in a motor car. The car sped away with the siren going and the two soldiers standing on each side of the car on the running boards with their guns. I met Sun Yat-sen and got nowhere. It was an act put up by his commissioner of finance. He was trying to ingratiate himself to Sun Yat-sen.

Fritz told his aunt in December 1922 about the convoluted negotiations with the Canton government, concluding that the regime faced imminent financial collapse and that, therefore, it proved "difficult to talk business with a drowning man." For this and other equally complex reasons, the American Metal Company never realized the whole of the debt it carried. The Kwangtung provincial government reported, after investigating the matter fully, that the company had "acted in good faith and fulfilled its obligations." The problem lay elsewhere: had the director of the mint "not speculated in foreign exchange" and had he not left his post "for six weeks at the Chinese New Year's season in 1920," the mint "could have fulfilled the contract."

During 1921-22, Sun Yat-sen, then presiding over a pretentious but shaky coalition based at Canton, reduced the obligation from $751,000 to $482,000. No further payment on the principal followed, so that by 1947 interest charges alone had soared to nearly $4,400,000. In 1947 the commissioner of finance for Kwangtung wrote Fritz that all future "responsibility for liquidating this debt should rest with the national government" and complained that the amount now seemed "unreasonably large." The American Metal Company responded that if the Chinese exhibited a serious interest in reaching a settlement, a "very substantial part of the total indebtedness" could be compromised. The Chinese reply, dated November 27, 1947, declared resolution must await "the time when China's financial situation takes a turn for the better." Of course, that return did not occur prior to the Communist revolution of 1949.

After trying unsuccessfully to collect the debt, Fritz moved to Shanghai. According to one contemporary account, Shanghai in the 1920s was...

> ...a jewel of many facets. She presents a cold mark to the traveler touching her shores for the first time and, although he may partake of certain pleasures and perquisites accorded the alive with a full pocketbook, in the main she reserves her treasure for the student and philosopher.

Located along the southeastern coast of China approximately 800 miles northeast of Hong Kong and 550 miles west of southern Japan, Shanghai today is one of the world's most populous cities. Shanghai is situated on the west back of the Whangpoo River about 12 miles upriver from the estuary of the Yangtze, China's principal commercial artery. Shanghai lies only a dozen feet above sea level on a level plain that once featured swamps. Between World War I and World War II, the city embraced a total of 5,584 acres with a circumference of about 11 miles. At its greatest length, the city stretched 7.5 miles; its greatest width did not exceed 2.27 miles.

Normally the climate at Shanghai is temperate. Subtropical conditions and the threat of typhoons arrive for three months during the summer, with the heaviest rainfall occurring in June and July. At the other extreme, January, the coldest month, experiences some snowfall but rarely witnesses temperatures below 35° Fahrenheit.

The emergence of Shanghai as the leading financial center of China dated from the first two decades of the twentieth century. Although Manchuria figured as the focus of foreign investment between 1902 and 1914, Shanghai thereafter surged in importance, until by 1931 fully one-third of all foreign investment in China was concentrated there.

Shanghai's existence as a free port with unrestricted foreign trade began with the treaty of Nanking in 1842. British, French, and American representatives quickly took possession of designated areas of the site under the concept of extraterritoriality. The Japanese received similar concessions in 1895 under terms of the treaty of Shimonoseki. Thus, Shanghai on the eve of the twentieth century stood poised as a cosmopolitan and international community, an autonomous city-state on the mainland of China. The 1890s witnessed some growth in light industries aided in part by the Sino-Japanese War of 1894-95. Following World War I, a sustained economic boom took place that eventually rendered the city the preeminent example of development under the treaty-port system. At that point, Shanghai ranked first in foreign trade, in foreign population, and in foreign investment; it was also the largest industrial and manufacturing center in China and its foremost transportation complex. Indeed, by 1926-27, Shanghai had won undisputed status among the leading six or seven ports of the world. First-time visitors were surprised by its size and density, its Western aspects, and the pervasive spirit of optimism that reigned there. Joseph W. Stilwell, American military attaché, thought the city resembled Philadelphia in many of its features.

As China's financial heart after 1925, Shanghai pulsated to a silver boom. There was more silver in Shanghai than any other city in the world, an estimated 400 million ounces at one point, and the concentration produced irregular fits of frenzy. Fritz recalled that both foreign and Chinese traders "would go to the telephone and call their broker who by now had the day's quotations from New York. They would put in their order, raise the limit, tell the broker to hold on to the silver, or sell it two and a half points above yesterday's course."

The decade of the 1920s and at least half of the 1930s were exciting, even exhilarating times to be involved in precious metals, foreign exchange, and banking. Shanghai took its place as one of four international silver markets around the globe with Bombay, London, and New York. Soon Shanghai also established a gold-bar exchange where the Chinese in particular traded with "reckless abandonment." The Chinese weakness for speculation applied to grain, hides, and other staples, in addition to gold and silver. Shanghai's banks thrived in this heady atmosphere of foreign exchange, compounded by the large volume of remittances forwarded from Chinese living abroad. By 1927, Shanghai boasted no fewer than 170 banks, excluding the branch banks representing foreign organizations. "Business is business, if you want to know," Fritz observed, "and in Shanghai it is a twenty-four-hours-a-day proposition."

Yet, by all contemporary standards, Shanghai could also be a difficult, even a dangerous place to live. One account reported that 20,000 bodies were picked up every year in the "dark alleys" by police, many of them tall, turbaned Sikhs imported from British India. Another report warned that the city was "no place for sissies," "no place to erect a house," and certainly "no place to raise a family." Stilwell felt certain that "This town would ruin anybody in no time." Conversely Shanghai generally was recommended as a good place "to go to, to grow rich, and to leave."

During his first years in Shanghai, Chester Fritz shared a home in the French Settlement with Robert Mishler. An American, a good horseman and active polo player, Mishler was also "very social." He numbered among his close friends Mei Ling-soong, who married Chiang Kai-shek in Shanghai in December 1927. Fritz remembered that she visited the house on several occasions, "spoke faultless English," and was "a very charming conversationalist." When Mishler died of leukemia, she telephoned Fritz to express an interest in purchasing Mishler's library.

Fritz abhorred and shunned the vice-ridden side of Shanghai's attractions, but, of course, he could not remain ignorant of it. He recalled especially a certain street near the waterfront popularly called "Blood Alley" in an area where foreign naval and merchant marine sailors gathered for an evening's entertainment or sport and the frequent fights and brawls. He also described the "badlands" section just outside the enclave as a "sorry section where there was much gambling and prostitutes were conspicuous." As a matter of fact, one contemporary story estimated that there were at least 25,000 prostitutes available in Shanghai. Beyond that, however, Fritz brusquely denied any special knowledge, insisting "I do not think I am competent to pass an opinion on the question of prostitution in Shanghai. It was a wide-open city and nightclubs flourished."

Most foreign residents found living in Shanghai comfortable. Salaries were good and the social life varied. Most Englishmen and Americans worked for large, home-based companies and corporations, usually on five-year assignments, which included as part of the contract a six- to ten-month paid vacation called "home leave." Compared to salaries received in the United States, those in Shanghai were higher in that dollars carried an additional increment of purchasing power. Moreover, passage of the China Trade Act in 1922, amended in 1925, provided for federal incorporation of firms engaged in business in China, and contained an exemption from federal taxation.

These advantages, however, did not necessarily mean that foreigners attained wealth. As Shanghai grew hot and humid each summer, spouses and children escaped to cooler vacation spots in the mountains or along the coastline. Many went to Tsingtao, a former German settlement with "suitable living quarters and a fine beach."

Socially, the foreign and Chinese populations mixed little. Indeed, the tendency was actively to engage in a social schedule among their own kind. Fritz profiled typical social behavior in this manner:

> The average foreigner lived well and had an abundance of servants. As entertaining was rather simple with good but inexpensive Chinese servants, there was a tendency to overdo it. The result was that many of them became overactive socially. Some men complained about these frequent dinner parties which were often booking guests two and three weeks ahead of time. The manager of the Italian bank told me that for three nights running at dinner parties he was seated beside the same lady and he was getting bored because he had run out of conversation.

Customarily one stopped at one of Shanghai's many nightclubs after the evening meal, which was usually consumed at home. A few clubs featured nightly shows, and all of them encouraged ballroom dancing. Popular clubs included the Astor House, across the Whangpoo River, the old Carleton, later the new Carleton, and its "huge ballroom." In summertime, the Majestic Hotel's open-air theater offered diversionary relief from the evening heat. The Majestic also accommodated gala occasions—for instance, the reception following General Chiang Kai-shek's marriage in 1927.

Locally, the term "taipan" denoted the head of an important business firm or agency. Actually, however, the word conveyed broader social and cultural implications:

> A Taipan is one whose monthly mah-jong accounts at the club run above one thousand taels, whose advice is sought on the best brand of cigars to import, who prides himself on being able to tell the difference between port and sherry blindfolded, who calls all the girls at Del Monte by their nicknames, who knows precious little Chinese and boasts that knowledge of the language is not necessary, whose name always figures prominently among the honorary presidents of all foreign charities, and who also owns a string of Mongolian ponies which he races twice a year. The reason he

remains in China is that he would rather be a big fish in a small puddle, where all his splashes and those of Mme. Taipan are chronicled faithfully in the press of the Treaty ports, than return home where his ego would be kept in a sling the year round. His success socially is measured by the number of wins his ponies achieve at any race meeting.

The Sassoon family, along with the Ezras, Hardoons, and Shamoons, epitomized the Shanghai taipan. Sassoon interests in Shanghai dated from the 1850s, when a modest outlet was established there for textiles produced in Bombay. Later expansion in the Far East, including shipping and the opium trade, gave the Shanghai office sufficient importance gradually to command the frequent visitation of a family representative. Property acquisitions followed in a piecemeal fashion. Yet Hong Kong remained the chief outpost of Sassoon interests in China.

Into the 1920s, the Sassoons began concentrating a major investment in Shanghai. On the Bund near the Custom House, Sir Victor Sassoon built the city's first skyscraper, the 10-story Sassoon House, completed in March 1930, and Sir Victor himself took up permanent residence in Shanghai in 1931. With his arrival, the image of the total taipan reached its zenith. Sir Victor, bearing mustache, monocle, ascot, and an awkward limp acquired in pilot training during World War I, was called the "most eccentric Englishman alive," and had long been noted for his fast-blooded horses, admiring women, and far-flung financial and property interests.

"He owned Shanghai," observed one commentator, with understandable exaggeration. "His home, Villa Eva on Hung jao Road, was a favorite place to dine and his garden parties were exquisite." Briefly stated, Sir Victor, the last and most flamboyant scion of a famous commercial family, contributed indelibly to Shanghai's interwar reputation as a city *sui generis*.

> I can still see Sir Victor with his monocle, a peculiar limp, as though he were weighed down by his millions. But limp or no limp, a group of young married ladies buzzed and hummed around him, oozing honey all over his shirt front. One of them stood out from the rest; at twenty-seven she had a record of five husbands, two below and three above. Grass roots, I mean, not bridge.

In addition, British officers and civil servants "paid him their respect with sickening deference."

All this supplied grist to the caustic pen of Edgar Snow, then a reporter for Shanghai's *China Weekly Review* who described the city for the *American Mercury* in December 1930 as the "most polyglot city in Asia" and the "most materialistic city in the world." It boasted of "more heathen, more sinners, more concubines," and "more missionaries" than any other place, amid an atmosphere "where a bank clerk can afford to keep a mistress" and where no one, Chinese or American, permitted the shallow nature of Sino-American understanding to interfere with the business of making money.

To Snow, the International Settlement functioned as "a poorly camouflaged British colony." There the typical American concentrated on trade and commerce "uncontaminated with the virus of city pride." He was at once "more likable, more interesting, more intelligent" than his counterpart back home, but also "more cosmopolitan, more tolerant, and more wicked."

Although Americans had claimed a section of the settlement and had been doing business in Shanghai for over eighty years, Snow found only four who could speak Chinese, excluding missionaries in whose schools the language did not carry the rank of a regular offering. Indeed, few Americans resident in Shanghai knew much of China itself or had heard of Mei Lan-fang before he was acclaimed by New York theater patrons. Typically, the Shanghai American, according to Snow, believed it...

> ...dangerous to travel outside of Shanghai..., he meticulously avoids Chinese food, screams when he hears Chinese music, assures visitors that all Chinese are potential criminals, and believes that the practice of "squeeze" or the accepting and giving of gratuities, is the cause of China's inferior position in the family of nations. In pidgin-English he holds solemn conversations with his houseboys and from them makes sweeping generalizations about the Chinese people.

Yet, to other, more charitable observers, Shanghai boasted freedoms and opportunities known in few other places. Long-time newspaper editor J. B. Powell, for instance, remembered the city as the "only port in the world where a passport was not necessary for landing privileges." Also, the free interplay of ideas and preferences could be pursued according to individual inclinations. Thus the spectacle of flags that in comparison made other cities "look naked." Everyone in Shanghai "leaned on the flag" and advertised his nationality. There were more flagpoles per capita in Shanghai than anywhere else, and the unprepared tourist might believe himself partaking of an eternal holiday.

Social clubs, organized according to business or nationality, abounded and provided a coherency that the city itself did not possess. Given the requisite resources, one could indulge one's interests (and passions) to an extent not entirely possible elsewhere, often in such expensive pursuits as art collecting and polo playing. The city's rapid growth and prosperity also gave it a prominence that attracted outsiders. By the mid-1920s, Shanghai could play host to many of the intellects and artists of the time, including Albert Einstein and Noel Coward. Few premeditated tours, either of the Far East or of the world, would be held complete without a visit to Shanghai.

The city was a monument to laissez-faire economics. The laws of supply and demand reigned supreme. The Horatio Alger ethic found few doubters. As a result, rapid, even sudden, fluctuations in one's comparative wealth were not simply commonplace; they were expected. Yet, paradoxically, one retained his dignity even when financially embarrassed. Not so in the event of bankruptcy, which met with low tolerance.

Chester Fritz shared in many aspects of Shanghai life, of course, but voluntarily rejected others. Economically, he enjoyed the comfortable lifestyle of his British and American peers, largely because his salary of $900 a month allowed him to indulge in a comfortable home, Chinese servants, and high society. He also took regular home leaves and usually visited Japan each August. His appetite for travel never waned.

Socially, Fritz could take it or leave it. He spurned alcohol and women as a general rule. Besides, Shanghai's population contained very few eligible foreign women; the majority lived there because of their husbands' employment. More importantly, Fritz continued his interest in Chinese culture. Although Shanghai was hardly his first experience in Chinese living, the city still offered opportunities to contrast and compete with those he had experienced elsewhere.

Above all, Fritz held a special position in that he sold silver bullion, the basis of Chinese coinage. His primary customers were Chinese and Japanese bankers, and he needed to know the people with whom he dealt. In fact, Fritz was among the few Americans in Shanghai who developed as a matter of course strong business and social connections with the Asian contingent in the city. It was an inescapable imperative.

Conversely, the majority of old, established Chinese families in Shanghai held most foreigners in low esteem, believing that Westerners had no manners and few social graces. On one occasion, for example, a Chinese couple wanted to invite Fritz to their home. The wife appealed to her father-in-law for tacit permission, only to be told that he had "never had a foreigner in my home and I never will. They are beasts with unbridled passions."

For his part, however, Fritz found Chinese social customs and ways intriguing, whether in Shanghai or elsewhere:

> If the hosts were Cantonese, they would after the meal usually start playing Choi-mui. It is a fingers game where they become quite excited. The idea is to simultaneously shout out the number of fingers being extended by the two players. It is very interesting. The sophisticated Chinese when he comes to the figure eight will shout, "bot-va!" That means eight horses. This game goes very fast. The loser has to drink a cup. It is about the size of a big thimble so it is not very dangerous unless you have repeated losses.

He recalled, on another occasion, that...

> ...in the old days in Shanghai when a host was giving a dinner party he sent out invitations which were accompanied by a large, red folding piece of cardboard. On the cardboard were printed the names of the guests who were invited and you were supposed to indicate whether you accepted or declined the invitation. But many of the sophisticated Chinese would delay their decision and simply write on the cardboard "noted." So the poor host never knew how many people were coming until the very dinner hour. In the meantime, different guests would ask each other, "Are you going to this dinner?" because no one wanted to attend a dinner that was a flop. If the dinner was a ceremonial one, it would include, if the hosts could afford it, bird's-nest soup, which is quite palatable. It is obtained from Sumatra, a near-by island. It was the mucous deposited by a cave swallow in making their nest.
>
> If you mention to a Chinese that you know Mr. Wong, he would reply, "Yes, I know him. He gave me a dinner." This

phrase was equivalent to the Westerner replying, "Oh yes, he is a good friend of mine." But the Chinese prefer the other phrase and more often than not, they were given a dinner.

Fritz also remembered his coping with a Chinese telephone directory in Shanghai:

> The Chinese language has no alphabet. So if you want to look up in the telephone book a Mr. Wong, you calculate the number of strokes in your hand and if it is eight strokes you then go to that section of the telephone book. But when you get there, however, there may be a number of other last names with the same number of strokes. If you have the person's address it is of some help, yet your problems have only started because the book simply says the residence of Mr. Wong. So you begin to try numbers and when the servant answers the telephone and he recognizes your foreign accent he has already decided not to understand you. So the conversation develops into a barking contest: "Who are you?" "Who are you?" and so it goes on. Finally on one occasion, when I had lost my patience, I said, "Whoo Pi Choo," which was the name of the warlord of the area, a real dictator, and quite demanding. When I said that name the servant hung up the phone and, I was told later, did not answer the telephone for several days.

Fritz established the branch office of the American Metal Company in Shanghai in the National City Bank Building, well within the city's growing financial district. Leading European, American, Japanese, and Chinese banking and financial institutions occupied the area, and all involved themselves in foreign exchange where silver contracts accounted for large commitments. Indeed, Fritz's office window overlooked the gold-bar exchange where Chinese proclivities toward speculation often supported important volume. The excitement and risk involved in trading futures contracts fascinated Fritz.

> Sometimes when some important news broke there would be a great roar coming up from the Exchange right in front of my office window. And you never knew at that moment what was the cause of the roar. You felt like a leaf in the wind! It affected your morale and influenced your thinking.

Ever Westward to the Far East: THE STORY OF CHESTER FRITZ

Thousands of Chinese speculators bought and sold Japanese yen or American dollars. Their buying of dollars meant they sold silver, while buying yen meant they bought silver.

> We should emphasize that China was the only country in the world on a silver monetary basis. The price of the Chinese dollar fluctuated with the value of silver in the primary markets of London and New York. At the same time, Shanghai and Bombay were the leading consuming markets of the world market in silver.

The intricacies of the foreign exchange markets became more understandable with time and experience. Too, the Shanghai markets, when the quotations were cabled to London and New York, increasingly influenced prices. In fact, every Shanghai bank depended on those daily quotations in order to establish the rates of exchange and employed runners who spent their day relaying information between bank offices and the exchange center. Bank officers in turn devoted considerable time to setting rates and meeting orders called in by brokers. Salaried foreign employees dealt less in these contracts than Chinese speculators.

Fritz paid particular attention to the Mitsui Bank, the important Japanese financial house, located directly across the street from the exchange. He observed that a long plank across the manager's desk held telephones connected to the various Shanghai brokers. Yet, no matter how often and long the phones rang, neither Mr. Hashasumi nor Mr. Kano, the first and second exchange officers respectively, ever bothered to answer the phone. The bank's business proceeded mostly on a personal level.

Therefore, Fritz cultivated the friendship of Mitsui's Shanghai manager. When Harold Hochschild visited China again briefly in 1926, Fritz organized a dinner party at the Majestic Gardens, arranging the seating so that the two guests of honor, Hochschild and Hashasumi, occupied adjacent chairs. Later, Hashasumi reciprocated with a sumptuous party of his own for Fritz and his boss, both of whom were sincerely interested in Japanese culture, and he sang Japanese songs in "a fine orthodox Japanese style for them." The party did not want for its lighter moments.

> It was a Japanese custom to take your shoes off. Unfortunately Harold was wearing a sock that had a noticeable hole in it. Later in the evening when we were talking about this, Mr. Kano said, "What a shame, he had that sock on with the hole

in it. He is such a nice man."

Fritz's silver business developed gradually. Initially, most transactions were accomplished through the Shanghai branch of the Hong Kong and Shanghai Bank. The earliest shipments passed smoothly through the Shanghai office. Soon, it was not at all unusual to see Fritz personally supervising the unloading of silver bars from trans-Pacific steamers for delivery to the custom house, where the bars were temporarily deposited on its green lawn for inspection. From there, Chinese coolies loaded the bars onto wheelbarrows for relay to the bank. The bars were then converted into "sycee shoe" ingots of 50 taels each in weight, and Fritz delivered Chinese taels to the various Chinese banks. He also sold silver separately to the several silver shops in Shanghai where the art of haggling reigned supreme. Here, however, sales depended on the exchange rates falling to the advantage of buyers.

Once familiar with the intricacies of foreign exchange, Fritz sought to offset this disadvantage by buying U.S. dollars two months forward, mainly from the Mitsui Bank because it dealt exclusively in the market. It was not long before Fritz held a large account with the bank, which continued until 1936 when China abandoned the silver standard in favor of a managed currency. Fritz himself best explained the complicated nature of the arrangement.

> I bought U.S. dollars two months forward, from Japanese banks. The Japanese banks were all located around the big gold bar exchange in Shanghai. That's where the great market was and so we could get rates higher than the usual rates of the market. The idea was to get the best rates for the day. Thus I was able to submit specific bids to American Metal in New York. This is why they liked it, because they had a firm offer from my side of the U.S. dollars, and against those dollars they could buy silver or use their own production. And they shipped the silver and two months later the bars arrived in Shanghai.

Having modified the risk of shifting exchange rates, Fritz undertook to improve his position through allied dealings in Shanghai. In time, he sold silver bars only to the Bank of China, which met the full cost of each delivery within a day. This eliminated the necessity of haggling with the various shops and, as Fritz explained,

> Mr. Ho, head of the Bank of China, was very cooperative and a good friend. He was an important link in our silver

business. It was through him that we delivered the silver upon landing and got a check the next morning. I immediately sent it to New York where it started from because we wanted to avoid interest charges and to show a profit. Otherwise I would be out of a job!

Tsuyee Pei inspired the Bank of China's policy of buying silver in the New York market. Fritz advised Hochschild in 1928 of the bank's new policy:

> As the Bank of China, because of its close working agreement with the Nanking and Hang Chow mints, is in a preferred position in the local bar silver market and as they are prepared to share with the New York seller a portion of the local premium obtainable from the mints. The Bank of China has become the best buyer for the China market and are paying prices which would not be profitable to others. The point I am leading up to is this: that under normal market conditions we will likely find it more expedient to sell silver in terms of U.S. currency because of the premium rather than to buy U.S. dollars and run the risk of receiving no premium in the event the mints are not operating. This procedure has its disadvantages, as you are aware, in that it handicaps us in our arbitrages and makes our position less liquid.

Custom orders accounted for most of the silver that American Metal Company sold in China between 1921 and 1936. The company bought ores and bullion from various mines and companies and smelted them in its refineries at Carteret, New Jersey, and Monterrey, Mexico. American Metal paid the market price for the silver, collecting only a small premium from the buyer of the refined product. The company realized a larger profit upon the sale of bullion produced from its own mines, of course; yet the custom order market contributed to the efficient, profitable operations of its refineries.

The American Metal Company merely bought and sold silver in China during the period 1921-1936; it did not acquire a direct investment either in mines or refineries. The company's business there gradually accounted for 10-15 percent of its whole. According to Harold Hochschild, the China market was "not our most important business," even though the company "made a lot more money than we had expected," which continued until China demonitized silver in 1936.

Fritz also functioned as an arbitrageur for the company in Shanghai.

Mr. Silver

International arbitrage is conducted in securities—silver certificates in this instance—which are traded in the markets of two or more countries. The object is to buy a security in one market and sell it in another at a higher price or, conversely, to sell a security in one market and cover the transaction with an acquisition in a second market at a lower price. The arbitrageur must know not only the rules and practices of various exchanges, he must also master the general trend of the market, as well as of his particular security, and anticipate the level of activity in it.

Hochschild summarized the company's collateral interest:

> The silver market was an international round-the-clock affair. The chief centers were New York, Shanghai, Bombay, and London. By the time the Shanghai market was closing, the Bombay market was opening. By the time the Bombay market was closing the London market was opening. By the time London was closing, New York was open. So it went around the clock and we had representatives in all these cities. It was arbitrage. We both sold silver outright and arbitraged. For example, we could often buy silver in Shanghai and sell it in London on the same day at a small profit or vice versa.

Company policy normally required two authorized signatures in order to effect its power of attorney. The sole exception was at the branch office in Shanghai, where Fritz was the only one in the organization of over 10,000 employees who had the sole right of power of attorney for the firm.

> In all other matters there had to be two signatures, but I was alone in Shanghai and it was considered expedient that I should have sole authority. The arrangement worked smoothly with the banks in Shanghai. There was never, as Harold Hochschild said, "a single hitch."
>
> I enjoyed a certain prestige as being the only silver man in China.

Fritz knew some disadvantages, too, such as the necessity of making immediate market decisions without the opportunity or benefit of second-party discussion. As a result, Fritz "received a tremendous amount of training and discipline in the silver market working for the American Metal Company. It was the most valuable lesson I learned in China. They were great traders." Little wonder that Fritz still regards Hochschild as his foremost "shenson," or teacher.

Similarly, Hochschild confided his reasons for having hired Fritz:
> I knew he was completely honest. I thought he was prudent and would not exceed his instructions. I had already heard of several cases of foreign exchange experts and arbitrators working for banks who exceeded their instructions hoping to make more money and often through this assumed unwarranted speculative positions. I knew this would not happen with Chester, that he would carry out our instructions.

Alone in a small, distant office except for one secretary, Fritz worked hard and long in order to build up accounts for the company. At times his loyalty to the company involved personal risk:
> The doctor told me I had very large, swollen tonsils, and that they should be removed. But I could not afford to be away from the office because it was a question of sending and receiving daily telegrams. So I went to the doctor's office on Saturday afternoon after our office was closed and he gave me a local anesthetic. The doctor injected Novocaine into my tonsils and I held an enamel jar underneath my jaw as the blood rushed out. Eventually the Novocaine wore off and I was in agony. I told him that was enough! For days afterwards, I ate ice cream because my throat was extremely sensitive. I would ask my secretary to take the telephone calls and I would write on a piece of paper replies to the calls as my voice was indistinct. So we sent our cables off to New York as usual.

Fritz had not yet turned 40 years of age in the late 1920s when he became known as "Mr. Silver" to the most important banks in Shanghai. He was a trusted, loyal, and successful representative of a leading American resource company, thoroughly trained in a variety of complicated aspects of foreign exchange and marketing. Socially, he joined the ambience of equestrian hunts and polo playing, even though his proudest victories date from the ensuing decade; and he qualified as one of Shanghai's most eligible bachelors.

In 1928, Fritz boldly turned his mind to even greater opportunities in China. Would Hochschild and the American Metal Company support additional, even indirect, ventures? Fritz knew that without their support, his chances for success lessened considerably.

In July 1928, Fritz outlined his proposal in a two-page letter to

Hochschild. The first part of the proposal recommended the company reduce its overhead at the Shanghai office, not by "changing the personnel," but by "merely altering the form of its present representation." Thereupon followed the second, more substantive suggestion:

> I have given much thoughtful consideration as to the advantages and disadvantages to all concerned of a proposal that the Metal Company discontinue its Shanghai office and arrange for its orders in the Shanghai market to be handled by the local firm of Swan, Culbertson Company, whom I have the opportunity of joining as an equal partner.

Fritz also acknowledged the personal advantages of such an arrangement and his dreams for the future:

> I would be lacking in candor, if I endeavored to have you believe that the Metal Company would be the sole one to benefit under this proposal. Frankly I feel that in becoming a member of S. C. & Co., I would be assisting in the building of a firm which will develop as the years go by into a substantial business, as the prospects of this firm with its connections are most encouraging, particularly in a financial center of the type of Shanghai, furthermore it is the pioneering group which would have the advantage in such fields. So that in the years to come I will be able to derive a certain satisfaction, both mental and material, in being a partner of a firm of this kind.

Hochschild's qualified endorsement came in August. The company, he said, could support Fritz's ambitions, provided three stipulations could be agreed to: Fritz would have to continue giving the company his "close and constant attention" according to the "confidential manner as heretofore"; there would have to be assurances that no conflict of interest would develop between accounts, notably with a competitor known as S. Japhet & Company; and, finally, assurances were called for that Fritz would not be influenced by other considerations "as to the safety limits in our exchange transactions with...Chinese banks."

Fritz's detailed reply of October 19 promised "the same degree of attention to business" and "at less cost." Thus, on January 1, 1929, the American Metal Company of New York agreed to pay an annual remuneration of $10,000 to Swan, Culbertson & Company (in monthly payments) to manage the company's account. On its part, the Shanghai firm of Swan, Culbertson & Company agreed to pay all cable charges, office expenses, salaries, while Fritz himself agreed to provide the same personal attention to the silver trade he had demonstrated over the previous seven and one-half years.

The firm of Swan, Culbertson and Fritz was born. Although the senior partner left the firm in 1936 and the two remaining members left China by 1951, the firm stood until World War II as one of the most important investment firms in the Far East.

V

Swan, Culbertson and Fritz

The partnership of Swan, Culbertson and Fritz, launched on January 1, 1929, marked the beginning of one of the most successful investment firms to operate in the Far East during the 1930s. By the time World War II curtailed its operations in 1941, it had experienced twelve years of steady growth and financial success in China. The firm centered its operation in Shanghai but gradually opened branch offices in Singapore, Hong Kong, and Manila. Ultimately it also expanded into South America.

The firm's success is perhaps best understood through the careers of each of its three capital partners: Joseph E. C. Swan, Charles D. Culbertson, and Chester Fritz. All three sought their fortunes in the Far East. All three had proven themselves at other endeavors before joining the partnership. All three possessed singular talents and aptitudes. And all three brought unique assets potentially advantageous to the success of the firm.

The firm's founding father and senior partner, Joseph Edwards Corson Swan, was born in Ocean City, New Jersey, on September 23,

Ever Westward to the Far East: THE STORY OF CHESTER FRITZ

1897. During World War I he served with the Princeton ambulance unit and later with the Army Ambulance Corps attached to the French Army. The French government awarded him the Croix de Guerre after the armistice.

Upon returning to the United States, Swan immediately went to work at the Guaranty Trust Company of New York. In the early 1920s, the bank cooperated with other American enterprises like American Metal and Eastman Kodak in developing new markets in the Far East. Through its newly created subsidiary, Asia Banking Corporation, Guaranty Trust established branch banks in Shanghai, Peking, Hong Kong, Hankow, Singapore, and Manila. Swan, freshly trained in bond transactions and young, single, and ambitious, requested and received an assignment to manage operations, alternately, in Hankow and Singapore between 1919 and 1923. Rather than return to the U.S. when Guaranty's Far East dreams waned, Swan readily accepted the post of manager of the Shanghai office of the American Oriental Banking Corporation. There he remained until forming his own brokerage and investment company in 1925.

Swan was less gregarious than Culbertson and more deliberate than Fritz. Business acquaintances found him even-tempered, studious, diplomatic, and preoccupied with business. Sir Victor Sassoon once refused to sit opposite Swan, explaining that "He is too winning. He is too smooth. I want to keep my pocketbook in my pocket." Swan had "a pleasing personality and was well received wherever he went," according to Fritz. "I had great respect for him."

Upon Swan's marriage in November 1923, he and his wife became known as mainstays of the foreign business establishment in the International Settlement. Kent Lutey, an American contemporary in Shanghai, remembered Swan as a friendly, handsome, and personable man, and his wife as an admired and attractive member of the American community there.

As others, the Swans participated in the modified British amenities and entertainments that flavored cultural and social life in Shanghai, including equestrian hunts and polo playing. Mrs. Swan was highly regarded for her ability in these sports. The Swans rode often, but not with the competitive passion that characterized Culbertson and Fritz, the latter of whom won several firsts in hunts and polo.

Having formed the Joseph Swan Company in Shanghai, Swan purchased a seat on the Shanghai Stock Exchange with an eye to concentrating on the Chinese bond market. At the time, the Chinese government sought to rehabilitate bonds issued earlier, notably those issued by the imperial government in the wake of the Boxer Uprising of 1900 and the reorganization bonds issued by the fledgling republic after the Revolution of 1912. Both issues, as well as others, had dropped in value, dragging China's international credit standing with them. The government hoped a re-purchase policy would reverse the trend. Swan, using his London contacts, profited sufficiently in the bond exchange so that by 1928, according to Culbertson, he decided to take on a partner with the idea of developing a market for equities listed on the New York Stock Exchange.

Swan's abilities and reputation were such that he gradually became an active board member in a variety of financial and banking institutions. He served as director of the International Investment Trust Company of China, Ltd., a Sassoon enterprise; the Underwriters Savings Bank of the Far East, Inc.; the Yangtse Finance Company; and the advisory board of the Shanghai Power Company. In addition, he represented the interests of American stockholders who lost $4 million when the Chinese American Bank of Commerce collapsed in 1930 and filed for bankruptcy. He was also one of a fifteen-member committee that drafted the constitution and by-laws for the American community, and a board member of the American Club.

Swan quit Shanghai in 1936 in order to establish his own firm in New York City. Personal and financial reasons prompted the decision, including his concern for the future of China. Between themselves, however, Culbertson and Fritz viewed the step differently, although both agreed that the firm probably then held the largest foreign account in New York.

Culbertson believed financial reasons best accounted for Swan's departure. "He got half of all our commissions, and there were other opportunities in New York." In effect, Swan seized the opportunity to manage Swan, Culbertson and Fritz's brokerage business through the new J. E. Swan Company and thus to supplant the former manager, Hayden, Stone and Company, with whom Swan worked out a 50-50 split on the fees. "Those fees put Joe in business," said Culbertson, "but they didn't harm our firm because we had to pay commissions anyway." It seemed to Fritz, on the other hand, that Swan left Shanghai mostly for family reasons. With three young children, the Swans felt strongly that the city was "no place for an American couple to raise a family," and for that matter, Mrs. Swan "never really liked Shanghai."

Culbertson and Fritz thought the firm's best years in Shanghai occurred before 1936. However, Ralph Stillman, later manager of the firm's operations in South America, believed that not only did Swan's departure not affect growth, the firm had not attained its peak at the time he left. It has been suggested that Swan's pessimism about China's future made up his mind. His "vision in establishing a brokerage firm in Shanghai had been shrewd," said a contemporary inclined to exploit hindsight, "but more correct was his wise decision to leave for New York City."

Swan, Culbertson and Fritz had been capitalized at $600,000 in 1929. The two remaining partners purchased Swan's one-third interest and increased the capitalization to $750,000, then to $1 million. Neither gave any serious thought to changing the name of a successful business.

Japan's military occupation of Shanghai in 1941 and the resulting curtailment of business levels forced Swan to close his company in New York in 1942. Fritz explained,

> Aside from the business we sent him, his activities produced very little revenue. He had high hopes of developing new underwriting activities, which did not produce sufficient revenues. Swan then joined E. F. Hutton & Company as a partner until subsequent developments eventually put him in the position where he gained control of the firm of Hayden, Stone Company. Joseph Swan was a senior partner in the firm when he died of a heart attack on June 21, 1960.

Charles D. Culbertson was born in Stanley, Wisconsin, on April 3, 1898, and was graduated from the University of Wisconsin in 1920 with a bachelor's degree in commerce. Almost immediately he joined several other college graduates in the first class of Eastman Kodak trainees in "a very generous program" that permitted each to select a preferred corporate department. Culbertson chose the sales department without hesitation.

Kodak first assigned him to its Chicago stock house. A retail store, it featured a complete line of the latest photographic supplies. Shortly, Culbertson was promoted to manager of the southern territory, one of the company's five regional divisions.

On May 13, 1924, he arrived in Shanghai bearing the impressive title of company manager for China. The chief advantage of the position was flexibility, an opportunity "to get out from under the routine and impediments of the head office, where I could be doing something on my own."

Prior to 1924 Kodak's operation in China had been simply a subsidiary of its London branch. For some in top management, China loomed large as a potential market; however, under the London-based distribution system, products and supplies suffered heat spoilage because of the long transit from England through the Suez Canal. Thus the new position was created, with this aspect of the export trade to be supervised directly from Kodak's home office in Rochester, New York.

Culbertson settled in Shanghai, already chosen as the company's distribution center for the region. Sales rose as anticipated, providing Culbertson with increased stature at home as well as in Shanghai, where the night life was "very busy and lively." On May 29, 1926, he was married to Lorraine Fleming, the daughter of one of the more prominent American attorneys there.

Swan and Culbertson met soon after Culbertson's arrival. Of about the same age, with shared interests in business and equally optimistic about opportunities in China, the two men grew to be personal friends, and their families grew close. "We used to see a lot of each other, family and so forth in those early years," Culbertson reminisced. Finally, in the summer of 1927, he gave Kodak a notice of resignation, effective six months hence. "I wanted to make it very clear that I wasn't bargaining for a higher salary. I was getting out. I did not want to make them think that I was going to fool around and carry on, hoping to get a bigger salary."

On January 1, 1928, Culbertson transferred his 100 shares of Eastman Kodak common stock (1928 high of 181-1/4) to become an equal partner in the re-named Swan and Culbertson Company. He resigned his Kodak position for two reasons: first, "I thought I saw a big opportunity," and second, "I used to say that I didn't want to have to explain to somebody why I was doing something."

American business acquaintances in Shanghai recalled the formation of the new company and assessed Culbertson's association with it. One suggested that while he lacked Swan's "warm personality," he was nonetheless "a good-looking man and obviously very ambitious." A second agreed, cautioning that Culbertson was "an aggressive partner and at times at odds with the others." Stillman, however, who probably knew him the longest, recognized Culbertson as "primarily a good businessman, not a broker. He could have been successful in anything. He was personable and had the type of personality which was valuable to a brokerage firm."

Originally, Swan and Culbertson occupied a small space in the annex of the old Russo-Asiatic Bank, which stood next door to the National City Bank building where Chester Fritz had his American Metal Company office. They shared an otherwise-unused bank vault and an office on the second floor advertised as "First Floor Up."

Culbertson's challenge in 1928 was to expand his equities sales on the New York Stock Exchange in a bull-market year, at a time when the demand for brokerage services in Shanghai was non-existent. Local newspapers carried only two American stock quotations (U.S. Steel and Anaconda Copper), both of which arrived weekly. Culbertson arranged with United Press for additional stock listings, eventually on a daily basis. The firm in turn published these quotations under their letterhead and circulated them as rapidly as possible about the city. Soon the daily delivery of stock prices by Chinese couriers on bicycles became a common sight on the crowded streets of Shanghai.

The comparable business interests and, to a lesser extent, social contacts which were the basis of the Swan-Culbertson alignment also accounted for Fritz joining the firm. Fritz initiated the discussion. Culbertson remembered the first mention to have been direct, even casual. "He came around one day and asked to join us, and we said, 'Come on in.'"

For Fritz to join the firm seemed the next logical step for all concerned. By 1929, Fritz had become an experienced foreign exchange trader and the best-known silver dealer in China. As previously arranged with Harold Hochschild, Fritz brought the large American Metal Company account to the firm and continued to manage it separately, while giving the partnership the benefit of his knowledge in foreign exchange and precious metals. Culbertson remembered his own enthusiasm for the arrangement because "silver was the key to financial knowledge in Shanghai." China held to a silver standard, Fritz was "Mr. Silver," and silver "told us about all the other exchanges we had to do business with."

Stillman advanced a further assessment of Fritz's place in the partnership and contrasted his role in the three-way relationship:

> He was involved in the day-to-day operations in precious metals and he supervised the daily trading in commodities and metals and in foreign exchange. In time the firm became very active in foreign exchange, largely remittances.
>
> I always thought of Chester compared to the other two as sort of a loner. He just wasn't social....But he was a good person to do business with. He was a tough trader and a very reliable one.

Swan, Culbertson and Fritz remained a partnership for several reasons, perhaps the most important being that the firm's membership on various exchanges could not be retained under corporation status. "It was an old ruling," according to Culbertson. The addition of Fritz meant the firm could demonstrate greater stability to customers. The partners believed, correctly, that "it would give more confidence to our clients if all our assets were available in case of financial trouble."

With the completion of the Sassoon House, Shanghai's first modern skyscraper, in 1930, the firm moved its offices there. The building was centrally located in the heart of the city's commercial district at the corner of Nanking Road and The Bund. As the firm's business grew, so did its quarters. By 1935 Swan, Culbertson and Fritz occupied three sides of the first floor above the street entrance. Two approaches to the firm's main door, one from either side, created a large lobby effect; the area outside the doorway featured two wood panels etched with the eastern and western hemispheres. Centered above the panels was a large, complicated clock acquired from Sir Victor, indicating the correct time in all the major cities of the world. The total effect conveyed an obvious message: the firm's business affairs, like the scope of the British Empire, knew no sunset. To reach its office, you could telephone 11200 or, depending on your nationality, cable "Sing Foong" or "Swanstock."

During the summer of 1929 the firm started promoting its expanded cable services. A specially prepared brochure, entitled "Facilities for Profitable Investment," acknowledged that in the past it had not been feasible for Shanghai residents to consider foreign stock and bond investments seriously. Now, however, that better connections existed, it had become "quite possible for people in China to deal in New York and London markets almost as readily as in those of a purely indigenous nature."

The resulting growth in the volume of stock, bond, and commodities transactions presented new problems. For example, the cost of the advertised cable service began to exceed $15,000 per month. The firm, to offset the escalating cost, developed a private code under Fritz's impetus. Eventually, it found application in cabling transactions between the firm, its principal correspondents in the United States and London, and its branch offices in port cities on two continents.

The sophistication of the code spoke not only for its creator's nimble mind, but also for the firm's wide-ranging interests and pursuits. The code book, consisting of more than 1,000 pages, used a five-letter combination to contact company offices and to transmit instructions for buying and selling virtually every stock, bond, commodity, or currency anywhere in the world. The operator first selected a five-letter symbol for each single digit from zero to 10,000, which increased by 25's to 25,000, by 100's to 45,000, by 1000's to one million, and by 10,000's to 100 million.

Specific instructions followed, again according to combinations of five letters. For example, BQOYA translated as "sell five contracts of May wheat in Winnipeg"; DZYTR meant "sell 500 shares of Valley Placer Mining." An amount of 300 yen would encode as FTJPL, 300 rupees as FTZRT. JGHEU meant New York City and JLUVN, the National City Bank of New York. The final section of the code book contained thousands of predetermined phrases: JRJNA meant "advise immediately if not accepted"; POSMY, "pay in pesos the equivalent of."

Naturally, the perfected code enhanced efficiency and cut costs. In the mid-1930s, the cable department of the central Shanghai office employed eight full-time operators who cabled orders around the world twenty hours a day, six days a week. The Roosevelt administration's 1933 decision to greatly modify U.S. adherence to the gold standard produced one of the busiest moments ever. "People were speculating," Fritz recalled. "The American dollar was going down and they bought commodities freely"; the result was "a flood of orders, five to six thousand a day."

The success of Swan, Culbertson and Fritz was due largely to the fact that it faced no competition in Shanghai for the first few years. To operate, the firm needed little capital to function as brokers for the New York Stock Exchange dealing in equities, bonds, and commodities. According to Culbertson, the firm "never had a losing month" between its start-up and December 1941. It attempted to offer sound advice when called upon, usually recommending a cautious, generally conservative approach to investing. Of itself, it took a dim view of speculative ventures and gambling. The same, however, could not be said for some of their clients, who in Culbertson's mind "were gamblers from nowhere. They were terrible gamblers!" Most customers were not Americans, but local Chinese and various nationalities within the International Settlement of Shanghai.

The firm's New York account was registered under Swan, Culbertson and Fritz according to whichever branch initiated any given transaction. Clients' names never appeared in any New York listing. The key was the creation of an omnibus account under the firm's name, which enabled it to buy and sell directly through its own name. This simplified business procedures at the New York end, but great complications arose in Shanghai itself, where Chinese investors rarely attached their actual names to their account. They preferred instead to use a "chop," a seal commonly bearing a Chinese character carved in ivory. Fritz recalled that this customary practice often confused newer members of the firm who had yet to complete their cultural re-orientation. It served primarily to conceal one's assets from prying eyes, whether of family, relatives, friends, or enemies.

> When a wealthy Chinese died his family immediately went through his personal effects and papers to try to locate any seals, or "chops," he might have had. With these they went to the different banks and asked if they had any accounts under this or that seal. The Chinese were very secretive. Most of them did not reveal even to members of their family the location of their assets.

The firm's steady success eventually encouraged competition. Culbertson believed that Swan, Culbertson and Fritz had been "lucky to get a good start before others began to get in." In fact, by 1941 six other firms provided comparable services. The S. E. Levy Company, opened in 1931, was the chief competitor and "a thorn in our side for many years." Fritz discussed the company's methods:

> Soon other people saw how well we were doing and a group of local Jewish brokers formed the S. E. Levy Company and they became our major competitors. It was a dog fight!
>
> At times they were so crooked that they would bribe our Chinese bookkeepers for the names of our clients. Then they would go to talk with these clients and say, "I see Swan, Culbertson and Fritz charged you $50 for a contract on cotton. We'll do it for $45."

Culbertson characterized Victor Gensburger, the leading personality behind the Levy operation, as "a very smart fellow and very aggressive," but possessed of "a bad reputation." Initially, according to Culbertson, the competition hurt the firm but...

> ...In this kind of business a fellow doesn't necessarily move his account. He may do business with them and have an account in two places, which cuts down the mischief. And then he gets advice from two places, you see, but that cuts

Ever Westward to the Far East: THE STORY OF CHESTER FRITZ

down on one's business.

The formation of a brokers' association capable of adopting regulations and setting fees ultimately stabilized the situation. The association elected Culbertson as its first president, although both he and Fritz worked to create it.

The advent of the Great Depression caused a more serious decline of the firm's affairs. "It was pretty tough going for us," Fritz recalled. "We were a young firm and it was a harrowing experience. Many of our clients failed to respond to our calls for more margins." Some Chinese clients vanished, prompting Fritz to offer this insight into their character:

> People talk about the integrity of the Chinese and how his word is as good as his bond. Look at his bonds! Let's accept the fact that he is as good as his bond. He is honest, if it is convenient to be so and if it is necessary, but not otherwise.
>
> In Shanghai, I cannot tell you the great number of Chinese investors who would disappear when their investment went sour. They had a local expression which explained their absence. The Chinese would say in pidgen English, "Where is Mr. Wong?" and one would reply "Have go Ning Po more far."—i.e., he has gone to Ning Po, a walled city, one day's journey from Shanghai.

And kidnapping, a tried and true tactic among Chinese, sometimes influenced the investment markets.

> One day the gold bars started to drop fast and I could not understand why. I learned later that three brothers, who were big traders in gold bars, were involved and one of them had been kidnapped. The two remaining brothers sold out the position of their kidnapped brother.
>
> When a Chinese was kidnapped, the family members were very reluctant to communicate with the police. They preferred to deal directly with the kidnappers and it was done in a very peculiar way. An ad would appear in the newspaper, usually referring to some classical Chinese expression. The Chinese have no courage and they pay up right away.

Fritz's expertise in foreign exchange and precious metals paid large returns for the firm during the international monetary crisis of the Depression. Great Britain suspended gold conversion in September 1931, and Japan abandoned the gold standard the following December.

Swan, Culbertson and Fritz presciently anticipated both developments—profitably. The firm did likewise in March 1933, when the United States greatly modified its adherence to the gold standard—even more profitably. Fritz relished his recollection of the dramatic moment. It proved the first of several memorable financial coups.

> Just think, gold used to be $16 an ounce!
> I made a large profit for the firm when America went off the gold standard. I anticipated that this would happen although a lot of people thought, "Oh, America is invincible!" I didn't.
> I sold American dollars short. They went down.

The Depression caused the firm's greatest volume of business. As long as customers buy and sell registered securities and investments, brokers will realize a return in commissions. The devaluation of the American dollar, for example, prompted thousands of foreign investors to buy U.S. stocks and commodities. Most Shanghai clients were interested in just two commodities—silver because it had long provided the intrinsic basis of Chinese currency and rubber because of the many companies operating plantations in the Federated Malay States. In time, the firm also acquired large accounts in the New York Cotton Exchange and an equally large account in the Chicago, Montreal, and Winnipeg grain trading pits. Fritz remembered the wheat futures account at the Chicago Board of Trade as being "huge," because the Chinese were "inveterate speculators." Culbertson added, "At one time, I can remember we had three quarters of the wheat contracts in a certain delivery on the Chicago Board of Trade."

The case of the Joseph brothers, for several years Swan, Culbertson and Fritz's largest single account, will serve to illustrate the point further. Ellis and Ray Joseph, members of the Baghdad Jewish community of Shanghai, were noted for their eccentricities. By avocation, they were also highly successful commodities speculators whose account Fritz brought to the firm. He termed the pair, respectfully, "the salt of the earth" and "a broker's dream." And why not? The Josephs made a fortune selling rubber futures short—that is, correctly anticipating that the price of raw rubber would drop.

> Day after day we sent orders to sell rubber short—six months forward. Ellis Joseph made a huge profit. In the meantime, as the market dropped, Hayden, Stone had to pay into our account the money resulting from the short sales. But we didn't have to turn it over to the Joseph brothers until

they liquidated their account. So that gave us a lot of cash because there was no air mail to China then and the mails were very slow and we had cash coming in from the rubber.

Fritz met the Joseph brothers through a close personal friend, Moyes Ezra, an employee of Ezra Shamoon, himself a wealthy Shanghai businessman and perhaps the preeminent Baghdad Jew in the city. For several years Fritz and Ezra had a direct telephone connection between their respective offices. "We frequently talked with each other daily about the various markets," Fritz stated, and also "operated a joint personal account at the gold bar market." "It was from Moyes that I met important people in the Jewish community from Baghdad," including the Hardoon family.

Hardoon was a Baghdad Jew who came to Shanghai in the employ of one of the Sassoon banking houses. He rose to be head of the property department. In that position, it is said he was one of the first to design a key-money episode, a form of gaining property and of renting it. He prospered.

Subsequently he married a very shrewd lady who was a Maconese—i.e., part Chinese and part Portuguese from Macao. They eventually acquired the equivalent of a long garden which they filled with Chinese style houses over a quarter-mile long. It was on Bubbling Well Road, the center of Shanghai.

As they had no children they followed the practice of adopting children until they reached seventeen and they included Chinese, Russian and Portuguese nationalities. In addition to that, they supported an additional 1,500 people in their big premises.

I was invited to attend Mrs. Hardoon's 60th birthday, a fascinating experience. She sat on a high pedestal surrounded by her entourage, and the various children came to do her homage which consisted of doing a kow-tow. These adopted children, most all of them wore Chinese clothes, and I recall how amusing it was to see two young blonde Russian girls of about six years of age wearing beautiful brocaded silk, Chinese-cut clothes and their two golden braids hanging out behind them. The affectionate relationship between the children and Mrs. Hardoon was quite touching, especially on her holiday.

On another occasion I called on Mrs. Hardoon, trying to interest her in buying some American stocks. She listened for awhile but her response was unfavorable. She stated "I only buy land!" and with that remark, vigorously stamped the ground with her foot. My plea was that she should diversify some of her assets. This was good advice because eventually the Hardoons lost most of their assets, which were in land, to the communists after 1949.

Swan, Culbertson and Fritz also performed as underwriters, mainly during the late 1920s and early 1930s. Ironically, the Depression heightened this business in Shanghai for reasons Culbertson placed in historical perspective.

The result of the Depression was that some American companies who needed money came to Shanghai.

With the price of silver going down and if you knew how to produce, China was the cheapest place to do it. There money was cheap, the labor was cheap, and it was very good. So these American firms came out to Shanghai and financed and we were a big part of all the underwriting. It was quite a big deal for awhile. We made 2 and 3 percent of the total bonds or shares we sold.

The firm's major role in underwriting occurred within a year of Fritz's becoming a partner. The Shanghai Municipal Council sold the electric power plant and network, then one of the world's largest, to the American and Foreign Power Company of New York, which formed a syndicate to raise the necessary capital by selling as many shares as possible locally. Once accomplished, the new company was re-named the Shanghai Power Company. Swan, Culbertson and Fritz underwrote the sale of the shares, amounting to $120 million in Chinese Nationalist funds.

We were all amazed when we discovered the results of the bids for the power plant. The Americans bid 81 million taels (Shanghai taels) for the plant whereas the British group bid 50 million taels.

Sam Murphy, who made the bid for the Americans, told me that he was instructed to buy the plant whatever the cost and stated, "I would not dare return to New York unless I had completed the purchase. But, if I had been able to learn what my opposite number was thinking, it would have been a tremendous savings."

In other words, when the American and Foreign Power Company made the successful bid to buy the power company from the Municipal Council, they proceeded to pay for it by selling securities to the Shanghai public. So actually they did not put out a great deal of money.

The American and Foreign Power Company brought out from America a number of engineers who made efficient changes which eventually made the power plant one of the brightest jewels in their foreign ownership.

The second and third such ventures proceeded from the success of the first and took much the same pattern. Soon after the sale of the Shanghai Power Company, the Shanghai Telephone Company was sold to the International Telephone and Telegraph Company of New York in competition with a Swedish corporation. ITT in turn created a new Shanghai Telephone Company, whose stock Swan, Culbertson and Fritz underwrote. The firm also performed a like service for the International Insurance Company of Shanghai. Although originally conceived as a joint venture with E. D. Sassoon Enterprises, Fritz said "they backed out" barely a week before the issue date. Joe Swan decided, "We'll do it ourselves." The stock issue was oversubscribed seven times the number of shares available.

During each of these underwriting ventures, the firm enjoyed the strong support of Li Ming, a leading Shanghai banker and the most prominent investment banker in China. He became general manager of the Chekiang Industrial Bank of Shanghai in 1922, and introduced many modern banking principles to the operation. According to one biographical account:

> The chief features of his management policy were concentration, liquidity and prudent investment. He followed a stringent loan policy, as he believed that, because China lacked a central banking system, it was necessary for commercial banks to maintain sufficient reserves to meet all obligations at any time. The bank was one of the first Chinese banks to engage in foreign exchange and international trade operations. It grew to become one of the five leading private banks in China.

Li Ming also promoted economic cooperation between China and foreign interests. He firmly believed that China needed foreign capital

Caricature by Miguel Covarrubias of Chester Fritz riding furiously in polo game in China; presented to Fritz by the artist as a Christmas present in 1938.

and technology in order to improve upon its rate of economic development. To this end, Li Ming formed a consortium of Chinese, British, and American banks to achieve the three expansions just discussed, with the assistance of Swan, Culbertson and Fritz. Li Ming was a "wonderful man," Fritz concluded, "one of our best Chinese banking friends."

Again in cooperation with local Chinese banks, the firm acquired ownership of a bakery, the Bakerite Company, and a brush manufacturer, the Bolton and Brissel Company. Located in the western district of Shanghai, the bakery made crackers, packed in square tin canisters for distribution over a wide area of eastern China, and bread and pastries for the urban market, including coffee shops. The bakery in turn controlled the Big Chocolate Shop on Nanking Road, a popular gathering place for Jewish refugees. The bakery reopened after the Japanese took control of it in 1941.

The Bolton and Brissel Company exported pig bristles and hair brushes to the United States. The pig bristles, used mainly for toothbrushes, came from Suifu, an inland city on the Yangtze River about 1,700 miles from Shanghai. The company started making hair brushes in 1937, according to Fritz, when Jewish refugees from Austria said they could do it. "We put them to work and they made excellent brushes. It was a thriving business until the war."

In the early 1930s, Swan, Culbertson and Fritz prepared an advisory brochure on the art of speculation and investing techniques. Written by Dickson G. Watts, a successful cotton trader, and printed in both Chinese and English, the brochure advised, necessarily, that success could not be guaranteed. "We do not undertake, and it would be folly to undertake, to show how money can be made." Still, the firm identified five essential qualities in a successful speculator, including self-reliance, judgment, courage, prudence, and resilience, the "application of which must depend on circumstances, the time, and the man."

The brochure recommended the following two categories of practical advice to prospective speculators: the "absolute laws" and "conditional rules." The first category admonished the reader against overtrading, doubling up or suddenly reversing direction, hesitating to withdraw, and moderating the risk when in doubt. The conditional rules recommended "averaging up" as opposed to "averaging down," stopping losses and letting profits run, admitting the power of public opinion, selling when markets turn quiet and weak, recognizing that "buying down" requires a reserve of nerve and resources, and that omitting the element of chance could not be permitted in forming an opinion of current conditions.

Successful operations in Shanghai and an inclination to risk enabled the firm to open branch outlets in Singapore (1930), Hong Kong (1932), and Manila (1934). The Singapore office proved the least rewarding and closed after only two years. Culbertson felt the disappointing response in Singapore could be attributed to shallow local interest in trading in the New York markets. Fritz agreed, adding that British hegemony there permitted "keen squeezing tactics." The Hong Kong branch performed sufficiently better to justify its continuance until World War II. The site proved more lucrative in the postwar era, when Fritz employed it as a base for trading in gold.

Higher gold prices provided the impetus for launching the Manila branch in 1934. Gold sold at $16 an ounce in 1933 when the U.S. modified the gold standard, and at $35 an ounce when it fixed the price the following year. Ralph Stillman, assistant manager at Manila from 1937 to 1939, explained the firm's reasoning:

> At that time (1934) there were a few substantial gold mines in the Philippines. But when the price of gold increased it brought into existence the establishment of a lot of low-grade mines that became profitable when the price of gold went to $35 an ounce.

The combination of higher gold prices and flourishing mining triggered a flurry of activity in the Philippines that lasted for several years. "There was a great deal of speculation in gold stocks," Stillman observed. "It was a very active market and a lot of them were penny stocks."

The Manila office acquired three hundred to four hundred accounts over the next three years, making it one of the larger brokerage houses in the city. In fact, according to Fritz, earnings there in 1935 or 1936 exceeded those of the central office. The bullish gold market interested most customers, including some of the firm's clients in Shanghai and Hong Kong, but the Manila branch normally did a fair business in the New York stock market.

The firm also seriously explored the pros and cons of financing its own gold mining venture in the Philippines. It hired a prominent U.S. geological consulting concern to perform a study. In view of the findings, however, Swan, Culbertson and Fritz decided against proceeding because the mines in question were not only of poor yield quality, but also because of the number of mines previously reactivated.

The Manila office built up several large sugar commodity accounts among Philippine cane growers. These were "legitimate hedging in the New York sugar market," according to Stillman, and became "a very important part of our business," owing partly to the preferential access Philippine goods and supplies enjoyed under American tariff laws. Most producers rarely took purely speculative positions; they simply sought to "hedge the commodity market on their own production."

Once under way, the Manila branch of Swan, Culbertson and Fritz remained the firm's second most important unit in the Far East until the Japanese invasion of the Philippines during World War II. It reopened again after the war, mainly on the strength of another short-lived surge in the gold market. But its business volume never recovered the levels attained in the prewar years.

As the firm widened its business interests in Shanghai and beyond, it added personnel of promising talents. Key persons included Dick Aitken, William Babb, Vern Claire, Charles Cumming, Emil Essig, Abijah Upson Fox, Dick Harris, W. I. Irle, Sam Judah, Sergius Klotz, Louis Quincy, Holt Ruffin, and Ralph Stillman. Many came from the foreign branch offices of the National City Bank Corporation. Others had backgrounds in insurance, commodities, and foreign exchange. A few became junior partners under the principle, as Culbertson phrased it, that "If they made $100,000, we made $300,000." Most departed the firm before the outbreak of World War II.

Events of 1936 and 1937 brought China to an economic and commercial crossroads. Silver, the historic monetary base of China's economy, fell victim in 1936 to inflation, a paper-managed currency; this eventually led to financial disaster. The Japanese invasion in 1937 damaged the country's ability to engage in foreign trade and accelerated the inflationary spiral. Naturally, the firm faced adjustments, some more premeditated than others. The departure of Joseph Swan, the firm's guiding mentor, in 1936 posed leadership problems for the remaining capital partners. In addition, many of the firm's most able junior members followed Swan's lead and left for either safer shores or greater opportunities.

Silver failed to survive the international monetary crisis of the Depression. Between 1925 and 1932 the world market price per ounce dropped from 73 cents to 25 cents. As early as 1926, India scrapped the silver standard in favor of gold, freeing a hoard of coins. Melted into bullion, the silver flooded the world's markets. Other countries deliberately debased coinage in order either to pay World War I debts or fend off rapid inflation. In 1928 alone, for example, Belgium, France, and Great Britain sold 40 million ounces of silver, ostensibly to raise revenue. Still, it remained for the United States, in the person of its leading silver spokesman, Senator Key Pittman of Nevada, to determine the future of silver and, therefore, the fate of China.

The Pittman Act of 1918 was the first major silver legislation adopted by the United States since 1890. The act established a temporary minimum at $1 per ounce, even though the current market value ranged substantially lower. The act also authorized the secretary of the treasury to melt down up to $350 million of American silver dollars and to sell the bullion ingots at not less than the newly stipulated price. Finally, the act ordered that the Treasury purchase domestically mined silver at the $1 price until it had replaced the exact amount of melted coinage.

In 1920, when the world price plummeted to less than half its high value of $1.37 per ounce, many congressmen and citizens had to wonder at the prospect of the United States buying millions of ounces at 40 cents per ounce higher than the prevailing rate. The answer lay, of course, in the recently adopted legislation and its promise to come to the relief of hard-pressed silver miners in the West.

With the expiration of the Pittman Act, silver production in Nevada declined from 9.4 million ounces in 1924 to 4.2 million in 1930. Some 2,500 unemployed miners in Nevada supplied the impetus for Pittman to launch a second campaign to elevate the price of silver by whatever means available. The senator worked tirelessly over the next four years, often standing alone, to rescue American producers by treating the issue as a world economic problem arising in the midst of the Great Depression.

Pittman achieved his goal in 1933 and 1934. The World Monetary and Economic Conference meeting in London in 1933 adopted practically all of Pittman's recommendations (he being President Franklin Roosevelt's appointed delegate to it). Ironically, the Pittman proposals represented the only real accomplishment of the conference. As approved, the proposals featured two base plans, both of which left the future of American silver producers to be determined by a newly formulated international policy toward the metal. First, the conference agreed to cease the late practice of melting or debasing silver coinage. Second, it agreed to substitute low-value paper currency with silver and to prevent passage of legislation tending to depress the price in the marketplace.

A formula established that the United States would purchase 24 million ounces of silver for the next four years, which represented 98.5 percent of the total American production in 1932. "Almost single-handed," wrote a Pittman biographer, the Nevada senator "had committed the United States to buy the yearly production of American silver for four years—an objective which silver producers had been agitating for since 1873." By presidential order of December 21, 1922, the secretary of the treasury began complying with the London Agreement, immediately arranging to purchase silver at 65-1/2 cents an ounce—or 22-1/2 cents higher than the current world price.

Pittman's second triumph came in 1934 with passage of the Silver Purchase Act. It prescribed domestic purchasing quotas after the manner prescribed at the London Conference, and declared it United States policy to increase the portion of silver to gold in government bullion stocks until silver reached one-fourth of the whole or until it attained a price of $1.29 per ounce. This meant, incredibly, that the federal government had been committed to purchasing more than one billion ounces of the white metal when average world production was less than 200 million ounces annually.

Pittman's political strategy to secure passage of the Purchase Act took form in 1930. As a member of the Senate Foreign Relations Committee, he won passage of a resolution "to examine and study conditions that may affect American trade and commerce with China." A year later, as chairman of a subcommittee with a $20,000 travel budget, Pittman left for China during the spring, where during a tour of several weeks, he met with Americans in Shanghai's international community.

The senator and his staff met Swan, Culbertson and Fritz individually at a gala dinner party at the Park Hotel. Both Culbertson and Fritz recalled the occasion vividly. According to Culbertson, the American entourage...

> ...were just whiskey drinkers from Nevada, that's all it was, Pittman and Company. They just rode the price of silver up. That's all. He came out with a bunch of drunks and barely got off the boat in Shanghai, but he made the round trip.
>
> Then they went back to the United States and said that it would be good for China to put the price of silver up. Well, of course, if you put the price of silver up, all those good economic advantages we had for many years in China

disappear.

Silver was down in the 20-cent-an-ounce level and Pittman drove China off the silver basis. The United States by passing the Silver Purchase Act of 1934 put the price of silver so high that China had to go off the silver standard and sell its silver.

Fritz recounted his conversation with Pittman during dinner, when he tried to impress upon the senator that raising the silver price for producers would likely have a harmful effect upon silver consumers.

I have a thought that might be interesting to you and that is this: the big point you make in America is that by raising the price of silver you will increase the purchasing power of the Chinese. In other words, by putting the price of silver up that increases the value of the Chinese dollar. But we look at the other side of the coin. The Chinese dollar, if it gets too high, it will make them non-competitive with others in the products they have to sell. After all, the Chinese don't have much to sell.

Did the Silver Purchase Act cause China to abandon the silver standard in November 1936? Culbertson and Fritz disagreed. Culbertson stated emphatically that the act "destroyed" China. Fritz, on the other hand, maintained that while American legislation raised the price at the expense of the Chinese economy, other factors also had to be considered:

The primary influence for China abandoning its silver monetary basis was Sir Frederick Leith Ross, governor of the Bank of Egypt. He was brought to China and he recommended that China go onto a managed currency. The Chinese government endeavored to hold the Chinese dollar at about the equivalent of 29 cents, which they did for a short while.

Then came the Japanese invasion of China and this was a contributing factor in the Chinese dollar giving way. The Japanese acquired the main ports in China and that's where the money came on imports which kept the Chinese government afloat. So the Japanese invasion weakened the position of the Chinese dollar.

In any event, China's drastic action of 1936 immediately closed the firm's reliable silver trade account. Suddenly, says Culbertson, the market for silver evaporated and the American Metal Company had no business in China. American consular reports at the close of the year confirmed that silver importations had virtually ceased regardless of source.

Inflation, already climbing, spiraled upward after 1937. Fritz recalls the following humorous yet revealing story about the consequences.

> There are various tales told about [Jewish refugees] and how they were able to get their money to Shanghai when they left Germany. They arrived in considerable numbers, as there were no visa requirements in Shanghai or China, whereas if they went to South America, it would cost a considerable amount of money and they had to show a certain amount of capital resources before they could obtain a visa.
>
> Shortly after the Jewish refugees arrived in Shanghai they established an open air market where they bought and sold various commodities. As the money was deteriorating rapidly, inflation took a firm hold and everybody tried to get rid of any money they had as if it was a hot potato and bought commodities, land, or gold bars, the few that were there. In this open-air market on Szechwan Road traders would concentrate for certain hours of the day and buy and sell anything that was available. One man bought twenty boxed cases filled with tins of sardines, but when he opened them they were not eatable. So the next time he saw the seller at the market, he said to him, "I could not eat those sardines when I opened the tins." The seller looked at him rather surprised and replied, "Those sardines were not for eating, they were for selling!"

For Swan, Culbertson and Fritz, there were compensatory opportunities, notwithstanding the deepening incursion of Japanese armies in China proper. The brokerage business continued, as did various investment ventures with local Chinese banks. The new opportunities, fueled by inflation, lay in commodities and gold. Also, the foreign element increased notably owing to uncertainties in Europe. Many Americans, however, departed under the strain and worry, with wives and children usually the first to leave.

Fritz admitted to having pondered his options seriously, but eventually arrived at the following rationale for staying in Shanghai:

> When China left the monetary silver standard, that stopped our trading in silver, which was done for the account of the American Metal Company, Ltd. But the bulk of our income by far came from our activity in New York shares and also in our

underwriting of companies in Shanghai. There was no valid reason why I should leave China at that time, as I have written in letters to [Kathrine Tiffany]. When she suggested I leave China, I pointed out to her that I felt I had an obligation to remain in China as that was where my roots were—my capital—my obligations to my partners, to our staff, and to our clients.

You don't walk out just because there is stormy weather ahead. The Joseph brothers' business, which was a very big item in our firm, continued until the outbreak of the Pacific war in 1941. At the time we were not very much concerned by what you call the *Panay* Incident in 1937.*

A number of our junior partners left during a period of several months prior to the outbreak of the war. No one knew definitely it was coming. The capital partners stayed on in Shanghai.

You ask, "Why risk internment?" By sitting in an armchair one can ask these questions, but when you are on the firing line and have obligations to others and the need for protection of your capital, it was a different problem. Also, you could not walk out of the door. We had roots there in investments of our own in local companies which we held jointly with Chinese bankers.

It is very easy to pass judgments after the event has occurred, but little did we think the Japanese would strike such a blow as a declaration of war against the United States, Britain, and France and other allies.

The Japanese took over Shanghai at the outbreak of the war. Prior to that they had troops that were operating in Northern China but they never invaded the International Settlement or the French Concession until Pearl Harbor was attacked. That is, it was not really a declaration of war, but a sneak attack while their diplomats were negotiating in Washington, D.C. That attack on Pearl Harbor was cleverly planned—in fact, I was told later by a Japanese friend that

---

*During fighting between Chinese and Japanese forces at the city of Nanking in 1937, Japanese bombers sank the American gunboat *Panay*. The Japanese government subsequently assented to U.S. demands for an apology and an indemnity as a result of the incident.

they had a rehearsal of their military attack by planes on one of the islands of Japan. It was a fantastic attack in that the Americans were completely surprised and unprepared.

You indicate that *we* should have left China, whereas here was the American government with all its sources of information and yet they were caught off balance—to put it mildly!

The events of December 1941 were a watershed in the history of the Far East. World War II profoundly influenced China's affairs and terminated the unique political and economic environment of Shanghai and its sister treaty ports. It closed down, at least for the duration, the main offices and branches of Swan, Culbertson and Fritz, and dashed the plans and visions of men such as Culbertson and Fritz who had come to regard the city as their home. Little did they suspect the difficulties which were to follow. The war presented them with the challenge of survival at the outset, while five years would lapse before the discontent and dislocation that resulted could be resolved.

VI

Sportsman

Life in China was not all work. Fritz took to things British. He learned their games and participated in their contests. In time, he became an accomplished rider and a competitive polo player. He trained hard and played to win. He purchased a stable of horses which stood second to none. His name became as well known in Shanghai for sports as it did for stocks. This daily activity kept him trim and in excellent physical health.

The Shanghai Paper Hunt Club, established in the 1860s, was one of the oldest and most active sporting clubs in Shanghai. Although the British provided the impetus in forming the club, its membership became more cosmopolitan as the International Settlement expanded. By the 1930s, twenty different nationalities were represented, including members of American, Austrian, Belgian, British, Chinese, Czechoslovakian, Danish, Dutch, French, German, Hungarian, Italian, Japanese, Norwegian, Polish, Portuguese, Russian, Swedish, and Swiss birth.

While the membership of the Shanghai Club was clearly international, the club officers were almost always British. According to Kent

Lutey, an American who was vice president of Henningsen Produce Company, a sportsman, and a contemporary friend of Chester Fritz in Shanghai, the British "enjoyed having clubs and the honor of being officers of these clubs. Americans rarely felt that way and were quite content to let them run the clubs. Besides, the British were in the majority."

The primary purpose of the Shanghai Paper Hunt Club was to sponsor "paper hunts"* and to foster interest in other equestrian events. Amid the turbulence and disorder of the Taiping Rebellion, British residents and officers stationed in Shanghai began to go paper hunting, as had been done in the Crimea and India as a substitute for fox hunting and wild pig sticking in India. An early comment in the *North China Herald* on paper hunting, in 1866, stated "the fact is that Anglo-Saxons alone can appreciate Anglo-Saxon enjoyments."

Initially the paper hunts started and ended at the race course that was located on the western boundary of the International Settlement. As Shanghai grew, however, the paper hunts moved further out into the country. Generally flat, the country was dotted with grave mounds and intersected with tidal creeks and lagoons. The small creeks provided the finest jumps and usually were nine to ten feet wide. In the early years, there were few participants and spectators. By the 1920s, however, annual hunts drew as many as 150 participants joined by hundreds of spectators. The majority of riders were British, followed by a dozen or more Americans, a few Chinese, and two or three Japanese. Women as well as men participated.

Moreover, by the 1920s, the Shanghai Paper Hunt Club offered much more than mere sponsorship of paper hunts. It became an important business and social institution in Shanghai. Many of the leading foreign businessmen as well as a substantial number of individuals from the Chinese commercial community were members. The club itself provided an attractive social environment where members discussed business in the relaxed atmosphere of social occasions and after the excitement of weekend competition.

The Hunt Handicap, usually held about the middle of the season, was the most prestigious race of the year. It was always more strenuously contested and no honor was more coveted than that of winning the Hunt

---

*A paper hunt is a horse race. The contestants follow a course marked by a mixture of small pieces of colored paper which are scattered on the ground by the master of the hunt before each race.

Handicap. According to the rules, only those ponies and riders who had competed in two hunts in the season were eligible. The Handicap was timed and "based on the record of both the pony and the rider during the season and the weight of the rider." The course was carefully selected to include all the best jumps and was usually about seven miles long. The Hunt Handicap severely tested both rider and pony.

The sport of paper hunting involved a certain amount of expense. Infrequent participants might rent or borrow a pony for a weekend hunt. But the regular participant maintained his own horses at some considerable expense. It was estimated that in the height of paper hunts in Shanghai, before 1937, that about $500,000 was spent annually on the purchase and upkeep of China ponies and in the employment of mafoos and riding boys in connection with the sport. In addition, proper wearing apparel was the rule and necessitated the purchase of breeches, coats, top hats, and saddles. A subscription fee and annual membership, although not excessive, when added to other costs, made paper hunting in Shanghai a sport for the affluent.

The selection and training of a pony for the paper hunt was taken very seriously. The rules provided that no pony could exceed 14 hands high. The idea was, of course, to get as close to 14 hands as possible. Most of the ponies were 13.3 hands high. There were three classifications of ponies: X indicated an unclassified pony; Y indicated a China pony; and Z indicated a cross-bred pony. All the ponies were geldings, as no mares were brought down from Mongolia. The majority of horsemen believed that the China or Mongolian pony was superior to the cross-breed, a cross between a Mongolian and Russian pony. The Mongolian pony was a direct descendant of the Tarpan, the wild horse of Mongolia. According to one contemporary work on China ponies:

> The Mongolian pony ranges in height from about 12 hands 3 inches to 14 hands and has the following characteristics:
>
> Large head, short ewe neck, deep chest, short legs, long body, thick hocks, shaping hind quarters, shaggy long winter coat, hairy fetlocks, heavy mane, and thick low-set tail.
>
> He shows an extraordinary variety of temperament, from the gentleness of a lamb to the ferocity of a tiger. He has speed, sturdiness, soundness and stamina, is a wonderful weight carrier, and can bear equally well torrid heat and arctic cold. He has all the qualities that sportsmen admire, undauntable pluck, staying power, amazing cleverness over

a country, and the true determination from start to finish to get home first, which is the mark of the true race horse.

The paper hunt season began at the end of November and lasted until late February or early March. It coincided with the agricultural cycle of the Chinese peasant, who by November had harvested his fall crop and by March would plant his spring crop. The preparation of the paper hunt was done with much tradition, all very British:

> On the eve before the hunt, when the meet is announced, the Master keeps open house at the race club for members, who discuss ponies and performances, speculate on the hunt, and chaff one another over tea. The Master lays the first hunt, and on the Saturday, an hour or two after noon, he and a few chosen friends, start with Ah Pau, the Head Paper Hunt Boy, and half a dozen of his satellites, carrying bags of paper, white or a mixture of colors, white, red, blue and yellow for the course, green for the bridges over which the hunt must stop, and purple for the wades. The course varies in length from about five to ten miles, but hunts of twelve to fifteen miles are occasionally laid. Checks are frequent, the paper is often lifted, and there are usually one or two halts at bridges. A patch of paper is thrown down every few yards, often on a grave mound or some prominent place to catch the eye. A good dry-cut or water jump is chosen for the finish and is always flagged, the finishing flags being set a short distance beyond the jump.

At 3 o'clock the field is ready. The ponies saddled and bridled. The spectators assembled. As the start of the race comes down to the last seconds, the senior steward initiates the hunt: "Gentlemen, the time is up, you may go!" With those words, the participants leap to their saddles and charge for the first jump in pursuit of the paper trail. As the race progresses, the strenuous terrain, with its series of jumps and pitfalls, causes many riders to fall from their mounts. For some of them, the hunt is over. For others, the baffling trail is lost and then again found as signaled by a rider raising his hat and the shout of "Tally-ho!" As one contemporary account described it:

> After half a dozen miles or so, the hunt quickens in expectation of the finish; the thrusters sit down, cram on their hats and ride, keeping a wary eye on one another. The quarry is elusive, bewildering, tantalizing, holding everyone up just

as they begin to get going, but suddenly a crowd appears in the distance, and then a desperate race and thrilling rush for the flags. The excitement among riders and spectators is intense, and as leaders come into view, their names are shouted, one by one. A cheer greets the winner as he passes the flags, quickly followed by the card, the first half dozen, and the field. Nothing remains but congratulations—and condolences—and crowd and ponies wind their way homeward.

After the hunt, participants and spectators adjourned to the race club for refreshments and oral replays on the events of the hunt. The veteran winner took his victory in stride, but for the maiden victor it was a special occasion. He was hoisted to the bar, asked to make a speech detailing his win, toasted, and presented with the ultimate symbol of victory—a pink riding coat.

Disdain for the sport of paper hunting, however, brought regular protests from the native Chinese who threw rocks at the participants as they rode through the countryside. Chinese peasants were always at the water jumps to watch the foreigners fall in the water which was a great excitement for them. More formal protests centered on compensation or the lack of it for damaged fields. The Shanghai Club responded by annually distributing $5,000 as compensation for any unavoidable damage. In addition, the Club built eight wooden bridges over large creeks in the country and presented them to the Chinese. By 1929, however, the issue became one of principle. The Kuomintang added paper hunting to their long list of unacceptable "special rights" granted to foreigners. They argued in protests to the British consul general and the Shanghai Consular Body that "the jurisdiction of the foreigners does not extend beyond the borders of the Settlements."

The success of Chester Fritz, the rider, paralleled the success of Chester Fritz, the silver trader. Together they met, matured, competed, and complemented each other in the sunset of Shanghai's golden years before the dawn of World War II.

In Hong Kong, Fritz played golf but found the game boring. In Shanghai, he took up riding and enrolled for lessons at the Russian Riding School. Under the watchful eye of Captain Gourovitich, formerly of the Russian cavalry, Fritz quickly demonstrated an unusual aptitude for horsemanship. Unlike most adult beginners, Fritz at age thirty-two seemed naturally blessed with a good pair of hands essential to being a

Sportsman

good rider. Short at five feet, seven inches, with an ideal riding weight of 158 pounds, Fritz was in prime physical condition. The thirst for competition and the desire to win were already well documented in his Shanghai business career; they soon would be evident in the hunts.

In January 1925, Fritz wrote to his aunt about his newly acquired interest in riding. On the one hand, he acknowledged it was only "an interesting diversion in the day's routine." Yet, in the same breath he expressed "hopes of participating in some of Shanghai's famous winter cross country hunts." The excitement of the hunt and the large number of spectators intrigued Fritz:

> I was out to the big hunt of the year—New Year's Day—some 180 riders taking part. A large number of foreigners had motored out from Shanghai to see the finish, which proved to be rather exciting, as the finish was placed just beyond a bad jump which brought about a number of spills.

During the 1925-1926 season, Fritz became an active participant in the paper hunts at the Shanghai Club. In fifteen races, Fritz appeared only once on the card, placing sixth on February 20, 1926. His horse, Don Carlos, the first pony he owned, was a Mongolian with unusual markings. He was pure black with a white mane but according to Fritz "didn't have a finish" and "pulled like a train and jumped like a stag."

In the next season, Fritz improved on his standing from the previous year. He placed fourth on November 27 and third on December 11. But on January 30, 1927, Chester Fritz took first in the prestigious Hunt Handicap for the 1926-1927 season. Winning on a borrowed pony, Petzite, Fritz covered the grueling course of eight miles in a winning time of 29 minutes and 5 seconds.

> Winning that race was the most exciting event in my life. I couldn't sleep for two nights! Eighty-five starters over eight miles and—full out—gallop all the way! I was young and desperate for success.

The winning of the "pink coat" provided the young American with a certain amount of prestige, particularly among his British companions. His American friends, however, treated his victory with humor and nicknamed Fritz "the Kiukiang Road Cowboy." Kiukiang Road represented the street where he achieved his financial success; and cowboy, of course, symbolized the home state of North Dakota. The latter comparison was totally erroneous. Fritz had ridden only an occasional farm workhorse while growing up in his native state.

Ever Westward to the Far East: THE STORY OF CHESTER FRITZ

Riding became a daily part of the Fritz schedule. "I used to ride every day," he said. "The pony had to be in good condition." When Fritz became more affluent, he purchased several horses and employed a Russian trainer. He added "drag hunts" with Shanghai hounds on Sunday mornings, and Wednesday afternoons to his weekend paper hunts. The early morning workouts agreed with Fritz's temperament. They were a constructive alternative to late night parties, alcohol, and excessive entertaining, which he shunned.

In February 1929, Fritz suffered a broken shoulder which put him out of action for most of that season:

> At the present time I am just recovering from a bad fall while riding across country some ten days ago. I happened to be riding an English hunter, which are not as sure-footed as the "China pony." At the time the accident happened, we were galloping "full out" across furrows, when the hunter made a misstep and we crashed with rather disastrous results to my left shoulder, which I have had to carry in a cast and now in a sling.

Chester Fritz continued to win or to place in the paper hunts from 1926 until the start of World War II. In total, he won or placed in twenty-two events. The acquisition, however, of a horse named Tempest in 1936 catapulted Fritz into the limelight of the Shanghai paper hunts. During the 1936-1937 season, Fritz and his horse Tempest took an unprecedented three "firsts." Spectators now outnumbered participants by twenty to one and lines of motor cars brought the elite of Shanghai to the club. Clearly the paper hunts had become the big social event of the weekend.

Local newspaper coverage confirmed the growing social importance of the weekend paper hunts. Banner headlines and lots of copy contributed to a growing notoriety for Fritz in the Shanghai community. He and his horse Tempest were featured in stories in the *North China Daily News* and the *Shanghai Times* under such headlines as "Chester Fritz Wins Exciting Race" and "Chester Fritz on Tempest First in Well-Bunched Finish, Spills and More Spills." The following interpretation was often repeated: "The popular combination of Chester Fritz and his hunter Tempest were again to the fore yesterday when the pair triumphed over a field of nearly sixty riders to win the fourth hunt of the season."

The number of hunts in the 1937-1938 season was reduced to four because of the increased hostilities of the Japanese-Chinese conflict.

By the start of the 1938-1939 season, however, Fritz and Tempest were clearly marked as the team to beat. During this hunt season, Fritz received as much coverage for losing or coming in second as he had for winning in the two previous seasons:

> The strong combination of Chester Fritz and Tempest finally met their match yesterday at the Christmas Hunt, when N. I. Krikoriantz on Danville got the better of him by two lengths after a grueling hunt of about eleven miles.

The same story was re-told later in the January 1, 1939, edition of the *North China Daily News*, when it reported that Krikoriantz had "just beat Mr. Chester Fritz on his famous pony, Tempest." When Fritz lost his mount in a collision with another rider, the same newspaper gave full coverage to the mishap, although this was a common occurrence for most riders. The paper reported that he fortunately was not injured, but "would have to buy himself a new pair of silk riding breeches." Even Fritz was mortal!

The winning combination of Fritz and Tempest produced a psychological effect on other contestants, as Fritz recalled:

> I remember a young German rider—his father, Tiefenbacker, was Master of the German Hunt during World War II—who came up to me at the start of the hunt and asked, "Is this Tempest?" I replied, "Yes." And he said with an obvious disappointment in his voice, "Oh, no chance for me." You see he wanted to win his pink coat.

Tempest had "a fantastic finish." But he was not an easy pony to ride. "If you didn't land on Tempest perfectly, when you came over a big jump, he would make a sharp swerve left or right and start bucking. So you had to be well down in your saddle." But more than that, Tempest was always extremely difficult to handle and dangerous.

> He killed his Russian trainer, a Tartar from Russia, who was a very kind and humble man. He killed him! If Tempest did not like the way you were riding him—he would let you know.

The firm of Swan, Culbertson and Fritz was clearly identified with the paper hunts. Each of the three capital partners as well as three other members of the firm won their "pink." The six pinks were "even more than the great British firm of Jardine, Mattson & Co." But Culbertson and Fritz were clearly the best riders. Of Fritz, Culbertson said, "He was a very fine horseman. He was a very good rider, he had a good seat and he looked very well on a horse in the country."

In comparison to polo, in which Fritz also excelled, the paper hunt was more of an individual achievement:

> You see, it was a personal triumph! In this way—in polo you have your teammates whom you have to play with and feed them with the ball when you think it is advisable. But in the paper hunt—it is you alone! Maybe I overexaggerate it, but it gave me a deep sense of satisfaction and a kind of identity.

At the close of the paper hunt season in March, Shanghai horsemen turned their attention to the sport of polo. The game was played each year from the last of May until the end of September. The polo season perfectly complemented the paper hunt season. Participants and spectators alike moved naturally from one sport to the other.

The Shanghai Polo Club, situated in the very heart of the settlement, sponsored most of the big matches. The club literature boasted of sixty playing members and two hundred non-playing members. The playing members paid a $25 per year subscription fee and a $10 entrance fee. With a central location, the Shanghai Club was the most popular and heavily used. The Kiangwan Polo Club, located five miles out of the city in the middle of the International Race Club, however, had the better field. Here the course was full size as opposed to the smaller one at the Shanghai Club. The Kiangwan Club required a $100 entrance fee, a $40 per year subscription fee and an additional fee of $20 to play polo.

Both clubs were international in membership. The Kiangwan Club members included many Chinese members. The polo clubs like the paper hunt club provided not only the opportunity to participate in sports but also a basis for socializing as well. The Kiangwan Club, in part, offered outstanding facilities:

> Any member is entitled to use the Club House or the Race Course, which is beautifully fitted up with every modern improvement, and with comfortable bedrooms for both married couples and bachelors who may wish to stay there for a weekend or longer. There is also a delightful Town Club, situated just opposite the Country Club in the Bubbling Well Road, which has recently been built, and has all the most up-to-date requirements, including a magnificent ballroom and a modern gymnasium.

The game of polo is difficult to play. There are four players on each team. Mounted on trained ponies and armed with a mallet, team members try to hit the ball through their opponents' goalpost. The playing field usually measures 300 by 150 or 160 yards and is bounded by a side board approximately one foot high. Play in polo is divided into six seven-minute chukkers.

Polo requires the coordination of three basic skills: horsemanship, hitting, and strategy. As in paper hunt riding, the skills of an experienced rider and a well-trained pony are essential to success. But abilities to hit the ball and play a team game required other skills. According to Kent Lutey, "Skill, training, and anticipation are vital in good polo. The best ponies cannot do much for you if you lack those qualities. It is always the rider plus the horse that wins a race or makes a polo winner."

On each team the players are assigned to specific positions, which are numbered one through four. Each position entails specific offensive and defensive duties.

The establishment of a player's handicap is an important procedure. The handicap, by Shanghai rules, was based on a player's estimated value to his team on six chukkers of play. Handicaps ranged from a low handicap of zero to a high handicap of six—the higher the handicap, the better the player. In handicap games the total handicap of all four players on one team is compared with that of the opposition. The difference between the two totals then is awarded as scored goals to the team with the combined lowest handicap. Handicaps varied from year to year according to constantly changing handicap committees, the general level of play, and the improvement or decline of individual players.

The Shanghai polo season attracted a wide variety of players. Polo generally was played daily from Tuesday through Saturday. Most players played two or three times a week with Tuesday and Saturdays reserved for players with a handicap of one or better. British Army officers stationed in Shanghai, with the Defense Forces, contributed to what Fritz labelled an "unusually high order" of polo. Challenge cups were awarded to the winners of major matches. Internationally known teams and players joined in spirited competition with local players when visiting the city. The Elizalde brothers, a polo team from Manila, played in Shanghai. Winston Guest, a top American player from Long Island, competed in Shanghai for several weeks while his wife was recovering from surgery for appendicitis. He won a cup which he later referred to as the "Appendicitis Cup." Guest was favorably impressed with the China polo pony and commented that "The mounts I used were great. They are brave little animals, full of spirit and willingness."

Chester Fritz played competitive polo in Shanghai from 1927 until the end of the 1941 season. According to Kent Lutey, Fritz's handicap of four was exceeded only by that of one Count DuRivau, a French officer who played for France on its International Team; "This comparison indicates how Chester's polo was rated by the other players," Lutey said. With the possible exception of Culbertson, who was selected as "Polo's Man of the Decade" in Shanghai in 1940, Fritz was the best American polo player in Shanghai.

Fritz applied the same enthusiasm for polo as he had for paper hunt riding. He played polo regularly three or four times a week. In 1929,

> I lived out at Kiangwan, some five miles out in the country, where I had an entire polo field to myself. I moved my polo ponies to Kiangwan and each morning at six I was out practicing getting in condition for the opening of the polo season....A polo pit was available where I put my saddle on a wooden horse and hit the returning ball from the wire domes in various directions. Truly it was delightful in the country; imagine, having your own exclusive polo field. Where could one do that in America, except at a very heavy expense?

Kent Lutey wrote:

> Chester had good polo ponies. I doubt that anyone had a better stable, but several had equally good horses.
>
> Chester played hard and well (as indicated by his numerical handicap). He played by the rules and he played to win.
>
> He was a dangerous opponent in a match.

Culbertson agreed: "Chester was a very brave fellow and he had lots of guts. Chester wasn't a mean winner but he sure wanted to win."

Newspaper clippings of Shanghai newspapers confirm Lutey's and Culbertson's assessments. On July 4, 1932, in the Independence Day Match between Fritz's team, the Cowboys, and the Troopers, the Cowboys scored an impressive victory with a 5 to 3 win. In this game Fritz played third position on the team. According to the *North China Daily News*, "Fritz missed at first, but settled down to brilliant play."

Between chukkers, the band of the First Battalion of the East Lancashire Regiment played light music. According to the newspaper account,

> Soon after the start of the last chukker Fritz got in one of those long shots which used to be a feature of his play in past

seasons. Unfortunately L. K. Taylor, watching the progress of the shot, failed to see Fritz carrying on after his shot, and a nasty collision occurred in which Taylor was unable to rise for several minutes and a substitute was called for. However, Taylor pluckily decided to carry on.

This annual match between the British and the Americans was, at least for American residents, the highlight of the polo season in Shanghai. The traveling British Cup was awarded to the winning team each year. In the early years of competition until the mid-1930s, the matches were not close. Fritz recalled that even with lopsided handicaps, the British usually won. In the last years of the 1930s, however, the Americans began to defeat their British opponents on occasion and the matches became very competitive.

> There was a lot of conversation before and after the annual match between the British and Americans. And one of them was quite bloody! The British captain and I met head on in the center of the field. The referee was British, which was an important point. McMichael, who was a veteran player and a good one, was on the ground unhorsed. I was still in the saddle so the referee called a foul on me. I have had a lot of fouls called on me.

During the same year newspaper accounts mentioned the firm of Swan, Culbertson and Fritz and the establishment of their own polo team, "Sing Fong." On July 24 in an Army Cup match between teams of veteran players with handicaps of two or more, the Sing Fong team "had things their own way and they set the pace after the first chukker," handily defeating the opposing team, Meadowbrook. The newspaper reported that "Fritz was the best mounted man on the field and his accurate and long hitting proved valuable." In this particular game there was a note of luck to one of Fritz's goals. At an opportune moment, Fritz failed to hit the ball into the goal so his pony kicked it in for him. Truly a well-mounted polo player!

In July 1935 Fritz and the Cowboys defeated the Good Companions. This was an impressive victory as the opposition boasted the best polo player in Shanghai—Count DuRivau. The newspaper reported that DuRivau "was spectacular" and that Fritz "scored the only goal in the first chukker." The game was rough and the newspaper assigned responsibility for that fact to the Cowboys. Fritz scored again in the third chukker and helped his team to victory.

Ever Westward to the Far East: THE STORY OF CHESTER FRITZ

The Japanese invasion of China in 1937 influenced the playing of polo in Shanghai. Many playing members left Shanghai permanently while others who stayed simply did not play as much. The Japanese occupation of the International Settlement in Shanghai in December 1941 ended the playing of polo. The last game held in 1941 was staged with a great deal of pageantry. The polo ponies, their tails bound, were led around the playing field by their mafoos. The flags of many countries fluttered over the grounds. One of the teams in the event was named "The World." Its membership was international: Count DuRivau of France, Luciano Riggio of Italy, Captain Krikorianz of Russia, and a Mr. Heyn of Germany who gallantly got up out of his sick bed to play. The World "played an Anglo-American team of Budgy, Moller, Colonel Hornby, Culbertson and Fritz." The pomp and ceremony ended the polo season. "The war came and we didn't speak to our new enemies—that is, openly."

In addition to paper hunts and polo, travel continued to occupy an important part of Fritz's leisure time. Japan, in particular, became a favorite place to visit.

> Whenever I was in Shanghai, for the summer, I always planned to go to Japan for a month. It was a very interesting experience. Rural Japan is delightful.

Fritz enjoyed the hospitality of the Japanese, the scenery, and the kabuki theater.

> The moment I would arrive in Tokyo, I would go to the kabuki theater. There they performed the old classic drama. There the same actors participated for life. The Japanese theater is fantastic. It is so realistic because of the use of lights, the movements, and the revolving stage.

The most memorable trip, however, for Fritz was the summer of 1936. He climbed Mt. Fuji.

> Mt. Fuji is idolized by the Japanese and enjoys over 50 different names. "The Sublime," "The Superb," "The Majestic," and so on.
>
> When you climb Mt. Fuji, there are nine stations from base to summit. Most pilgrims take along a large staff about eight feet long which is octagonal in shape, and on the sides are burnt the name and design of each station.
>
> It is preferable to arrive at the last station at night so you can be up when the sun rises, which is down below you. If it is foggy you have had it. If it is clear, you have a wonderful

view. Thus the proverb:
> There are two kinds of fools.
> He who has never climbed Fuji.
> And he who has climbed it twice.

Riding and travel were important leisure activities for Chester Fritz between World War I and World War II. But the military conflict between Japan and China permanently altered these forms of recreation. After World War II Fritz rode only on rare occasions and became a spectator of international polo matches when business permitted it. Fritz did not visit Japan after 1937. Travel after the war, however, included South America, the Middle East, and Europe. And he approached each of these activities with the same curiosity and interest he felt the first time he sailed for China in 1915.

VII

Between Two Worlds

In 1929, Fritz made two all-important decisions. The first, already discussed, involved joining Swan and Culbertson as a capital partner, which commenced his golden opportunity in China for the ensuing dozen years. The second was his marriage to Bernardine Szold, an American journalist. Their life together through mid-1936 and the personal happiness he derived from it paralleled his growing influence and success with the firm.

Bernardine Szold and Barbara Harrison, the daughter of President Warren G. Harding's governor-general of the Philippine Islands, were on a trip around the world when they arrived in Shanghai in early 1929. Both women had been living in Paris, and they had reached China by way of the Trans-Siberian Railroad. During their two-week stay in Shanghai, Fritz met the travelers and was quite taken with Bernardine. Fritz proposed marriage by cable upon her return to Paris, and she accepted by the same means. He welcomed her back to China at Dairen, Manchuria, eastern terminus of the Trans-Siberian route, and by pre-arrangement the couple was married at the American consulate on June 18, 1929. Chester

Between Two Worlds

was 37 years of age, Bernardine 33.

When he had announced his intent to marry, Fritz's partners and his aunt were surprised. He was "no babe in arms," according to one friend; he had lady friends, "most of them quite attractive. It never occurred to me that he'd taken Bernardine seriously." His Aunt Kathrine desired to know as much as possible about the bride-to-be, and questioned him at length in her letters. Fritz, in a letter of May 24, replied in great detail, including responses to what he called "a vast array of questions about my fiancée."

Bernardine Szold Liveright was born in Illinois of Hungarian parentage. Her mother and father now live in Florida. Szold is her maiden name and Liveright is her married name. Her previous husband is an American publisher who is still living in New York.

Bernardine speaks English without a foreign accent, perhaps with a slight English accent as a result of her student days at Cambridge, England. She has lived the past four years in Paris with a brief residence in London. She is not a Roman Catholic. She has not inherited wealth. She has had considerable journalistic work in Chicago and particularly in New York, where she has a large circle of friends. She is now working on a novel which is about three quarters finished. It may be called "The Dove." I am told by others that she comes from a family of scholars. Regardless of the foregoing, she is a most fascinating lady, and I am in love with her not for what she has accomplished, or her family, but because of herself. As a conversationalist, she is brilliant, thus arises the mystery as to why she should be interested in me.

She has been moving in most interesting circles in Paris and New York, her friends are largely people of literary tendencies or rather those who are interested in the arts. You state that two months is a short time to know anyone, then "only on a social basis," what other basis would you prefer? I do not believe that I would care to live with anyone that I work with, particularly in my line, where there are no ladies. You ask as to what my Chinese friends think of her. Those of them who have met her are very much taken with her, however this is not an argument in Bernardine's favor, as after all what difference does that make. Furthermore, there is little social intercourse between the Chinese and the foreigners. Bernardine is in love with me not for what I have got (which is but little) but for what I am. The question of finances has never been discussed, in fact she does not have any idea as to how I am fixed in that regard.

Bernardine, who is now in Paris, will be traveling via Siberia to Manchuria, where I will go to meet her. We expect to be married in Dairen, the port of Manchuria, sometime next month. As it will be impossible for me to get away from the office for but a brief period, we will likely return to Shanghai immediately. I had planned to go to Japan for a honeymoon, but Bernardine prefers to get settled in Shanghai as promptly as possible in order that we may get down to our regular routine as soon as possible. Furthermore she has been traveling most of the past two years and is "fed up" with living in trunks. She prefers a quiet wedding in Dairen to a large wedding in Shanghai, where I have so many friends. Here she has no friends or relatives, thus a wedding does not afford that same pleasure were she being married in her hometown or surrounded by friends and relatives. Furthermore we have a horror of being the actors in a spectacle for our friends' entertainment. After all we are the ones who are getting married....

Bernardine is not beautiful but very striking in appearance with unusual and distinctive ideas as to dress, etc. She has most original ideas that are not always conventional, she does not follow the herd. She has a young daughter at a girl's school at Lausanne, Switzerland. Rosemary will continue at Lausanne for the time being, as here schools are of a different order.

Fritz's letter remains the best biographical profile of his first wife. Obtaining more information, especially on her life with Fritz, is difficult because she has refused to consent to an interview and he believes that further detail is "not essential."

This much is known, however: Bernardine was born in Peoria, Illinois, of a large family of Hungarian descent. An aunt, Henrietta Szold, was a prominent Jewish educator and international Zionist until her death in 1945. Bernardine had been married three times prior to her marriage to Fritz, a fact he claims he did not learn until later. Her third husband had been Herman Liveright, son of Horace Liveright, the founder of the Boni and Liveright Publishing Company of New York (today a subsidiary of W. W. Norton and Company) and an activist on behalf of anti-discrimination causes. She and Herman were divorced in 1925.

Bernardine's career in journalism is sketchy. She was a friend of Janet Flanner, Paris correspondent for the *New Yorker* magazine, who wrote under the pen name "Genet." Bernardine, according to the publishers of the magazine, never served in the same capacity, although she did contribute one article under the name "Argus," which appeared in the issue of July 11, 1925. There is no indication of other articles in the *New Yorker* or other magazines, nor that she finished her projected book.

Several telephone conversations in 1980 between Bernardine Szold Fritz and Dan Rylance revealed that she still planned "my own book"; that it was his love of travel and adventure that first drew her to Chester; that her years in Shanghai counted as "the best of my life," and that Fritz's donations to the University of North Dakota hardly surprised her. Also, virtually every friend, acquaintance, or business associate of Fritz's has an opinion about either her or the marriage. None wished to be quoted out of consideration for Fritz; it is safe to say, however, that nearly all found her interesting.

Many recalled vividly her distinctive dress and gregarious personality. She favored striking clothes, described as "Hollywood-like" or having a "Bohemian touch." The accessories she invariably wore included wide head bands, turbans, and long earrings. "I think she would have been an attractive woman if she hadn't overdone it," commented one male acquaintance. But to another, less deterred by her eccentric wardrobe, she appeared "attractive" and, although "not sexy," endowed with "lots of figure."

Many Shanghai contemporaries commented on Bernardine's personality. She spoke rapidly and enthusiastically, one observed, and seemed of a decided mind on almost every topic. Another commented on how she sought to be the center of any group or conversation, oftentimes discussing unusual subjects, sometimes deriving enjoyment from shocking a listener. Still another described Bernardine as "very bright, self-centered, and rather affected," even if a "genuine bluestocking."

The relationship between the Fritzes did not pass undissected. Most agreed that in personalities, the couple seemed opposites. One associate described the contrast: "There isn't one iota of affectation about Chester. He is a very plain-spoken person, while Bernardine seemed somewhat affected." However, others suggested that her social aptitudes provided a "perfect balance" for her husband, "who tended to be more reserved." A few thought Bernardine appealed to Fritz because he preferred "conspicuous women." All agreed, nevertheless, that she operated as aggressively in social circles as her husband did in business.

The *China Weekly Review* welcomed the newly married couple to Shanghai on July 13, 1929, reporting that the Fritzes would be "at home, after Wednesday, July 10, at their residence at No. 9 Rue Kaufmann." The residence, a handsome rented home in the fashionable French Concession of the International Settlement, was their only home while in Shanghai. Fritz purchased property near the sporting reserve outside the settlement. There, he said, "we were going to build a house with a Chinese-style roof." The war stymied the plan. "Fortunately, I sold the lot for gold bars."

By 1936, Bernardine had achieved great success as a patron of the arts and a social hostess. Harold Hochschild, upon his second extended visit to China, admiringly acknowledged that the Fritzes numbered among the minority of foreigners striving for social contact with the Chinese. Fritz concurred, crediting much to his wife.

> I'll give her credit for this. She was one of the first foreigners in Shanghai to entertain Chinese socially. The British stood aloof from the Chinese, but not Bernardine.
>
> We had many fine Chinese friends. One couple was Dr. and Mrs. Lin Yu Tang. He was the most successful Chinese writer in English. He wrote a number of books in English, including *The Importance of Living, My Country and My People,* and *A Moment in Peking.*

Other prominent people invited to the Fritz home included Mei Lan Fang, an actor; Anna Mae Wong, the movie actress; the American novelists Kathleen Norris and Emily Hahn; Sir Victor Sassoon and his sister-in-law Princess Ottoboni; and Mr. and Mrs. Miguel Covarrubias, he a successful Mexican painter and caricaturist, and an authority on Balinese culture. According to the *North China Herald,* "Inevitably distinguished young women of letters are drawn to Mrs. Chester Fritz's charmed circle." Her husband's annual birthday always proved a delight because "just about every nationality in Shanghai" was represented, "the majority of them with some claim to fame in artistic and other fields." Her husband proudly admitted that his wife certainly qualified as "a great hostess."

Travel also interested the couple. The Fritzes took extended fall vacations every other year. They toured Japan and the United States in 1930, and a large portion of China in 1932. The year 1932 found them visiting Bali with the Covarrubiases before sailing to Europe and the United States. A second visit to Japan took place in 1935. Peking fascinated them during the summer of 1936.

The launching of the International Arts Theatre stands as Bernardine's chief accomplishment in Shanghai. The *North China Herald* profiled the group in July 1935:

> The International Arts Theatre is an "emphatically Sino-foreign effort" started two years ago by a small group headed by Mrs. Fritz. Their first production failed; it hoped to mix Chinese and Western musical forms. Mrs. Fritz then left for a year to study little theater in other countries. Things changed and improved as of January 1935. The first production of the reorganized group, "Lady Precious Stream," is a huge success.

Fritz took pride in Bernardine's involvement in the theater and its most successful production, "Lady Precious Stream." In August 1935, he sent his aunt the program and explained the success of the play:

> You will likely recall that this play ran for some months in London where it had considerable success. The play was produced in Shanghai by the International Arts Theatre, an organization recently organized by Bernardine, with international membership, chiefly Chinese. The play was given in English by Chinese actors and was a curious blending of the Western theater and the highly styled Chinese theater.

The theater brought Bernardine considerable notoriety. Her husband had no objection until Bernardine's sister, Aline Sholes, and her husband arrived for a visit from Omaha, Nebraska. The visitors, however, became permanent residents when Bernardine hired the couple as the executive directors of the theater group.

The marriage between Chester and Bernardine produced no children. Fritz explained:

> I saw all the problems other people were having with their

> children—terrible!
> And raising children in the Far East...only a few of them made good. Most were spoiled because there were too many servants picking up their things.
> I wasn't keen on having children, and Bernardine had one.

Culbertson recalled that Fritz once bluntly declared that there were two things of this world that he never wanted, "babies and dogs."

At the last of a flurry of farewell parties, Bernardine left Shanghai permanently in August 1936. Her personal safety, Fritz explained, was the principal concern in their joint decision that she should return to the United States.

> You see, the Japanese were moving down. They started in Manchuria and kept moving down towards the treaty ports. We were afraid of it. There were a lot of Japanese troops outside the International Settlement and finally they came in [in December 1941].

Within the year, Fritz bought Bernardine an elegant residence in Hollywood.

> I bought her a very beautiful home in Hollywood at 8170 Laurel View Drive. The home was built by Mr. and Mrs. Richard Wallace, an American movie director, who brought oak woodwork from England to do the interior of the dining room and one of the other rooms. The house was on the side of a hill and it had three floors. And I built a swimming pool.

Fritz himself spent very little time there—a brief visit in 1940, and three months upon his return from China in 1943, until he and Bernardine separated in March of 1944.

Chester Fritz left China for the United States on the Dollar Line's *President Coolidge* on January 16, 1940. It was his first visit to his home country in many years. Fritz had not seen Bernardine since she left China almost three and one-half years earlier. Nor had he seen their new home in Hollywood. "Great relief to be away and homeward bound at last!" he noted in his diary; "Free from office worries." Two weeks later, Fritz arrived in Los Angeles with his Chinese cook and his servant boy. He paid $540 import duties on items purchased in Japan, arranged for visa permits for his entourage, and reached the new house after midnight. "Then followed a thrilling experience in unpacking. How B. and I enjoyed [it]. She was elated over all the gifts that I brought to the house."

Fritz's introduction to Hollywood's high society occurred the very next evening. He and Bernardine had received an invitation to a dinner party in honor of Arthur Rubenstein and Leopold Stokowski. The guest list of forty-eight included Olivia de Havilland, Greer Garson, Marlene Dietrich, Charlie Chaplin, Bette Davis, John Bromfield, Norma Shearer, Errol Flynn, Princess Pignatelli, and the editor of *Vogue*. This was but the first of many such invitations Fritz received from actors, directors, editors, and artists in southern California during his stay.

Sir Victor Sassoon arrived in Hollywood two days later. He stayed at the Fritz home. The two friends toured the movie industry, once as guests of Edward G. Robinson, a personal friend of Bernardine, who took them to the premiere of the film "Dr. Ehrlich's Magic Bullet." Fritz and Sir Victor lunched at the MGM and Paramount studios. At Paramount they watched "The Ghost Breakers" starring Paulette Goddard and later visited with Basil Rathbone and Anna Mae Wong. The next evening the Fritzes held a cocktail party for eighty people in honor of Sir Victor. The tour continued the next day. Fritz and Sir Victor watched the filming of "Waterloo Bridge" with Robert Taylor and Virginia Fields, ate lunch with Sir Herbert Phillips, Billie Burke, and Mary Carlyle, and during the afternoon met Laurence Olivier and Greer Garson on the set of "Pride and Prejudice."

Ensuing weeks found Fritz motoring to Santa Anita and the races, playing polo, entertaining and being entertained by a cluster of Hollywood notables. His diary of the trip lists meeting Hedda Hopper, Melvyn Douglas, Mary Pickford, Jeanette MacDonald, Claudette Colbert, Jesse Lasky, the Marx Brothers, and Claude Rains.

An extended tour of Mexico began in early April. Fritz was accompanied by Sergius Klotz, manager of the Manila office of Swan, Culbertson and Fritz. Driving east from Palm Springs and across the desert to Phoenix, Fritz marveled at shifting phases and moods of the desert landscape. They spent a night in El Paso. The town of Juarez, across the border, impressed Fritz as "dreary, sordid, and dilapidated."

Fritz and Klotz continued on an eastward course paralleling the border. They spent the evening of April 10 at Eagle Pass, Texas, reaching Piedras Negras the next day, where they ate supper and attended a boxing match that ended in a riot. Throughout Fritz jotted notes about the local markets, entertainment, and customs.

The following day at Tuxedo, Texas, Fritz applied for a Mexican tourist pass and an auto permit. Reluctant authorities recommended the pair not persist in their plans for a journey through Mexico, however, because of continuing anti-American demonstrations in support of the nationalization of foreign holdings of oil and other property.

Fritz and Klotz pushed on in spite of this news, however, and arrived in Mexico City on Sunday, April 14. Fritz spent the next three days sightseeing and renewing former business acquaintances. He met Monroe Wheeler, who was assembling material for a Mexican exhibition at the New York Museum of Modern Art. Fritz shopped for primitive Mexican art objects, silver figurines, pottery, and masks while enjoying the hospitality of several friends' homes.

Wheeler joined Fritz and Klotz for the trip south to Puebla. On the outskirts of Tlaxcala, the group stopped to tour a sanctuary and an ancient pyramid. Fritz remarked on the exquisite workmanship of both and claimed that guidebooks mentioned neither one. He considered Puebla, "The City of Tiles," to be "colonial Spain at its best." The city's buildings, cathedrals, and museums were most impressive. After a brief visit to Zetacuaro and Patzuaro to observe Indian artisans crafting silver lacquer work, the three returned to Mexico City.

Fritz left alone for Guatemala on May 8. The Pan American flight provided him with a superb view of the volcanic peaks that dominate the mountain chain. He found Guatemala City a delightful surprise. Traffic moved freely and easily through the clean, safe urban quarters. Colonial architecture and brightly colored indigenous costumes competed for attention in a visual extravaganza. He toured a Franciscan monastery and convent and visited a luxury resort on the shores of Lake Amatitlan. He also wandered through the Indian markets and managed short trips to the Indian villages at Quiche and San Antonia.

Fritz returned to Mexico City five days later, and much to his surprise and shock found Sergius Klotz ill with malaria. A long drive back to California seemed impossible, and the local physician strongly recommended that Klotz return on the next available airplane flight. Fritz set out alone the next morning, driving continuously for the next two days except for gasoline stops. Visiting friends near the U.S. border on May 15, he learned that German armies had occupied Holland and Belgium. Customs inspection at the border the next morning took less than an hour. He stopped regularly for the remainder of the trip passing through Texas, New Mexico, and Arizona, arriving in Hollywood tired but relieved, and in time for dinner at the Edward G. Robinson home on May 26.

Uncertainty and hesitation haunted Fritz as he pondered whether to

Chester Fritz before his climb of Mt. Fuji, 1936.

American and British polo teams in Shanghai, mid-1930s. Fritz third from left.

Fritz making the near-side forehand shot—one of the most difficult in polo.

Chester on "Sail Away," which he rode to victory in the 1937 nine-mile cross country hunt.

Chester winning paper hunts in the 1930s.

A harbinger of even worse to come: Refugees fleeing Shanghai in August 1937.

Fritz in Hollywood with Sir Victor Sassoon (middle) and Basil Rathbone, 1940.

Fritz aboard the Gripsholm *in 1943 during his World War II repatriation voyage.*

Chester Fritz (front) and Ralph Stillman in Uruguay, 1945. Stillman headed the firm's interests in Latin American from 1939 to 1951.

Heinz Rothschild, valuable associate of Swan, Culbertson and Fritz in Latin American (1981 photo).

Dai Lam (left) and Ho Sing Hang, associates and friends during Fritz's years of gold trading in Hong Kong, 1946-1951.

Keizo and Mrs. Tsuchiya, close friends during Fritz's dealings in the Japanese bond markets in the 1950s.

Vera Fritz.

Chester and Vera watching a polo match in Rome, 1957.

Chester Fritz, 1958.

Fritz and Mrs. George Starcher at the 1961 University of North Dakota Homecoming football game.

Fritz speaks with then University of North Dakota President George W. Starcher on the steps of the library, October 1961.

Chester Fritz Library dedication, October 1961: left to right, Don Pearce, Head Librarian; William L. Guy, Governor of North Dakota; George W. Starcher, President of the University; Chester Fritz.

Chester Fritz speaking at the Library dedication, October 1961.

The Chester Fritz Library.

Night view of the 2,300-seat auditorium at the University of North Dakota, named in honor of Chester Fritz in 1972.

Chalet Vera in Gstaad, Switzerland, sold in 1977 for $2.7 million.

Chester and Vera Fritz, 1980.

Chester, 1980.

Between Two Worlds

return to China in 1940. German blitzkrieg victories in Europe stunned the world, while the fate of the Far East seemed unclear. Fritz waited, spending most of the summer on the West Coast and the fall in New York. By late October, he had decided to return to China. He explained his motives in a letter to his aunt:

> You inquire if it is not an "inauspicious" time to return to Shanghai. Personally I would prefer not to return. However, our roots are in China and after all one has obligations to others, viz., partners, clients, staff, etc. One cannot desert the ship just because it happens to be entering heavy weather. At the moment the situation is not critical in Shanghai. However, it is rather hazardous to forecast possible political developments in China. An increase of Japanese aggressiveness depends largely on the Russian attitude and the trend of the Battle of Britain. I am inclined to believe the American press has rather exaggerated the situation in the Far East with the Japanese. The State Department's request for the return of American women and children to the United States is largely a precautionary measure. However, as I have said before, no one can foresee what the future has in store as regards political developments between Japan and the United States.

Privately, however, Fritz was not so sure. On an emotional level, there was much to be said for living in a new home with Bernardine and enjoying the whirl of Hollywood society. Yet, his business was in Shanghai. He had explored alternative possibilities with Joseph Swan, his former partner, in New York, but none seemed as promising. He recalled discussing his indecision with Culbertson: "I was ready to call it a day, physically and mentally. A year before the war started I told Culbertson I wanted to resign. He pleaded with me to stay for one more year. I did and then I ended up in a Japanese internment camp."

The Japanese seizure and occupation of Shanghai occurred in two phases, and had its beginnings in the Sino-Japanese conflict which began nearly ten years before the Japanese attacked the U.S. naval base at Pearl Harbor, Hawaii, in December 1941.

In those years, many Japanese leaders became convinced that a powerful, united China under the leadership of Chiang Kai-shek would compromise their present position and possibly frustrate their expectations of greater economic expansion in the years ahead. China was already a vital source of raw materials for Japanese industry and was

Ever Westward to the Far East: THE STORY OF CHESTER FRITZ

also a major export market. Accordingly, the Japanese invaded Manchuria in September 1931, and by January 1932 had occupied all of Manchuria. Japanese provocations and attacks on Chinese territory continued until 1937, when the Japanese launched a determined southern penetration of China proper. Despite a few early Chinese victories, Japanese armies soon overran the major ports, cities, and lines of communication along China's coastline and arterial rivers. In fact, within eighteen months, Japan controlled all that it wanted in the eastern third of China. These conquests included most of the city of Shanghai.

The geographically distinct area of Shanghai where the International Settlement was located was initially spared. When most of the city was occupied following the Japanese conquest of the city on November 21, 1937, the special status of the foreign enclave was respected, and the Japanese stayed out.

At the time of their attack on Pearl Harbor on December 7, 1941, the Japanese struck simultaneously at Hong Kong and Manila—and at the International Settlement area of Shanghai. The foreign enclave was seized on December 20; Hong Kong fell on Christmas Day.

At the time he convinced Fritz to return to China fourteen months before, Culbertson had spoken reassuringly of the security of the International Settlement, and its permanence as a sanctuary. The Japanese "wouldn't be stupid enough to attack" the settlement; more pointedly, the two men's partnership had to be considered.

Culbertson recalled his reasons in persuading Fritz to return: "We always made money. We had all those clients, we had big positions in New York, and we had big positions in the local stock exchange. We had a vault full of securities. You just don't quit and leave that kind of stuff." Fritz had agreed, the arguments were powerful.

But the events of the five years between 1941 and 1946 dramatically altered the fortunes of the firm and both men; the period remains indelibly impressed on Fritz's memory as "the years of our discontent." Both his financial career and his personal life seemed in inexorable decline. The seizure of the International Settlement terminated normal business activities at the central office of Swan, Culbertson and Fritz; forcible internment followed in due course. Fritz's repatriation in late 1943 finally reunited him with Bernardine, but the joy accompanying his return was brief—the couple's fourteen-year marriage ended shortly afterward in separation and, ultimately, divorce.

The story of those unhappy years began with the Japanese seizure of

Between Two Worlds

the International Settlement, ending years of comfortable isolation enjoyed by the enclave's occupants: 1,500 Americans, a like number of Germans, 35,000 Russians, 12,000 Portuguese, 8,000 Britons, and 500 Italians.

The takeover by occupation forces initially went quite smoothly for the majority of the foreigners. Most were shocked at the attack on Pearl Harbor; American and British citizens, in particular, fathomed the deeper implications of the attack. Shanghai experienced a spate of institutional changes, but the daily routine of life in the city was mostly unchanged. In time, the Japanese garrison assigned to the city eroded to a small force, hardly large enough to manage an unruly mob.

American and British civilians were subject to some restrictions and regulations. In late December, the Japanese began a process of gradual internment and required all Americans and British to don numbered red arm bands designed "A" and "B" by nationality; this was to impress the Chinese "with the humiliation of the white man," Fritz said. In addition, theaters, cabarets, restaurants, and other places of amusement were closed to them.

The Japanese took immediate control of Shanghai's existing political structure, notably the city's special police and its municipal council. The monthly salaries of all "foreign enemy officials" were reduced to a flat rate of $2,000 Wang China-wei money denominated in Central Reserve bank notes (about $70 U.S.). The military confiscated all "sinews of war," including metal stocks, autos, rubber and chemicals. British department stores were placed under Japanese supervision. Chinese accounts in all American and British banks were liquidated. Japanese naval personnel occupied the American Club and the British Shanghai Club. Bicycles replaced cars. Pedicabs substituted for taxis.

Yet much remained the same. Prostitution remained a flourishing trade, thanks to the influx of Japanese civilian and military personnel. The British-owned Horse & Hounds Bar still served drinks at the rear of the Cathay Hotel. American and British engineers continued to operate the city's large public works, although now under Japanese command, with profits directed to the Koin, Japan's Asian board of development. A combination of newspapers, radio stations, and movie theaters funneled news into the city, including Japanese-produced newsreels. The Russian *Daily News*, which devoted one page per issue to English language items, even carried reports of Japanese military setbacks.

Fritz had prepared for the possibility of Japanese occupation long before a Chinese friend, editor of a financial paper, called him at 4 a.m. on December 7 to alert him to the Japanese attack. The man told Fritz, "You know the Japanese gunboat is shooting in the Whangpoo River. I can't make out what's all going on here." Fritz in turn woke Emil Essig, a Swiss partner in the firm, to request that he immediately drive to the office, "get those bags of money out of the vault, and put them in your house, so that we will have them in case the need arises."

> We were very apprehensive about when the axe would fall. In fact, as a precaution, I had bought a lot of Japanese yen currency and had them in suitcases in our big vaults in case of an emergency. When the Japanese moved down into the Yangtze Valley they issued paper monies called C.R.B. I even bought some of those and had them in suitcases.

Fritz's instructions to Essig and his plan of action revealed much foresight. The early morning precaution worked well except for one thing—a client saw Essig leaving the office with the jammed suitcases. The client and his Viennese wife complained to Japanese authorities, demanding that their money ($1,000 deposited as collateral security) be returned. The Japanese quickly located Fritz and brought him in for questioning. He told them the office had already been sealed by other Japanese officials, but his interrogators persisted. "Where is the money?" they repeated. "We don't have access to it," Fritz insisted. The Japanese then threatened Fritz by saying, "If you don't pay up we will put you in the Bridge House." (This was the facility where the Japanese tortured people in Shanghai.) Finally, Fritz agreed to personally pay the couple $100 per month until the $1,000 had been repaid.

The ordered suspension of business activities in Shanghai followed the Essig incident. Within a few days, according to Fritz, the Japanese "locked our office and blocked our bank accounts." Ironically, however, the same treatment did not necessarily befall competing investment firms. An etched brass sign riveted to the main door of the offices of Swan, Culbertson and Fritz, below the firm's name, read "American Metal Company." This caught the eye of a young Japanese naval officer on patrol. His report created an immediate sensation among higher-ups who concluded an important American concession had been located. The sign meant nothing of the sort, of course, being merely a remnant of earlier days when China operated on the silver monetary standard and when Swan, Culbertson and Fritz represented the parent New York firm in silver transactions.

Nevertheless, the Japanese consulate seized the firm's offices. Fritz worried about the welfare of former employees.

> We had 134 people of many nationalities working in our Shanghai offices when the Japanese occupied the International Settlement in 1941. Many of the employees looked to me and asked, "How do we eat now?" When I say 134 people, it was really much more, as many of them had families and dependents.
>
> We eventually made separation allowances to the employees and a few of them obtained jobs in the Swiss Consulate. There Emil Essig, one of our partners, who was a Swiss citizen, became the financial officer when the Swiss government became the protecting power for the Americans, British, Hollanders and Belgians.

For a brief time prior to his formal internment, Fritz traveled freely about the International Settlement. A bicycle took the place of his car, and a red arm band conveyed his new identity. Internment loomed, however, and his anxiety increased.

> In the early morning the Japanese gendarmerie would come around at 3 or 4 and arrest some of the Internationals. I recall in my home, I kept a bag already packed with clean clothes if such a removal materialized. Unfortunately, in the early hours a motor truck would also come along to collect garbage and you never knew for sure if it was the Japanese coming for you.

It happened during August 1942. He was placed in the Chapei internment camp.

> This was the former campus of the Great China University. There were two large buildings. I was interned in a room with thirteen other Americans and we lived on camp cots which we brought to the camp. Everyone was supposed to have a job. The former undertaker in Shanghai became the barber. There was a standing joke that he likely would only be able to cut your hair if you were lying down.

The Japanese had established several internment camps in the Shanghai area. The Chapei camp, one of the better ones, contained primarily British, Americans, and a few Belgians and Dutch, with married couples making up a high percentage of the camp's population of 1,500. Fritz reflected:

> We were well treated in the camp. There was no physical punishment but we were warned not to try to escape. This would have been foolish because once you got into the countryside you could not lose your identity, i.e., you were not Chinese by dress and face, especially your eyes.

Naturally, he suffered some physical discomfort during his fourteen months of captivity. The poor diet alone was responsible for a twenty-pound weight loss.

> The food was not very palatable. It was delivered to us daily by trucks and consisted of third or fourth grade rice and ribbon fish which was very thin. On very rare occasions we ate water bufflo meat.

Some fared better than others. Indeed, the general condition of a few actually improved because "they couldn't get any alcohol. They began to lose weight and look healthier."

The Chapei camp ran itself. The self-appointed leadership simply conscripted people and assigned them regular tasks, the most important of which was the daily preparation of food, which arrived early every morning. Fritz, impressed by the organization, said, "I give full marks to the men who got the people to work."

Kent Lutey recalled conversations he had with his younger brother Paul, also interned at Chapei. Paul,...

> ...now deceased, was passenger agent for the Dollar Steamship Line in Shanghai. He was interned in the Japanese prison camp, as was Chester. Paul often spoke of how prison hardships showed up the real traits of men. For example, food was inadequate but one of the men who managed to get one of the cook's jobs grew plump. The others became skin and bones. Some men and women, especially those whose place in the community was unimportant, were the most difficult to deal with and caused additional trouble and grief to the others. Chester, according to my brother, was probably the leading U.S. citizen in the camp yet he would take no special position or favors. He always had a good word for the others and did his part.
>
> The worst job in the camp was the cleaning of the crude latrines and the offal. One day my brother saw Chester hard at work cleaning out these stinking troughs and gave him a commiserating comment, but there was no complaint from

Chester. He grinned back his agreement that it was not a good job. "No future in it."

The lack of privacy and surfeit of congestion in the camp wore thin on everyone. Rumors ran rampant, and to Fritz this was a particular source of irritation. Although he possessed no additional information, Fritz was frequently approached as a prominent businessman with access to informed channels. "Who is going to win the war, Chester?" "How am I going to get my money back?"

Disgruntled clients frequently became the most irritating of all. "I had clients bothering me all the time." "You have my shares!" some would repeatedly remind him, apparently in the belief that a stockbroker could function anywhere and anytime. One of General Chiang's concubines, for example, pestered Fritz to dispose of her lot of Shanghai dock shares. She became persistent and created a scene when he alluded to the restrictions at hand. Another former client, a shrewd Austrian woman with a large bond account, demanded Fritz arrange some safer trade of her securities. Better prepared in this instance, he not only reminded her of where they were, but also that the war had altered their relationship: "I cannot deal with you. You are the enemy!"

Repatriation occurred in the fall of 1943, when the International Red Cross completed arrangements for exchanging Japanese government officials and civilians caught by the war in the United States for a contingent of 1,500 Americans, some Canadians, and an assortment of seventeen other nationalities trapped in the Far East. The long, monotonous journey from Shanghai to New York, accomplished in two stages, required seventy-two days in transit and four separate crossings of the equator. Mormugao, Goa, a Portuguese colony on the west coast of India, served as exchange center. The 1,500 American civilians emanated from Japanese internment camps in Manila and Saigon, as well as from Japan, North China, Shanghai, Canton, and Hong Kong. Fritz and the Shanghai contingent boarded the *Teia Maru,* formerly the French steamer *Cambodia,* on September 21, 1943.

> After leaving Shanghai we went to the outer fringes of the harbor of Hong Kong where we picked up some Americans. We then went to Manila, or near Manila, and accommodated a few more Americans. We then passed through the Straits of Sunda near the equator and made a big circle to the right where we came near Ceylon and the ship finally landed in Mormugao, Portuguese India.

Ever Westward to the Far East: THE STORY OF CHESTER FRITZ

Although Fritz and the others were happy to leave the confines of captivity, the *Teia Maru* woefully lacked suitable accommodations for so many passengers. The available cabin space went to the women, while the hold became the men's domain, where each slept on a narrow mattress no more than eighteen inches wide. The number and types of Americans on board amazed Fritz. Many looked like beachcombers or vagabonds; their crudity and dissolution tended to confirm the impression.

Fritz took steps to protect his privacy during the second day out. A Mr. Melo, a Portuguese consul general being recalled for reassignment, held two cabins. At the last minute his Russian common-law wife and young son did not join him. Fritz paid Melo for the unoccupied cabin, and for the first time in more than a year knew the luxury of private quarters. A little bribery helped, too. In exchange for a modest payment, the Japanese chief steward gave Fritz access to the main dining room.

Melo and Fritz debarked together after the *Teia Maru* docked at Mormugao. John Morris, manager of United Press in Asia, had flown in to cover the exchange. "When he saw me coming down the gangplank, he shouted at me from the dock, 'Chester, you have a piece of Oklahoma.' I thought he said Yokohama but I was delighted to hear the details later."

The details which later came to light were these: before Swan left Shanghai several years earlier, Culbertson and Fritz had made an informal agreement with him concerning future investments. The essence of the agreement was that if any of the partners spotted an attractive opportunity, he should feel free to invest a small percentage in the names of the others. In New York, Swan soon became interested in the Theatre Guild Associates and eventually took on the role of a financial advisor. Through Swan's efforts, Culbertson and Fritz were to take a ten percent interest in every play or musical comedy the company produced, although most early efforts yielded little revenue. The pattern changed when the musical "Oklahoma" opened in April 1943. From the first it proved an instant and lucrative success. "I got $1,000 a month out of it for quite awhile. It was like an annuity for me during the years of my discontent," Fritz said.

At Goa, the 1,500 American repatriates boarded the Swedish liner *Gripsholm* on October 19. The U.S. Department of State had chartered the ship for the round trip; it carried stranded Japanese citizens homeward on the outward voyage from the United States. The government charged each American passenger $525 for the ship's return fare and advanced another $85 for expenses en route. *Life* magazine carried a photo essay of the journey in its December 20, 1943 issue. One photograph captured the refugees' first meal aboard the *Gripsholm,* and Fritz recalled, "I can still see the two lines of passengers moving in single file from one ship to another. What a contrast when we got on the *Gripsholm.* It was a gastronomical delight: roast turkey, milk chocolates, roast beef, vegetables. Many people, of course, got sick."

The return trip to New York took six weeks. At Durban, South Africa, the first port of call, the British community entertained the repatriates in a unique building called the Feather Hall, once the scene of auction sales of ostrich feathers. The ship then rounded the Cape and docked at Rio de Janeiro, where another gala dinner awaited the passengers. According to *Life,* to a good many of the group "it meant something to be able to have a hangover."

After crossing the equator for the fourth and last time, the *Gripsholm* berthed at New York City on December 1, 1943. *The New York Times* observed editorially that the voyage "already has an air almost of legend." After docking, Fritz noted:

> We were subject to considerable questioning by American officials, especially the FBI and the Treasury Department.
>
> It was wonderful to be a free man again on one's homeland. Although the ship arrived at sunrise in New York, I did not get to my hotel after all the questioning until 10 p.m. There I met my wife and had a real family reunion.

The Forum of Fargo, North Dakota, had dispatched its own reporter to cover the story of the returnees who were North Dakotans; their adventures were told in the paper's December 5 edition. These returnees included Helen Burton, for many years a resident of Peking prior to her internment at Woisshien, an old Presbyterian mission; Paul J. Kops, a lawyer in Shanghai who spent his internment at Pootung, the worst of the Japanese camps; and Mrs. Kops and their two young sons, who had been held at Santo Tomas, in the Philippines. The reporter either did not know about or failed to find Fritz among the happy crowd.

Joseph Swan, Fritz's former partner and now a resident of New York City, threw a gala party at the Plaza Hotel to celebrate the return of Culbertson and Fritz. Chester and Bernardine enjoyed a week at the Ambassador Hotel before departing for their Hollywood home. There the relationship encountered heavy weather; life "got too thick," in Fritz's view.

> Bernardine was very social and her picture was always appearing in the paper and always with the label, "Socialite." I once asked her, what does a socialite do?
>
> Bernardine was very proud of the fact that she had made a lot of progress socially with the movie crowd. She became a good friend of Mary Pickford and Mr. and Mrs. Edward G. Robinson. She was a very good hostess but she overdid it when she got to Hollywood.
>
> Our house became a clubhouse! Her friends and relatives just came there and stayed, some of whom I did not approve of. I came home on one occasion and felt absolutely out of it.
>
> I said to myself: this is where I get out!

The couple separated in March 1944, having agreed to a temporary property division and a monthly support payment. Some days later, Bernardine filed for divorce on the grounds of "extreme cruelty." Her complaint alleged that she had suffered under debilitating conditions "a long time prior to the date of separation," and that the separation had not lessened them. Fritz in his response of five days later denied all allegations and requested dismissal of the complaint and suppression of all claims for relief.

Since suitable grounds for divorce were limited in those years, a charge of mental cruelty sufficed for a generic category. The previously decided property division opened the door to final settlement. Bernardine obtained three benefits: alimony of $450 monthly, clear title to the Hollywood house, and title to three undeveloped lots in Los Angeles County. On August 28, 1945, the court increased the alimony to $600 per month while reaffirming the other original provisions. An interlocutory decree of divorce was granted on September 3, 1946.

Fritz explained the circumstances of the divorce to his aunt in a letter:

> I regret that I have to tell you that Bernardine and I most unfortunately are obtaining a divorce. During the last eight years we have lived apart in totally different environments and during that time we have grown apart. It would seem that the step was unavoidable under the circumstances. We are both quite unhappy about it as old associations are not easily dissolved.

Bernardine never remarried. She sold the Hollywood residence several years later. Learning of it, Fritz agreed with her decision because "no one person could live there" efficiently and safely. He was irritated, however, that she would not tell him "how much she got for it."

Subsequently, after Bernardine complained to her former husband about the high cost of living in California, he purchased for her another home in Beverly Hills, although he was under no legal obligation to do so. "I bought the house in my name, but gave her life occupancy," Fritz explained. "I promised it." No less voluntarily, he also raised his alimony contribution and assumed her medical expenses.

Since 1977 the combination of a "boiling" real estate market and Fritz's personal desire to liquidate all his assets "while I am still around" prompted him to try to sell the house in Beverly Hills. He offered Bernardine increased alimony if she would consider moving into a retirement complex. She refused for reasons known only to her. Fritz, however, did realize $40,000 from the sale of a lot adjoining the house. In later years until her death on February 15, 1982, Bernardine suffered from acute pulmonary emphysema and associated complications. Family and friends were pleased to remember her to others as one of the cast of "witnesses" in the 1981 movie "Reds," a film biography of the American radicals John Reed and Louise Bryant.

Fritz's divorce from Bernardine in 1946 ended his years of discontent. With an Allied victory secured and peace achieved, Fritz waited nervously on the West Coast for the first opportunity to return to Shanghai. The past five years had been very difficult, the worst since his first two years in Seattle. He had few illusions about what he would find in Shanghai, but he retained a firm resolve to pick up the pieces and settle all accounts. Unexpectedly, however, the next five years proved personally rewarding and financially successful. Amidst the tumult, uncertainty, and high inflation of postwar China, Fritz discerned another career trading in an even more volatile metal. Mr. Silver became Mr. Gold.

VIII

Mr. Gold

Dramatic changes affected the Far East in the post-World War II era. In China, there was no return after 1945 to the prewar ambience so friendly to free enterprise. Both the Nationalist and Communist leadership sought permanently to excise all instruments of foreign economic penetration and control. Extraterritoriality, including the unique political-economic autonomy of the several treaty ports, became the first casualty. Ultimately only Hong Kong survived. Other restraints soon followed, until it could rightly be said that World War II and its consequences had forever altered the economic life of China.

The demise of Swan, Culbertson and Fritz, one of the largest foreign brokerage firms in the Far East prior to 1941, profiles the dramatically changed circumstances. The firm's central office in Shanghai never recovered from the war. Even after the return to peace, the firm's business with the New York Stock Exchange practically evaporated, a victim of spiraling inflation and foreign exchange controls. Shanghai functioned briefly on a meager diet of local shares, foreign remittances, and bullion demand. The beleaguered Nationalist government re-

Mr. Gold

sponded with ever-more-ambitious rules of economic stricture. Finally, in the spring of 1947 the firm closed its doors in the face of alleged violations of the accumulating regulations.

Isolated from the Far East after their repatriation in late 1943, Culbertson and Fritz grasped their first opportunity to return in the fall of 1945. They first tried, without success, to get seating on an army supply plane. Then they learned that Shanghai had not yet opened to passenger ships. Fritz, growing anxious, wondered if the "reconstruction of our affairs in China" would ever commence.

The pair finally obtained passage on the *Fly Away*, which was a vintage freighter docked at San Francisco. The ship carried fewer than twelve passengers in order to circumvent the regulation requiring a staff physician. When at last it lifted anchor a month later, it headed for Manila, not Shanghai, where twenty-nine other ships preceded its turn at berthing.

Yet, the month-long wait in San Francisco had been profitable. One day Fritz noticed the price quotations for three or four Philippine gold mining companies. He immediately cabled Walter Wolff at the firm's Manila branch office to verify a suspected difference in the stocks' price on the two exchanges. He took the initiative.

> I instructed Manila to start buying the gold mining shares and to arrange for the proper endorsement so that the purchases would be in acceptable form for delivery on the San Francisco Exchange.
>
> The profits were unbelievable! I made $50,000 or $60,000 in arbitrage. Culbertson got half of the profits but it was my idea. I continued to use our private code while aboard the *Fly Away*.

Culbertson and Fritz spent most of January and February 1946 in Manila. With no housing available, Fritz slept on Wolff's couch in his living room. He also described his impressions of the city in a letter to his aunt:

> There is a great scarcity of housing and people are crowded into a limited number of houses which are still habitable. The Japanese rigorously followed a plan of destruction before the city was captured by American troops. Prices are very high, but not as high as those a few months ago as imports are beginning to arrive. An egg costs 20 cents. In the harbor there are over a hundred freighters, tankers and vessels of all types, many of them waiting to be unloaded,

and due to a shortage of docking facilities, most of them could not be discharged promptly....

There is practically no transportation as the trams and trucks were destroyed....With destruction in evidence everywhere, one feels very close to the ravages of war. Large numbers of Filipinos have lost their lives and the stories of Japanese atrocities and cruelty are unbelievable.

Walter Wolff re-established the Manila branch in October 1945, while Emil Essig reopened the Shanghai office on November 1. Wolff relocated in the same building, one of the few little damaged by war. Essig had a worse time of it. The Japanese had looted the premises and commandeered all the furniture, office equipment, and accounting machines. In fact, the U.S. Army had occupied the firm's former office space in the Sassoon House, denying access to all vaults and financial records. Not until May 1946 did Culbertson and Fritz regain possession.

Fritz found Shanghai in 1946 still "a truly fantastic place," despite the strain of the past five years. Japanese residents were being deported to the home islands. Most buildings lacked heat, largely because of a short coal supply and the absence of radiators. The Japanese army had been ordered to seize all scrap iron, and Communist control of north China interrupted regular coal shipments. The cost of food climbed as the value of the Chinese dollar dropped against the greenback. Hyperinflation was sure to follow; it was only a matter of time. Wearing a Parker pen in one's outside coat pocket was a popular sign of affluence.

Before the war, Fritz was a collector of antique Chinese plates, which were usually in pairs—male and female. After the war it became very difficult to obtain good specimens and the prices had increased to high levels. Fritz complained that the last lot of dishes he bought were recent models and not really antiques. His Chinese dealer replied, "Why should you complain, the workmanship of these recent plates is better than that of the ancient Chin Lung period."

Fritz and Culbertson rented a twelfth-floor apartment at the Grosvenor Hotel, which lacked heat but featured hot water once a day. The partners' first concern, however, was "trying to recover as much lost ground as possible." They began by hiring an accountant from the New York firm of Marshall Granger for the summer. His efforts to rehabilitate the firm's records resulted in the recovery of many securities, most of which had been piled in large wicker baskets at the Bank of China. He also satisfied a lengthy investigation by the Internal Revenue Service, which questioned Culbertson's and Fritz's personal tax returns for the war years. Otherwise the results were mixed.

The Shanghai office never again recovered its prewar business volume. Chinese clients could no longer afford to deal in American stocks and bonds. The Chinese dollar came under rising inflationary pressure. Local shares provided the bulk of brokerage fees, according to Culbertson.

> There were hundreds of people in front of our office where we posted the prices. We had thirty-two salesmen, mostly Chinese selling local shares. We had five seats on the Shanghai stock exchange. It was a big business in local shares but not a very profitable one. Many of the stocks were ridiculous in value but the Chinese wanted to get rid of them.

The firm also profited for a time from an active foreign exchange market. Initially, the Nationalist government prohibited Shanghai banks from dealing in foreign exchange, but the new rule said nothing about securities brokers. To handle this unexpected volume of business, the partners hired Frederick Mysberg to manage the trade. A Dutch national, he had most recently been manager of Handel's branch bank in Tokyo, and agreed to a good salary plus 10 percent commission. Fritz characterized Mysberg as "a damn shrewd trader but very avaricious."

The firm's Manila and Hong Kong branches proved more successful. Until the resumption of direct and adequate communications, the Manila office realized good profits from the arbitrage of gold mining shares between the Philippine and American exchanges. Hong Kong, however, emerged as by far the more important center. Here the firm captured large profits in a short time by selling gold bullion in the volatile international markets. Yet, by the spring of 1950 this also ended, partly because of increased competition, but mainly because of British and American official disapproval.

These last years in China also strained the relationship between Culbertson and Fritz. The short-term success of the Hong Kong gold trade and the failure of the Shanghai office forced another look at the long-standing business arrangement between the two men. Indeed, only the welfare of a newly founded operation in South America postponed an early and complete liquidation of the partnership. Age, conflicting lifestyles, and the frustrations inherent in the ever-narrowing economic opportunities in China accounted for the problems.

Fritz claimed a measure of independence. He spotted one last opportunity in silver and began exploring the possibilities of importing gold ingots. In fact, although he had returned to China to collect the broken pieces of his former business interests, he inadvertently "got into the gold business" as well. "It was so profitable."

Although China converted to fully managed currency in 1936, Fritz remained "Mr. Silver" in the Far East for several years following World War II. He consummated his last major silver transaction in 1947, during the civil war raging between the Nationalists under Chiang Kai-shek and Mao Tse-tung's Communist forces. The transaction, involving the acquisition and transfer of 10 million refined ounces, demonstrated the solitary and highly personal character of Fritz's business activities in later years, and hinted at the private initiatives a bullion trader utilizes in coordinating contacts developed in the course of a lengthy career.

Early in 1947, Fritz proposed to the Nationalists an idea he believed would help win the war. Having observed that Chiang's armies lacked esprit de corps and tenacity, he concluded the reason lay partly in that they were paid with inflated paper money. He conceived a plan which he recommended to O. K. Wui, minister of finance, at a private meeting in Canton, to have them paid in silver, China's ancient medium. Wui agreed in principle to the proposal, including a provision to have Chinese silver dollars minted in America. Wui thought the silver, however, should be obtained through the New York market. Fritz objected, suggesting instead a private purchase directly from the Mexican government. He knew this source as the more practical and private—that is, the prospect of such a sale would not adversely influence the price of silver prior to its completion. Wui, no stranger himself to the volatile bullion market, appreciated the point.

The two men could not agree, however, on the amount of silver to purchase. Wui wanted a series of acquisitions, starting with an initial order of 500,000 ounces. Fritz discerned the strategy. Should the transaction proceed smoothly, Wui could place orders without the services of Fritz. Fritz, of course, knew this and refused to divulge any further details until the minister agreed to a much larger order. They talked further. Finally, Wui relented in favor of purchasing 10 million ounces.

Once the details with the Chinese were decided, Fritz turned his attention to the sensitive problem of arranging for his financing. He knew from experience that the Mexican government without exception dealt on cash-and-carry terms. He also knew from experience that the Chinese government never relinquished payment until it was in possession of the silver. Fritz contacted the Bank of America in San Francisco, requesting financing and the accessibility of its representative in Mexico City to place the order. The bank cooperated, extending Fritz credit for $7.2 million or the equivalent of 72 cents per ounce. It also agreed to help safeguard his interest in the deal by attaching 1/2 cent per ounce to the transfer price or $50,000.

The bank secured the purchase and had the silver shipped to San Francisco. In the meantime, Fritz advised the Chinese government when to loan its engraved dies to the mint where the bullion was to be struck into silver dollars. When completed, the Chinese paid the Bank of America and took charge of transporting the silver to Canton. Fritz charged the Chinese an additional commission of 1/2 percent or $36,000.

The entire transaction proceeded without a hitch. Its eventual discovery, however, triggered an interesting commentary within American banking circles. Hearing about it, a vice-president in a leading New York bank asked rhetorically, "What the hell does the Bank of America know about silver? Not a damn thing," he answered himself. "I'll bet it's that so and so Chester Fritz. I'll bet it was him."

Fritz took pride in the fact that the "big deal was consummated outside the usual market channels and did not disturb the world price of silver," which held steady at between 72 and 74 cents per ounce. He correctly assumed, too, that the Chinese government might thereafter dispense with his services. Tsi Ti Mo, head of the Bank of China, negotiated directly with the Mexican government and purchased an additional 30 million ounces. Nevertheless, Fritz concluded, "My simple, direct purchase plan proved of great financial benefit to the Chinese." And, of course, Fritz had realized $86,000 for himself. Not a bad profit for an idea that cost him nothing beyond a little "assertiveness."

As Chinese confidence in the value of their managed currency ebbed, they turned increasingly to gold for protection. By 1946 the Chinese dollar had declined to a ratio of 1,800 to 1 against its American equivalent, a far cry from the 3 to 1 exchange rate that revailed prior to 1936, when China abandoned its traditional silver standard. Even so, the worst lay ahead. Before Fritz left China permanently in 1950, a single greenback commanded at least 90,000 Chinese dollars. One of the world's terrible experiences in hyperinflation had set in.

Speculators took note and plotted. But in fact, only a handful of practiced traders in precious metals knew the nature of gold markets anywhere. These traders combined skills in arbitrage and currency conversions with knowledge of trusted contacts in national banks. Even then, the most important ingredients were lacking—daring and nerve. Chester Fritz emerged as the first and the most successful gold trader in China between 1946 and 1950.

Milton Marmor, a correspondent for the Associated Press in China, once attempted to explain the furtive world of gold trading and the men who controlled it. He identified four conditions necessary to become an established personage in the business: "A million dollars deposited in a New York bank, membership in a worldwide syndicate with access to the right connections, sharp business brains and a world of nerve."

Although Marmor could not exactly indicate how the gold trader obtained the raw commodity, he knew it could be bought practically anywhere if the price was right. Large international airlines ship gold bars on order, and most transactions require less than two weeks to complete. Traders seldom realize more than two percent on any single transaction but, of course, two percent of a sale involving a million dollars or more is scarcely a paltry profit.

Marmor divulged no names. Instead, he offered a profile of the typical trader.

> They come from every part of the world, although their number is few and their occupation, for obvious reasons, is a select one. Gold is the tissue of their lives. They get a real kick out of handling the metal and waiting for the giant airliners to come down with the wooden boxes loaded with heavy metal and handled just like any other piece of goods....
>
> These men who trade in gold, who have the unusual thrill of handling millions of dollars worth of the precious metal as if it were eggs, who know the excitement of being at the wrong end of a U.S. $2,000,000 gold robbery as some of them were recently—these men don't like to talk too much about their occupation.

When the British government prohibited the importation of gold bars into Hong Kong after World War II, operations simply moved across the bay to Macao, itself a well used conduit for precious commodities and assorted illicit substances. Macao continued to provide direct access to the mainland, but its small land area made it difficult for international air carriers to use. Bangkok and Saigon assumed the place of intermediate stops in the supply chain. Both airports could easily accommodate the

Mr. Gold

largest carriers but, more importantly, lay within the practical range of Catalina seaplanes to accomplish the six-hour flying time to Macao.

Once the gold arrived in Macao, the trader finalized his transaction, usually with Hong Kong bankers who crossed the bay by ferry. The trader had no interest in the shipment beyond this point, but Marmor, the Associated Press correspondent, suggested, "It's no secret that those who buy gold in Macao proceed to smuggle it into China and other parts of the world for resale at big profits to wealthy merchants who prefer bullion to their own shaky paper currency."

Fritz maintained he was the first trader to import gold into Hong Kong after the war. He recalled:

> It was after my return in 1946 that we initiated the gold business. No other person in our firm understood it. I had all the connections.
>
> I imported the first gold to Hong Kong after the war. I worked through the Hang Seng bank in Hong Kong. They obtained an import license to import gold into Hong Kong for jewelry purposes. It worked for two shipments. Then the practice of issuing import licenses was stopped by the influence of the American government, who put pressure on Hong Kong via London to discontinue import licenses.

He accomplished his first transaction under manifold complexities, all requiring a full measure of financial credit, personal contacts, snap judgment, and nerve. Three of his contacts proved invaluable. He obtained information through his former employer in New York, the American Metal Company, that a customer in the Shanghai area had ordered the smelting of 20,000 ounces of gold into bars. He also learned that the customer counted on a handsome profit based on newspaper reports that gold then sold for $60 an ounce in China.

Fritz took immediate action. He first attempted to confirm whether the author of the order had already found an outlet in Shanghai. He went to Red Reed, manager of the Shanghai branch of the First National City Bank, telling him about the purported shipment and asking him to verify it if possible. Reed cabled his New York office, which replied in the affirmative, "Yes, there is a shipment and we are going to consign it to you in Shanghai." Reed, dumbfounded, turned to Fritz. According to Fritz the ensuing dialogue ran this way:

Reed: They had no right to do that without con-

	sulting me. You cannot import gold into China.
Fritz:	I will buy the gold from you.
Reed:	What price?
Fritz:	I will think it over.
Reed:	You have to give me a good price or I will ship it back to New York.
Fritz:	You can't bring it into China but I have a way.
Reed:	Tell me tomorrow morning what you will bid and I will say yes or no. I will show those bastards in New York that they cannot do that to me.
Fritz:	I bid $42 an ounce for the entire shipment. I will take delivery in Hong Kong.
Reed:	Oh! You cannot take it there.
Fritz:	You let me worry about that!

A third contact shortly secured a gold import license in Hong Kong. According to Fritz, "I telegraphed my friend Dai Lam and Mr. Ho Sing Hang of the Hang Seng Bank in Hong Kong. 'Can you arrange to obtain a gold import license?' To the wonder of all things, they obtained it. It worked for two shipments."

Dai Lam, "Big Lam" in the Shanghai dialect, figured among the founders of the Hang Seng Bank in Hong Kong. He and Fritz had known each other in Shanghai before World War II, when Dai Lam worked in banking and knew Fritz as a reliable businessman, a capable silver trader, and a foreigner who was sincerely interested in Chinese culture. To Fritz, Dai Lam was a "big man physically and in the community. He looked like Mussolini and acted like him. He was an autocrat." Competitors knew Dai Lam as a "man who did his own thinking." His knowledge of English was limited to one word, "no." When Dai Lam died in 1948, Fritz attended the funeral as an honored guest.

> When he passed away his family asked me to walk in the funeral procession down through the main streets in Hong Kong. Fortunately it was on a Sunday when there was little traffic.
>
> I was one of only two foreigners in that long procession. About half way along the route was a temporary shrine built holding a giant size enlarged photo of Dai Lam, where we

stopped and bowed three times.

This funeral was an important event as evidenced by the fact that there were twenty-nine bands in the funeral procession, various and sometimes strange uniforms blowing loud western wind instruments, and some of the bands were donated by his friends.

There are three important events in the life of every Chinese—birth, wedding, and funeral. Many Chinese families have been known to mortgage their future in order to produce an impressive funeral.

Ho Sing Hang, like Dai Lam, had been a banker in Shanghai before the war, chiefly as director and general manager of the Seng Dah Trust Company, Ltd. Although he was a Catholic, jokingly referred to by his colleagues as "the Pope," Mr. Ho lived in the traditional manner. At the outbreak of the Sino-Japanese War, he quit Shanghai for Hong Kong and devoted himself to founding and managing the Hang Seng Bank. He took refuge in Macao for the duration of hostilities after 1941. In a letter to Dan Rylance, Mr. Ho described the frenzied activity in gold after 1945, when China's currency was "subjected to wild fluctuations."

About his business relationship with Fritz, Ho said,

> Mr. Fritz also came to Hong Kong after the war to set up office here and the Hang Seng Bank dealt with him in gold transactions, as a result of which he became our friend as well as valued customer. He was honest and frank and our dealings were mutually beneficial as we trusted each other unreservedly....
>
> Mr. Fritz had a great sense of appreciation for oriental art, which probably was the result of his in-depth knowledge about China and her people while living in that country....Although I might not correspond with Mr. Fritz too often, we are always in each other's thoughts.

Fritz's second gold contract was also his last. Learning of his dealings, the London-based company of Samuel Montague, veteran dealers in precious metals, likewise obtained an import license.

> For this gold deal we joined with our main competitor, the large bullion dealer in London. We each had been negotiating independently for the gold held by the government of Colombia, South America. Together we purchased from them 40,000 ounces of gold. Since one could not obtain bank

financing in the gold business, your capital had to be liquid. Our 50 percent share of this shipment required $800,000, all in cash.

Fritz then moved his office to Macao. There, under the name of Federal, Inc., U.S.A., a legal subsidiary of Swan, Culbertson and Fritz, he applied for and received an import license from the Portuguese colony—the first international gold trader to do so. But, because of runway limitations at the airport, Fritz consigned his gold shipments to Manila, Bangkok, or Saigon. He would meet the flight at one of the cities with a chartered Catalina flying boat obtained in Okinawa to freight the cargo back to Macao. As Fritz described the last stage of the transaction,

In Macao, the Chinese banks, to whom I sold the gold, took control of the gold and brought it to the Hong Kong market. How they got it there I don't know. I did not inquire! At that time the import of gold could not be consummated. It was against the law.

I have no reliable information as to the amount of gold that we imported into Macao. The gold business was not illegal as our books were audited by the leading chartered accountants in Hong Kong and we paid taxes on our profits accordingly. This type of business, however, was totally different from our prewar activities. I was actively engaged entirely with gold, trying to convert stumbling blocks into stepping stones.

Later the law, of course, was changed. Today gold shipments can go directly to Hong Kong. The Hong Kong gold exchange is the first gold exchange to open each market day. It has considerable influence on the next opening exchange markets in Zurich and London and, later, the New York and Chicago markets.

Lloyd's of London carried the insurance on each contract. The famous company covered all risks save one—changes in government regulations. On one occasion, while a 40,000 ounce shipment was en route over India via KLM Dutch Airlines, a bloodless coup took place in Bangkok. The new inspector general of customs confiscated the shipment upon its arrival, even though the bill of lading read "Destination Bangkok—en route to Macao." Fritz, in Hong Kong, telegraphed the shipping agent to protect his $1.6 million investment and "to ship at all costs." Fritz explained how the gold shipment eventually left Bangkok:

When I talked to the shipping agent later in Hong Kong he told me he even got down on his knees and kowtowed to the customs inspector but with no success. The following morning there was a brand new, red Peugeot automobile standing in front of the inspector general's home. Our shipment of gold left for Macao later that afternoon. Purely coincidental, as they say in Hollywood!

Later, when asked about the gift and the fact that it seemed out of character, Fritz quipped, "I would remind you that in the bazaars of the Far East, on frequent occasions the law of the jungle prevails, and you cannot follow the rules as you learned them from Sunday school in North Dakota." Nor did the incident end there. When he was in Amsterdam to purchase another gold contract, Fritz raised the matter of the red Peugeot, insisting to KLM's management, then preoccupied with the Berlin Airlift, that it had guaranteed shipment to Macao. After considerable haggling, the airline reluctantly agreed to pay the price of the car.

Purchasing gold often required more investment of time than did the selling of it. Fritz wrote his aunt about his dealings when he stopped briefly in New York in early 1947. "I just arrived by TWA plane from Cairo. We left at 3:00 a.m., had breakfast at Athens, lunch in Rome, tea in Madrid and dinner in Lisbon." In a second letter, Aunt Kathrine received a full report of her nephew's activities as he commenced his second full year in postwar China.

> Our bullion activities have expanded considerably and we are flying gold to four different world markets. Business is extremely complicated, owing to the various exchange regulations prevailing in other countries.
>
> The situation in Shanghai continues to be most confused and it is my belief that it will continue to deteriorate before there will be any improvement. Our former business activities in Shanghai are greatly curtailed and we have been devoting ourselves to other types of business in other countries.

Bad as they were, conditions in Shanghai worsened still further. On March 3, 1947, agents of the Shanghai-Woosung Garrison Headquarters raided the offices of the Abis Federal Company, Inc., U.S.A., another legal subsidiary. They seized 38 ten-ounce gold bars and quantities of four foreign currency notes and arrested Frederick Mysberg, the office manager, for dealing in gold and currency in contravention of the Emergency

Economic Measures promulgated by the Executive Yuan in February 1947. Denied bail, Mysberg was jailed and shackled with forty other prisoners. The Netherlands consul general successfully protested this treatment, but failed to win bail for his countryman.

Mysberg's trial began on March 22, with Judge Meng Ting Ku of the Shanghai District Court presiding. The court inspected the company office on April 5, and nine days later announced its decision. The judge sentenced Mysberg to one year in prison and ordered confiscation of all American and British currency. Mysberg and his employer were acquitted of the second charge, dealing in gold bars.

Dr. George Sellet, an American lawyer in Shanghai and a former assistant U.S. attorney, represented the defendant. He argued that since penal provisions had never been enacted by the Legislative Yuan, a prison term could not be applied. He also contended that although Article 7 of the Emergency Orders prohibited transactions in foreign currency, the transactions involving telegraphic transfers and demand drafts that constituted the bulk of the Swan, Culbertson and Fritz business were not prohibited.

The American and Dutch consuls general also lodged protests with the Chinese government. The Dutchman raised the question of Mysberg's arrest when no warrant had been issued; the American desired an explanation for violation of private property without appropriate papers. Both consuls, in addition, challenged the garrison's authority under Chinese criminal codes to issue such warrants.

Under prewar privileges of extraterritoriality, Mysberg could not have been arrested or convicted. In 1947, however, China no longer recognized the old order, and the judge dismissed all foreign national claims to it in deciding the case. He based his decision solely on the new economic policy adopted by the Nationalist government, which stipulated authority "to take emergency steps to stabilize economic conditions." Whatever Mysberg did or admitted to proved sufficient to cast Abis Federal's affairs within the pale of these provisions as a banking house.

Colonel Chang Ya Ming, an officer at the garrison headquarters, disrupted the proceedings on several occasions, interrogating witnesses, haranguing the court, and accusing one Chinese defense attorney of questionable patriotism in acting on behalf of foreigners charged with infractions of Chinese law. He later threatened a Chinese employee at the American consulate in Shanghai. The embassy's protest went for naught.

On appeal, a higher court annulled the decision in late 1947 and remanded the case to the Shanghai High Court. The court's verdict, handed down in February 1948, reduced Mysberg's prison term to four months and released a portion of the confiscated money. The court, however, sustained the emergency orders. Meanwhile, Mysberg's health had deteriorated, resulting in his being freed on bail of $100 million Chinese Nationalist currency and the assurances of two "reputable citizens" that he would not skip Shanghai.

The Mysberg incident aggravated Fritz's growing dissatisfaction with Culbertson's place in their partnership. Culbertson continued to receive 50 percent of the profits, even though the volume of business had declined significantly, and Mysberg had been hired to manage the temporarily lucrative foreign exchange operation. Also, Sellet's being retained as the firm's legal advisor after the trial supplied, according to Fritz, "invaluable assistance to Culbertson, who called him constantly day after day." Conversely, Fritz not only had established and developed the gold business independently but "had no one to consult. I did not have any lawyer at my right hand!" Two reasons, however, justified his stifling these thoughts for the moment: he had not yet conceived a feasible solution, and he lacked the opportunity to do so.

Actually, his permanent move to Hong Kong in the spring of 1947 had been prompted only partly by the demands of the gold trade. The publicity given the Mysberg trial and the clear signals of changed economic conditions contributed importantly to the departure. The Mysberg matter had truly embarrassed him. Like it nor not, the Shanghai of the past no longer existed. In view of the deepening political crisis within China itself, moreover, British Hong Kong seemed secure indeed. At 55 years of age, Fritz had become cautious at the prospect of spending a second stint in an internment camp. Those days of discontent, he promised himself, would not be repeated.

The Hong Kong of the postwar Far East reflected the uncertainty and confusion that reigned on the mainland. Housing and office space were at a premium, largely as a consequence of the great influx of refugee Chinese families of wealth who sought the comparative safety of the colony. A good contact, however, solved part of the problem for Culbertson and Fritz. The Sassoon family "gave us some of their office space," Fritz gratefully remembers. The refurbished office in the Holland House not only proved "very comfortable," certainly better than "operating a business from a briefcase," but also contained two window air conditioners.

There a March 1947 letter from his aunt finally caught up with him in July. He noted in his reply that the letter had been forwarded alternately to India, Egypt, New York, then returned to Shanghai whence it was lastly sent to Hong Kong. He confided to her that...

> ...There is a certain kind of pleasure in living in this British Colony, where there is a definite sense of well-being and orderliness...The people are disciplined.
>
> Culbertson and I live at Repulse Bay Hotel, which is on the opposite side of the Island, facing the open sea and ten miles from town. The view from our room is superb as there are many green-colored islands of all shapes and sizes reaching far off into the distance. Across the bay, at times, fleets of the Kwangtung junks with their brown bat-wing sails are frequently moving out to sea or returning in the late afternoon from the fishing grounds. We have a beach at the hotel which is situated at the foot of the mountains a few hundred yards off the beach. I thought we were especially fortunate to be able to get into the Repulse Bay Hotel, where there is a long waiting list. Chuck and I were able to get a new Super Deluxe Ford sedan at ceiling prices without having to wait.

Bombay, India, the third center in the bullion circuit, was also the most complicated. Although chronology is now beyond recovery, its importance belongs to the period between late 1946 and early 1947, and its success was due mainly to the close personal relationship that existed between Fritz and the firm of Premchand Roychand & Sons, a powerful Parsee family resident there for nearly a century.

The pattern of Fritz's affairs corresponded to his operations in Hong Kong and Macao, where Fritz initiated the buying and selling of gold bullion until institutional competition and governmental regulations forced him out. The Bombay episode, besides being the most profitable, reveals better the enormous complexity of the business and exhibits the talents of one of its most astute practitioners.

During Fritz's earlier career as Mr. Silver in China, Harold Hochschild encouraged him to learn more about the international network in silver trading. To this end, Fritz visited Bombay occasionally, then one of four leading silver markets in the world. There, through prearranged contacts with his New York office, the young American dealer acquired invaluable lessons and insights into the operations of a recognizably large silver center. Fritz recalled his first trip to Bombay in the early 1920s, which serves to suggest the selective and highly personal character of transactions normally closed to a person of his origin and background.

Through the good offices of Mr. Bomanjee of the Parsee firm of Newanjee, I was granted a visitor's permit to visit the huge Bombay bullion bazaar, where a white man rarely if ever enters. Mawaris Indians dominated that bazaar. Bombay and Shanghai were the leading consuming markets in the world. Generally speaking, the Indian merchants possess a certain kind of dignity and respect for others. But when I entered the building I was immediately surrounded by the Indian dealers and their assistants. One Indian, who was a member of the Executive Committee, approached me and without any preliminary discussion said, "So you are a silver man?" I replied, "That is how I fill my rice bowl in China." He said, "I'll tell you what I will do. 200,000 ounces of silver, you tell me the price; then I will tell you if I buy or sell!"

All the eyes of the market now turned on the white man to learn what was his reply. I explained to him that I was on a holiday and that the silver sold by our company, the American Metal Company, came from Mexico, the largest silver producer in the world. I said that to relieve the moment and then moved on.

For the second visit in the 1920s, Fritz carried a letter of introduction to Premchand Roychand & Sons from a representative of the Irving Bank, New York.

I was very impressed with Mr. Maneklal Premchand and his knowledge of the bullion trade. I kept in touch with him and his brother Sir Kikabhai Premchand through the years. I thought, someday there may be an opportunity when we could work together. It came years later, after the war, and it was very profitable. It was a damn clever move. I planned it years in advance.

Established in 1856, Premchand Roychand & Sons counted among the oldest and most respected investment firms in Bombay. Premchand Roychand attended Elphinstone College, after which he joined the Bank of Bombay as a clerk. Opportunity announced itself in the form of the American Civil War. English textile mills turned to Indian cotton for supply when their American source failed. Premchand amassed a fortune only to lose it when the South re-entered the market in 1865. Never-

Ever Westward to the Far East: THE STORY OF CHESTER FRITZ

theless, Premchand possessed the "Midas touch" in his acknowledged ability to "turn script into wealth." In time he controlled the Bank of Bombay and his "imprimatur was sufficient to obtain almost unlimited credit." He was a prime mover in the founding of the Bombay Stock Exchange.

Upon his death in 1906, his two sons, Kikabhai and Maneklal, succeeded as co-directors. Both were well educated and nearly as talented as their father. The firm continued to prosper under their leadership, growing both in size and influence until it achieved the enviable rank of India's leading financial house. In their heyday the brothers served as trusted advisors to several Indian states, while the firm strove to become the largest single entity in the bullion market. Under Maneklal's guidance, Bombay competed with Shanghai for title to being the world's largest consumer of silver. Kikabhai entered politics, emerging as a leading spokesman in the Indian legislative assembly. His role in stabilizing the Indian rupee during the Great Depression brought him great distinction. King George V knighted him in 1931. He died in 1953.

Fritz's early and happy success in China's gold market suggested that a similar demand might exist elsewhere as well. Indeed, competition and frequent changes in governmental regulations strongly indicated that a market for imported gold might develop practically anywhere at any time. Accordingly, he turned his attention to the Indian subcontinent, where he knew that World War II had generated a huge surplus of sterling stocks.

Hoping to renew business contacts in Bombay, Fritz approached the Premchands in late 1946 with a loosely formulated proposition about importing gold. Nothing came of it—at first. Shortly, however, Maneklal responded in an interested fashion, simultaneously acknowledging Fritz's past personal acquaintance and his long experience and demonstrated expertise in the silver bullion exchange. In other words, Fritz had been invited to explain the details of his idea.

Indian government regulations did not prohibit the importation of gold in 1947 because no such business yet existed. The regulations came later, after India had become aware of the trade and had determined its effect upon its own monetary exchange policies. Again, as a pioneer, Fritz had to surmount some special problems. The four most difficult were the acquisition of an import license, the means for selling the gold, the manner and medium of payment, and the transference of the income to his China account.

Fritz saw less difficulty with the first two problems than with the last two. Above all he had to sell the gold for an internationally desirable and convertible currency. To accept Indian rupees would gain him little since he knew the world demand for them to be thin and irregular. He needed chiefly U.S. dollars with which to purchase the next gold shipment. Moreover, an internationally desirable currency meant nothing if Indian government regulations prohibited its legal export from the country.

As predicted, obtaining the necessary import license presented no difficulty. The Premchands' assistance, however, proved instrumental in satisfying the other three conditions. The firm bought the gold in exchange for pounds sterling which it acquired from Bombay bazaar dealers by selling them rupees. According to Fritz...

...When the gold arrived by plane at the airfield the Premchands arranged to meet the plane. It frequently arrived before daylight. They rushed the gold to the Bombay Mint where it was converted into Bombay Mint bars. The bars were then delivered to the buyers because we did not want them to know it was foreign gold. They were sensitive buyers and they might consider that as a bearish point. It worked very smoothly. But while I was there the Premchands did not want me to appear in the bullion bazaar or to talk to any other Indians.

The Premchands also arranged for the transfer of Fritz's sterling to his private accounts elsewhere through the National Bank of India. This guaranteed Fritz the needed flexibility to purchase the next shipment of gold. The Indian government did not want to sell sterling in order to obtain gold from abroad. It preferred that the sterling be applied to more productive purposes like industrial development. It may have been, too, that the government was unaware that sterling went to buy gold. In any event, Fritz told his partner in Shanghai of the success of the operation:

I told Culbertson how fortunate we were because our capital was being used in a business which in a few weeks was liquidated, i.e., when you bought a shipment of gold in a brief time and you sold on arrival you got your capital back plus a very comfortable profit. When I showed Culbertson the results he was very pleased. He did not know any of the gold dealers in India or elsewhere.

Yet, with each gold sale, Fritz was obliged to find a customer for the sterling received:

> There were various complications due to the changing foreign exchange regulation by the British government in London. I seemed to stumble from one crisis to another. I started out selling my sterling to British firms in Shanghai. But when I got to Bombay, my good friends the Premchands obtained permission from the National Bank, the federal reserve bank of India, to transfer my sterling to Russian account. The sterling was sold to pay for Russian furs bought in the Leningrad marketplace. Later that was changed so I had to find another buyer. In the meantime, I had to get the dollars to pay for the next shipment of gold that was booked and so there was a certain amount of apprehension. Fortunately a big bank in Amsterdam then bought my sterling. I noticed that the instructions to buy were to the Anglo-Palestine Bank in London to the Hadassah in Jerusalem. But there was no quotation available so it was just a blind guess as to the correct financial quotation. So I started out quoting them and after each sale, I raised the cross-rate, two cents or more and they kept accepting it. Finally they said this has gone far enough. Later when I called on this bank in Amsterdam they were very friendly and indicated it was a very satisfactory business for them. I replied, "I hope it was profitable!" and he replied, "Oh, it was very profitable."
>
> Later some of the sterling was also sold to buyers and transferred into Siamese account. But luckily that arrangement did not last very long as it took several weeks for it to go through and I felt very apprehensive. I said, "This is not the place for me to be!"

Once Fritz tested his advantage of being able to transfer sterling out of India, he sought to improve upon the procedure for obtaining import licenses. Normally, gold traders applied for one license at a time—that is, a license to import a contract usually already in the process of shipment. Each license required a substantial application fee and stipulated a definite expiration date. Fritz hoped for two reasons that once established in Bombay, he might apply for several licenses simultaneously. First, in this manner he might better protect himself against predictable competition and thus remain an active trader for a longer

176

time. Second, increased competition usually prompted government intervention or even prohibition. Still, he knew from experience that governments would honor their issued licenses, even after policy had been changed.

After several months of uninterrupted gold sales in India, the news reached other interested parties whose preliminary objectives were simply to contact Fritz in Bombay. Here is a sample cable exchange of one such effort:

—We heard Chester Fritz is in Bombay.
—He is not here!
—We insist he is there!
—No. Why do you inquire?
—We have a client who has an import license to import gold into Bombay which expires in ten days. He wants to sell it.
—How much?
—$10,000.
—We will offer $5,000.
—Sold.

It remained for these other parties—namely Louis Franck, a junior partner in Samuel Montague—to confirm the actual limits of the gold import market in India. He discovered in checking customs returns sizable quantities of gold passing through Karachi, Pakistan. At that point, Franck's employer sent him to India where he obtained a license to import 50,000 ounces in a single shipment. By comparison, Fritz had been handling shipments of 10,000-20,000 ounces. The effect of Franck's maneuver was to alert Indian authorities, who shortly discontinued all import permits. When Fritz later saw Franck in Hong Kong, he quipped, "Louis, you killed it!"

Unfortunately, there is but one document for this period that provides any insight into the Indian trade. It is Fritz's pocket journal containing the daily arbitrage of gold price quotations and sporadic purchases. In 1947, Fritz operated mostly out of a suitcase, so that, although virtually undecipherable to the unknowing, Fritz himself supplied an explanatory translation of its jotted entries.

> The Diary itself was bought in Cairo and begins as of the 1st of January 1947 when I was in Cairo arbitraging principally in the purchase of gold in New York and other world markets and selling to Bombay. You will notice that on the page for

January 2nd, at the top of the page, are the cabled quotations received in Cairo around 1 o'clock, covering gold and silver quotations in the Bombay bullion exchange in terms of rupees per tola. Of course, all transactions were by cable. My firm offers and their bids were in terms of English shillings per troy ounce. "Rupee" is the cable address of Premchand Roychand & Sons, Ltd., Bombay. All of the offers and bids were for gold and one for silver.

You will observe that I flew to New York after continuous delays owing to storms in Gander [Newfoundland]. In New York the transactions were particularly the sale of gold in Bombay with purchases in Switzerland and New York. Also, I bought silver in New York, and you will note that on 25th January I sold 200,000 ounces of silver at 61 pence per ounce. C.I.F. Bombay. As you will see, there was cabled activity each market day. The cable word "ELIAS" was our organization for whom we made offers to Bombay under certain conditions.

Subsequently I proceeded to Bombay where I arrived on 8th March. The cabled arbitrage transactions followed me and were executed by me wherever I happened to be. You will observe that a number of sterling transactions versus U.S. dollar transactions begin to appear, as for example 24th March, when I offered New York 50,000 at $3.26 to the pound sterling. Subsequently I left Bombay and after a brief stop in Calcutta and another in Canton, I arrived in Hong Kong in April. Bullion transactions continued.

You will note (from June onwards) that in Hong Kong the daily work page has a number of new quotations. The lower half gives the fluctuating changes for "bars" (gold price in Hong Kong dollars on the Hong Kong Exchange). T/T is the Hong Kong market price for U.S. dollars in terms of Hong Kong dollars. In October you will note large amounts mentioned, e.g., one transaction for one billion Chinese dollars. The amounts are impressive but the actual value is quite small as the Chinese dollar was then experiencing galloping inflation.

Fritz enjoyed a warm personal as well as business connection with his Bombay associates. When in the city during the week, he stayed at the Taj Mahal Hotel. On weekends, however, Sir Kikabhai Premchand commonly invited him to his spacious home at Tuju about twenty miles outside the city, across the channel and on the mainland. The beautiful mansion and its flowered gardens had been built originally for the Maharajah of Patiala. Here Fritz willingly absorbed the culture of both his host and the Indian ambience.

Sir Kikabhai Premchand arrived at his office every morning in a Rolls-Royce. He was carefully dressed as if he had just come out of a tailor shop in Bond Street. But when he returned home in the evening, he put on the comfortable native Indian dress and conversed for a couple of hours with his guru.

I would go to his home every Friday night and spend Saturday and Sunday there. I lived in the guest house and at lunch and dinner there were usually other guests, especially on Sunday. During the week I sat on Lady Premchand's right, but when the Rajas and Maharajahs came on Sunday my position shifted down the table.

One day the British Chief Justice and his wife were invited to Sunday tiffin. They served them with knife and fork. Rita, the wife of Sir Kikabhai, was very charming and very Indian. She resented some of the Western customs. I felt she watched me carefully to see if I continued to eat with my fingers as they did. There was a certain way to manipulate the dry food with your fingers. When she saw that I ate Indian style even in the presence of the British guests she took a different attitude toward me.

Fritz had learned long ago the truth of the old adage—"When in Rome, do as the Romans do."

The profitability of the gold trade could not offset the declining state of affairs in Shanghai. The central office of Swan, Culbertson and Fritz never recovered from the Mysberg trial and had to be closed by the end of 1947. It fell to Culbertson to oversee the closing. He notified all clients to transfer their accounts to the company's branch office in Manila or to take physical possession of their stocks and securities. Nevertheless, putting the office's affairs in final order involved "one hell of a mess," according to Culbertson, owing to staff disloyalties and their hawking of selected confidential cable information.

The closing also carried broader implications for Fritz and his partner personally and for their future in the Far East. They treated matters with utter realism, conducted a comprehensive inventory, and reached two important decisions. They recognized that except for the modest outlet in Manila and Fritz's high-risk gold ventures, there seemed no promising future for the parent firm in the Far East.

Accordingly, in early 1948, the partners agreed to phase out the Manila branch over the next three years. Their equally shared holdings in the branch as of January 1, 1949 totaled 200,000 Philippine pesos, or $157,000 American. During the course of the year Culbertson and Fritz sold 25 percent of their shares to Roy Ewing and A. B. Carson, two junior partners, and sold off the remaining 75 percent by 1950. Finally, in February 1951, they sold their seat on the Manila Stock Exchange to a third junior partner, Walter Wolff. At that point, the Manila office of Swan, Culbertson and Fritz became Wolff and Company, Inc. It continues today as a successful investment firm owned and operated by Luis Ongpin, whose business career began in 1935 as an employee of the original Manila branch of Swan, Culbertson and Fritz.

Personal and professional differences between Fritz and Culbertson reached their climax during the Christmas season of 1948. Fritz informed his partner that as of the turn of the year all profits realized from his gold trading would be divided 70-30 percent in Fritz's favor. Fritz afterward explained his view of the matter and its significance.

> The 70-30 percent relationship between Culbertson and myself related only to the company that did the gold business. I was well informed and equipped to handle that business. I initiated and developed it. In fact, Culbertson never touched any phase of it. The other business which was at a low ebb continued on a 50-50 basis.

Likewise, in a Christmas letter to his aunt, Fritz offered a pungent analysis of the rapidly deteriorating situation in mainland China:

> It would appear that Mme. Chiang Kai-shek's visit to the States will not be the triumphal tour it was a few years ago. The Americans are a gullible people, trusting and very generous, but I think by this time they are beginning to have a more correct perspective of the Nanking regime. The Chinese people are richly deserving of our assistance; however, when a large portion of that assistance goes into the pockets of the "favoured families" and the leading Chinese officials, that is another matter. It is the opinion of many that if Chiang Kai-shek and his crowd would resign, it would be much

easier to reach a solution and so end this costly and unnecessary civil war, but the Generalissimo and his group are greedy for power and money.

As for Culbertson, he left China permanently in February of 1949 for Buenos Aires and the United States. As Culbertson recalled, "I left China in February of 1949 when we received a cable from Ralph Stillman, manager of our office in Buenos Aires, that there was a break-up of the stock exchange. We were in a lot of trouble and Stillman needed money. So we sent him $250,000 and I said, "I'm coming right away!" Fritz himself remained in Hong Kong to pursue his trade in gold for so long as it proved profitable. March 1949 found him commenting again on the crisis in China:

> As you will have observed from the American press, financial chaos continues in China and the new currency is experiencing galloping inflation. There has been no serious fighting for some three months, but it appears that the Communists are becoming impatient and will soon endeavor to cross the Yangtze. Trade in China is at a standstill, and it is having its effect on Hong Kong which is filled with refugees and evacuees from North and Central China.

Fritz revealed his intention to leave China in April 1950.

> Owing to the changing economic and political conditions in the China trade area, we have decided that our firm in Hong Kong should suspend business activities and therefore we are closing this office within the next couple of weeks.
>
> As you may imagine, I am leaving China with mixed feelings. After all, during 35 years in China one's roots grow deeply and I have a warm affection for the Chinese people and Chinese culture.

The decision did not come easily. The Communist triumph notwithstanding, Fritz considered China his home, and he especially admired its culture. Moreover, he knew of no other place he preferred to live, and he certainly did not relish the thought of retirement. Privately, his closest friends urged just that upon him—retirement at age 58 in a comfortable and enjoyable corner of the world. After all, the China he had known and loved no longer existed, and regardless of what the future might hold, the new China could not realistically be seen as a land of opportunity.

Still, dreams and habits die hard. Ever Westward to the Far East had been his life's realization and success. It had soothed the emotional scars of childhood, his yearning for travel, and his quest for a productive occupation.

Mr. Ho, general manager of the Hang Seng Bank, who talked often with his American friend, presented Fritz with a pair of carved jade cuff links as a parting present. He had selected this particular gift, Ho explained, because symbolically, "It reflects the firm link of our pleasant relationship." In a personal note to Fritz, accompanying the gift, Ho wrote:

> On the eve of your departure, we wish to take this opportunity to express to you our sincere appreciation of the past business which you entrusted to us. It has been, indeed, a rare privilege for this bank to have enjoyed your esteemed patronage let alone the benefits of the sound advices which you so generously imparted to us.

Chester Fritz left China with total assets of $1.8 million. This was a substantial fortune. It represented 35 years of hard work in the Far East, but most of it had been accumulated independently, by Fritz, in the gold trade in only four years, between 1946 and 1950.

Popular stories exist, however, which suggest Fritz left China with a larger fortune and that he simply retired. These accounts are not accurate. The China account was only the base upon which he built a greater fortune after 1951, and he never retired. Acting alone on the New York Stock Exchange and in the precious metal markets he knew so well, Fritz made substantially more money as a private investor after 1950.

IX

The South American Connection

An American consular report completed on the eve of World War II identified Swan, Culbertson and Fritz as the oldest of four brokerage firms in Shanghai. The firm had a central office in Shanghai and two branch offices in Hong Kong and Manila. No plans existed to open a third branch, least of all in South America. Yet that is what occurred in the fall of 1939, indirectly as a result of the outbreak of World War II. The idea belonged neither to Culbertson nor Fritz, but to Ralph Stillman, a junior partner and assistant manager of the Manila office.

Ralph Stillman is a brilliant, soft-spoken investment banker who only recently retired. In 1954 he became president of the Grace National Bank in New York and in 1965 chairman of the board of the merged Marine Midland Grace Trust Company. He was born in upstate New York in 1906 and attended Phillips Academy in Andover, the Alumni Academy in Albany, and the Christian Brothers Academy in Troy. He dropped pre-medical studies after two years at Union College in favor of enrolling as a trainee in the newly launched bond school sponsored by the Guaranty

Trust Company—the same route by which Joseph Swan found his career. Stillman joined the City Bank of New York in 1927 as assistant manager, hoping to obtain an overseas position. The company assigned him to its Tokyo branch in 1929.

Stillman transferred to Swan, Culbertson and Fritz in April 1937, because of "its reputation and portfolio investment banking." This appealed to him, he recalled, as did the offer of a junior partnership and the success enjoyed by several former colleagues then working for the firm. Stillman went directly to the Manila branch as assistant manager, where he remained for two years.

In April 1939, Culbertson and Fritz dispatched him to Liverpool, England, the center of the international wool market, to learn the intricacies of the wool futures market. The idea was to train Stillman in anticipation of opening a branch office in Sydney, Australia, which would deal in raw and cured wool. Yet, when he completed his preparation in June 1939, war seemed all too imminent. "We decided to abandon the Australian project," said Stillman.

In New York and between assignments, Stillman proposed to his partners that he "take a look at Argentina." Culbertson and Fritz approved the idea, whereupon he sailed in September aboard a ship of the Ernst Prince Line that followed a giant zigzag course between Recife and Rio de Janeiro, Brazil, that at one point nearly touched the African west coast. Even as the ship reached Rio, the German navy had already sunk one British man-of-war off the coastline. Indeed, the British battle cruisers *Ajax, Exeter,* and *Archilles*—the famous trio that subsequently trapped the *Graf Spee* in Montevideo harbor until its captain scuttled it—escorted his ship into the estuary of the Rio de la Plata.

The decision to "try Argentina" had not been made casually. Stillman had talked at some length with Joseph Swan about it in New York, since Swan had already started a pilot operation in Buenos Aires on a capital base of $100,000. Together, the two men concluded that Argentina presented a potentially attractive opportunity for the Shanghai concern. Swan and Stillman noted that Argentina had experienced a large influx of European refugees whose financial standing might well provide a pool of customers; that the country seemed likely to benefit from the war; and that the economy seemed committed to free enterprise, shunning restrictions on the exchange of foreign currency. If, in addition, Argentina remained neutral in World War II as it had during World War I, the prospects of its acquiring a surplus of hard currency reserves brightened expectations all the more.

Once in Buenos Aires, Stillman rented a small office at the corner of Bartolome Mitre and 25 de Mayo streets, near the main business district. At first he aimed his advertising at those inclined toward New York stocks and securities. Gradually, however, he widened the appeal to American equity investments more generally, and, for the benefit of prospective European customers, an enticingly low commission rate on foreign exchange transactions. It worked. The business grew sufficiently to justify incorporating the office under the parent name and, within the year, to establishing a second registered outlet in Montevideo, also incorporated under Argentine law.

These two South American branches established by 1941 were to be the company's only operations outside the Far East, which remained its principal and preferred focus. The capital partners were never directly involved in the daily management of affairs in South America. Of the two, however, Culbertson took a more active interest. He visited South America regularly and dealt more closely with branch managers in developing collateral business ventures. For his part, Fritz visited Buenos Aires only once, for several months in the spring of 1945, arriving there after stopping at a number of sites along the way, including La Paz, Bolivia. He also spent a month in Rio, visiting Kent Lutey, his good friend from prewar Shanghai days. Of course, Fritz's partners sought his financial and advisory assistance, but these contributions represented the extent of his involvement in South American matters.

Stillman hired his first employee in April 1940, in the person of B. Heinz Rothschild, a German Jew. Rothschild proved an excellent choice. The young emigre possessed a quick mind and recent practical experience in handling securities. The Stillman-Rothschild relationship continued until 1951, when Stillman resigned in order to realize greater opportunities in New York and American educational advantages for his children.

Born in Frankfurt on the Main in 1913, Rothschild's law studies had been cut short by the Nazi ban against Jews attending German universities. He spent 1935 in Paris. He returned to Germany to work two years with a large exporting company, "hoping all the while that Hitler would not endure." He emigrated to Argentina in 1937, where he gained employment with the United Bank of Holland as an assistant manager and secretary of its securities arbitrage department. Rothschild said he joined the fledgling Buenos Aires branch of Swan, Culbertson and Fritz because the "possibilities for advancement at the bank were very limited."

Rothschild's duties centered on attracting and servicing customers' accounts and preparing a short market letter. Stillman and Rothschild worked well together. To Rothschild, Stillman seemed "an ideal employer" who "generously recognized services rendered" and possessed the ability to delegate responsibilities. Stillman remembers Rothschild as "a key person in the firm."

Argentine citizens comprised the majority of customers. Even so, the office developed a clientele among the large and growing Jewish immigrant community. There the name Rothschild conveyed strength and credibility, especially when business could be conducted in fluent German and French.

World War II spawned conditions and consequences that guided the firm's early activities. In the first place, Argentina itself prospered handsomely from the war because its raw commodities and goods, suddenly in steady demand, commanded high prices in international turmoil. Also, its wealthier citizens and resident immigrants looked to New York for the safest and most profitable investments. As a result the firm's stock brokerage volume grew "slowly but solidly" during the war years. The abandonment of commercial cable using a private code at the midpoint in favor of direct telephone orders indicated as much. Joseph Swan, having become a ranking officer in the brokerage department of Hayden, Stone and Company of New York, facilitated creation of an omnibus account in the same manner previously done for the Shanghai central office.

Use of the Montevideo office grew with the United States' entry into the war. It represented the Buenos Aires office's quick move to protect its lately established Argentine accounts, or, in Rothschild's words, "to forestall all eventual blocking of Argentine accounts in the U.S. due to Argentina's sympathy with the Axis powers." Indeed, Argentina's neutrality continued until the spring of 1945 and constantly perplexed Roosevelt administration policymakers who dreamed of the whole hemisphere united against the Axis enemy. America's considerable diplomatic pressure, however, did not translate into economic sanctions, so that the value of the Montevideo office did not become evident until the postwar years.

Unexpectedly, the untapped bond market proved to be the firm's most profitable interest. Stillman, the bond specialist, discovered the existence of two domestic bonds—*creditos*, liabilities owed directly by the government, and *seguros*, mortgages upon its assets and securities. The Argentine government had issued the bonds during the 1920s as an attractive investment medium for citizens who sought alternatives to agricultural land and speculative real estate. Backing for these bond issues had come from United States banks which had floated dollar bonds to a welter of Latin American governments during the decade. Some of these issues had been designated for specific purposes, of course, but most were generally defined. The United States, upon realizing its new-found status as the world's banking center following the dislocations of World War I, had sought by this means, among others, to supplant Europe's financial predominance in the Western Hemisphere.

Stillman's research into the subject produced two findings: that these bonds had traded in a limited market and that with the depression of the 1930s, "The market became very soft, with the result that most of these bonds went to very low prices and very high discounts." In other words, the value of the bonds deteriorated in direct proportion to a government's rate of debt default. Pursuing the matter further, Stillman found that Argentina's *creditos* and *seguros* sold in Buenos Aires at 4 percent, even though the stipulated interest rate ranged between 6, 7 and 8 percent. Even at that, the bonds found few buyers for the simple reason that the Argentine government could not pay anything on the principal or interest until all requirements for liquidating its foreign debt had been satisfied.

Stillman read the future correctly. The war-borne prosperity would enable Argentina eventually to redeem these bonds at par value. If he could corner the bond markets meantime, the firm could interpose itself as Buenos Aires' controlling agent in them. Stillman recounted the tactics he used to accomplish this:

> After great care, the firm checked out the possibility of these bonds by using all the services and recommendations of Hayden Stone, who purchased most of these bonds for us.
>
> We then purchased millions of these bonds for both large and small customers. We identified these bonds and created the business. This bond business ended shortly after the close of World War II, when the Argentine government repaid those bonds in full.
>
> For example, a customer came into our office to buy $100,000 of a 6 percent bond. (I forget the exact discounts

that they were sold at but they were around $60 or $70 in New York). A 6 percent bond selling at a 40 percent discount produced a yield of about 10 percent. Hypothetically, on a purchase of $100,000 of par value bonds, the customer would pay cash of $60,000 and have a 10 percent yield. But in actuality many of our customers purchased those bonds on margin. They paid only $20,000 or $25,000 in cash and borrowed funds from us at 3 or 4 percent. This, of course, increased the yield to 12 or 15 percent. These bonds were mostly Argentine *creditos.* They did not issue Argentine *seguros,* mortgage bonds, in foreign currency.

The foreign exchange trade also took an active turn after the war. British sterling in particular was a heavily traded currency. Stillman observed that his office "used to execute big orders" amounting to "millions of dollars daily" for the South American account of the Bank of London. The firm charged lower commissions than even the bank's own New York branch because the Bank of London was...

...always competing with their New York office for a larger share of the profits and they could buy through us through a New York bank, which was the Bank of Manhattan Company. We had a very fine relationship with them. We could buy the foreign currency that the Bank of London in South America found necessary to purchase cheaper than they could purchase it from their own New York office or even their own London office. It was a rather peculiar situation. But in a big bank, trading between different offices becomes political.

Large volume did not necessarily mean inordinate profits, however. Foreign exchange provided more of a service than a return. It more than paid for itself, to be sure, but in Stillman's words, "It was not an important item in the Buenos Aires operation."

The boom in Argentina lasted nearly a decade, until 1949. At that point, the depleted condition of the national treasury demanded corrective measures. The government of President Juan D. Peron had spent enormous sums acquiring war surplus material and armaments from the United States and Great Britain. In addition, the government lavished luxury-liner orders on British shipbuilders and created an air force practically out of whole cloth. Export demand for agricultural commodities eased steadily all the while. During 1949, therefore, the Argentine government decided to adopt currency exchange and export controls

The South American Connection

which, naturally, carried serious implications for a private firm dealing in New York and other international exchanges. As Stillman explained the situation:

> It became very difficult to purchase American dollars at that time. You had to advise the government for what purpose they were to be used. And they were not interested in giving encouragement to purchase dollars for the purpose of investing in stocks or speculating in overseas markets.

The imposition of currency controls dictated a revamping of the Buenos Aires operations of Swan, Culbertson and Fritz. Stillman insisted, nevertheless, that the "loss of foreign exchange dollars, not Peron, was the major deterrent in the change of the company's focus." Rothschild views the problem differently:

> Peron was a man of great charm but fascist ideology. With increased power he became increasingly corrupt. He was a brilliant Latin American demagogue who found fertile ground for his thinking among the lower classes and their relatively low standard of living, unprotected by social security. His ill-conceived state capitalism disguised as national socialism is the cause of the first slow, then accelerated decline of Argentina's economic, social, and political structure. If my recollection is correct, Peron came to power [in 1946] when four pesos equalled one U.S. dollar. When he left [in 1955] the exchange rate was forty to one, and today [1980] the dollar is selling at 1.4 million pesos.

Stillman, after consulting with senior partners, effected two basic changes. The first involved closing the Buenos Aires office and consolidating the firm's South American operations in Montevideo. Montevideo had historically been an early beneficiary and index of unsettled affairs in either Argentina or Brazil. The second change, accomplished more gradually, involved a diversification of interests in the direction of insurance, underwriting, and cosponsoring the construction of a large office building elsewhere in South America.

The move to Uruguay initially slowed the volume of equities trading through the firm, especially on the New York Stock Exchange. As Stillman phrased it, "our New York...business simply became very restricted at that time." The reverse occurred, however, once the severity of exchange controls took effect. Indeed, the number of new accounts as well as trading volume rose as Argentines themselves realized their country's economic desperation. Rothschild offered this succinct summary of conditions:

> The Peron government introduced exchange controls. As it always happens in such cases, this started capital flight in a big way. We did not operate in the black market, but a lot of money and new accounts came to us. Peron was the best customer man we ever had.

Meanwhile, in 1949, the Montevideo branch launched two insurance companies in Argentina, "Insignia" and "Prudencia." Swan, Culbertson and Fritz owned the whole of Insignia and 50 percent of Prudencia. (The other 50 percent was controlled by Bunge and Born, a multinational corporation best known to the public at large as grain dealers and shippers.) The Argentine government adopted regulations not long after this regarding foreign ownership of nationally incorporated companies. The regulations limited nonresident ownership to one-third of each insurance company, with the result that the balance of shares had to be sold to Argentine partners. Both Culbertson and Fritz sold their personal interest in the companies in the mid-1960s; according to Stillman, the companies continue to operate today and are "well-known, successful, and reliable firms."

The Montevideo branch also assisted the Coca Cola Company in establishing a distributorship in Cordoba, Argentina, an interior city about 500 miles west of Buenos Aires. The firm sold Coca Cola preferred stock to local investors; the parent corporation retained ownership of the equity or common stock. Culbertson and Fritz personally bought 7 percent of the issue (about 60,000 shares) from the original owners of the franchise, Bobby Jones, American golfing great, and Cliff Roberts, developer of the famed Augusta, Georgia, golf course. Their joint interest continues at present, in part because profits from the sale of their shares could not, under Argentine law, be transferred out of that country. Of late, they receive regular dividends; the stock's current total value is estimated at $1 million.

Venezuelan opportunities attracted Swan, Culbertson and Fritz investments during the 1940s. In the first phase, according to Culbertson, the company acquired draft notes from various financial organizations in Caracas through White, Weld and Company of New York:

> You could loan money at very high, very profitable rates and people could buy what they called Spanish *giros*. *Giros* yielded 12 to 14 percent and were considered quite strong.

Later, a second venture in Venezuela turned sour. Culbertson, captivated by the idea of financing an office building in the promising capital, committed the company to the proposition. It turned out to be "a bad deal," the worst the company experienced in South America. Culbertson said it was a beautiful office building and would have been a good investment, "but the government got kicked out and everything changed. There were bad times in Venezuela."

Time proved the idea more premature than ill-considered. The urban development of Caracas occurred, but about a decade later than Culbertson planned. Exactly how much money was lost is unclear, as is indicated in the following Fritz reminiscence.

> We lost a considerable amount of money from Swan, Culbertson and Fritz in Hong Kong on a large office building in South America after we left China.
>
> We were part owners in a new building which we [Culbertson and Fritz] and a group built in Caracas, Venezuela. The transaction was negotiated by Culbertson and a few of our astute South American partners. I never was familiar with the arrangement; in fact, I never went to Venezuela. Eventually it was a financial loss, chiefly because it was underfinanced and it was difficult to obtain tenants as there was an economic crisis going on. I never complained about this event although the deal was engineered by my other associates.

Culbertson suggests with more precision that the loss involved "around $750,000." Even so, Swan, Culbertson and Fritz in South America proved a profitable extension of the partners' interests, as well as for Stillman and Rothschild. Fritz and Culbertson each realized perhaps a million dollars after taxes. Stillman received $500,000 in severance pay upon his resignation in 1951, not to mention a wealth of practical experience that he lucratively applied to a long career in New York banking. Rothschild, Stillman's talented and resourceful apprentice, advanced through three separate brokerage houses and even today continues to devote conscientious attention to accounts still in force from the World War II era, even though they have all been transferred (as of 1969) to the Clariden Bank, a subsidiary of the Swiss financial firm Credit Suisse.

The success stemming from the changes of 1949 not only strained the existing reciprocal relationship between the parent company and Hayden, Stone, but it also piqued the self-interests of Stillman and Rothschild. Growth in the brokerage business in the Montevideo office "had reached such an important volume," Rothschild stated, that both "institutional customers and private investors" demanded an option to deal with Hayden, Stone directly—that is, "without paying an overriding commission to Swan, Culbertson and Fritz." Accordingly, Hayden, Stone established its own brokerage branch office in Montevideo in 1949, hiring Rothschild to manage it. New York Stock Exchange regulations obliged him to resign his previous position. Yet, because all company accounts were held in an omnibus account with Hayden, Stone, Rothschild continued in an "unofficial way" to supervise them.

This anomalous arrangement lasted until 1968, when Rothschild joined White, Weld and Company, taking "all the River Plate accounts with us," including those held by Swan, Culbertson and Fritz. Hayden, Stone, in apparent decline as a strong New York brokerage house, failed to find a comparably astute successor to Joseph Swan, its senior vice president, who died in June, 1960. As for Stillman, he resigned in 1951 to return to the United States after the changes had been made, efficient operation was restored, and the business had been stabilized. Although the South American operation was not personally an enterprise managed by Fritz, his capital of 50 percent helped establish it. His money and the talents of Stillman and Rothschild proved another winning combination. The South American venture was an important and successful investment for Chester Fritz during and after World War II.

X

To Give With a Warm Hand

Alumni are special people. They are the elders of a university. They provide a separate and unique constituency of the institution, different from each generation of students, faculty, and administrators. In 1925 University of North Dakota President Thomas Kane expressed the unique relationship of the alumni to the University:

> We all know but we do not always realize that a university is made up of faculty, students and alumni. This, after all, is the same thing as saying that the university is made up of its teachers and students which is obvious. The term students includes alumni and former students. Alumni are members of the household the same as married children never lose their ties with the old home. The same holds true for all former students, whether graduating or not, that they keep up the old home ties.

Most alumni, however, remain obscure to later generations of the university family. Their experiences as students remain largely personalized and for the most part private. Most alumni graduate. Some transfer to other institutions. Others establish outstanding academic records. All learn, and a few fail. A substantial minority achieve international, national, regional, or local recognition, but the majority do not. A select few reward their institution with newsworthy contributions. A still higher percentage give generously, each according to his or her means, but the greatest number donate nothing. Many alumni, later, as parents, give encouragement to their sons and daughters to follow in their footsteps.

Chester Fritz attended the University of North Dakota for just two years, from 1908 to 1910. Yet, between 1950 and 1969 Fritz donated more than $2.25 million to the University. At that time, his was the largest amount ever given by a single alumnus of the University, and today remains second only to W. Kenneth Hyslop's gift in 1979 and 1981 of rich Red River Valley farm land and other properties valued at $8 million.

Fritz's generosity to the University of North Dakota is not easily explained. He knew an unhappy childhood and left the state permanently in 1910. He returned only twice, once in June 1951, and again briefly in October 1961. Evidently, however, from the beginning Fritz carried the essence of his later philanthropies and a highly developed sense of stewardship. Three aspects of Fritz's character contributed to this attitude: a special love and respect for his foster parents, Neil and Kathrine Macdonald; a personal debt of gratitude to North Dakota, its people and institutions; and a poignant sensitivity toward hard-working youth, intelligent, with high moral standards, but lacking financial support needed to enroll at college.

Prewar Japanese expansionism, World War II, and the Revolution in China in 1949 forced major changes in the life of Chester Fritz. Before those events, he had little time or interest in seeking out the University on his own terms. His attitude is best revealed in a letter to his aunt written in 1950:

> I hope to be able to attend the UND alumni dinner in New York on November 13, if I am not able to...I will not be disappointed. I have never attended one in my life so I could still miss them without regrets. In China I never met a single UND alumnus. Furthermore it is likely I would not know any of them at such a dinner—such functions to me are not interesting but only a duty.

Fritz, however, for whatever reason, attended the dinner that year. Years later Edna Twamley, a classmate of Kathrine Macdonald Tiffany at the University, recalled his presence at the New York alumni gathering.

> I very distinctly recall the night you visited the UND Club in New York. You told us of your long residence abroad and how you had become intensively interested in the financial situation and the business opportunities in China. Perhaps even on that night or before you were already formulating the great project that now has become a reality.

A month had not passed before Fritz mailed a check for $10,000 to the University Development Fund. In his letter to J. Lloyd Stone, the University's alumni association director, Fritz observed that the contribution "affords me a certain kind of pleasure and genuine satisfaction in that I am now able to express my gratitude for the benefits which I received as a student at the University of North Dakota. I have not visited the campus since my departure as a student nearly 40 years ago....This expression of gratitude may be somewhat tardy, but is nonetheless genuine."

The gift caught University officials by surprise. Who was Chester Fritz? John Hancock, a member of the class of 1903 and president of the Jewel Tea Company, epitomized the ultimate in success among UND graduates. He attended the New York alumni meeting and wrote to Fritz:

> I was sorry there had not been more chance to spend some time with you, but I hope the opportunity arises in the future. When next your trail crosses mine, won't you let me know of your presence?
>
> I have been giving any spare funds to the University for several years past and my feelings about it are the same as yours. In addition, I feel that a dollar given to that territory will be spent wisely and that it will go much farther than a dollar spent in any of our Eastern institutions.

In June 1951, Fritz returned to the campus he had left in 1910, to accept the University's honorary degree of Doctor of Laws in recognition of his recently discovered achievements in financial and international affairs. Fritz immediately pledged an additional $20,000, payable over a five-year period, to the University Development Fund. He also discussed, in general terms, provisions of his will with Alumni Association Director Stone, with the intent of establishing a scholarship program upon his death. Not long thereafter, Fritz wrote UND President John C. West of his wholly positive impressions of the campus: "For the first time in over forty years I visited the University in 1951. I was pleased to observe the marvelous growth of the physical plant and more especially the facilities for training the young people to live a better balanced life."

University officials, developing an obvious enthusiasm for the newly found donor, appointed Fritz to the Alumni Board of Directors as a "sort of roving representative." Fritz did not attend Board meetings, but at Stone's urging, he contacted a fellow alumnus in Europe on behalf of the University. This was Charles Boise, class of 1908, who according to Stone, seemed predisposed "to make a substantial contribution to the University but finds it impossible to get his money out of England." Fritz called on Boise in London, but to no avail. "Boise never made a donation!" Fritz later noted. In 1952, President West also invited Fritz to represent the University at the Sesquicentennial festivities for the U.S. Military Academy at West Point. Fritz did so with pleasure.

For Fritz, these early unencumbered donations, as well as the traditional University reciprocal gestures of recognition and service, proved congenial to his personal lifestyle following his departure from China. Restless, bored with life in New York City, and indignant in the face of gratuitous advice to resign himself to retirement based on accumulated assets, Fritz took to Europe, chiefly Switzerland. There he would remarry, build a permanent home, and set about augmenting his wealth. In the interim he sought out the University and acknowledged his respect.

It might all have ended there. Neither Fritz nor the University could rightly have expected more. Fritz did not possess the wealth, and the University lacked a practical proposal. Indeed, events after 1954 might not have occurred at all if it had not been for the happy combination of Fritz's progressive financial successes, the advent of a new University president given to expansive dreams, and the passionate commitment of a most unforgettable woman. Theirs was a relationship at once delicate and determined. A unique milieu set between the age of Eisenhower and the tragedy of Vietnam.

The years following World War II brought many dramatic changes to the nation, state, and the University. The war economy, not the New Deal, ended the Great Depression. Adequate rain and higher crop prices, not the antics of Governor William Langer's administration, saved North Dakota agriculture. At the University, a new day had dawned. Louis Geiger, in his history of the University, summarized it in these words:

> The opening of the fall term of 1946 was perhaps the most memorable occasion of its kind since that September day in 1884 when the university welcomed its first students. War veterans alone numbered 1,550, a figure within a few hundred of the previous enrollment figure of 1,960 set in 1939.

To Give With a Warm Hand

The total enrollment exceeded that earlier mark by nearly a thousand and in 1947-1948 the figure soared to 3,077, a record that stook until 1955-1956.

Between 1946 and 1954, however, the University drifted. The mere existence of changing economic times did not produce new institutional goals. It remained difficult to "think big" after living through twenty years of despair. The Alumni Association, revitalized under the leadership of J. Lloyd Stone, adapted more quickly to the post-World War II era than did the University administration. The association's seven major goals, which included a state medical center, a new gymnasium, a student union, better alumni records, a stronger *Alumni Review,* increased contributions, and a new University alumni development fund, spoke to the future rather than the past. Yet in the twilight of the West presidency, the University waned.

New leadership did not come until July 1954, when Dr. George W. Starcher assumed the presidency of the University of North Dakota. With more than twenty years experience as a professor and administrator at Ohio University, Starcher brought to the state a deep understanding "of what a university is and ought to be." Youthful at 48, the new president possessed an abundance of energy, idealism, and leadership. He accomplished much of his leadership through a real concern for the needs of individual students and a toleration of the varied, sometimes competing, viewpoints of faculty.

His new institutional goals were first published in a 1955 University statement called "To Grow Toward Greatness." Funded by the Campbell Foundation, the brochure emphasized Starcher's ideas for a greater University and challenged members of the University alumni family to "think big." It promoted stewardship and stated that "the sum of man's highest obligations to his fellow man could be expressed in the one word: education. For in knowledge lies the surest hopes of man's achieving his highest purposes."

The brochure featured four major goals: cultural and intellectual stimulation, research, general needs, and physical plant. The latter, "Monuments to Ideals," seemed the most unrealistic for North Dakota. Starcher proposed four buildings to function as living symbols of a greater university. These included an auditorium, a fine arts center, a library, and a chapel. The pamphlet also made a strong pitch for a new library by stating that the existing one "is already overcrowded and becoming inadequate. The truth is—the University of North Dakota has an inadequate library." A good library was essential to Starcher's conception of a greater university because "the soul of a university is its library, and a university is often measured by its library facilites."

The new president first met Kathrine Macdonald Tiffany in the fall of 1954, at a Chicago gathering of UND alumni held in an upstairs dining room of the Carson, Pirie & Scott department store across the street from the Palmer House. In a well-prepared address (a Starcher trademark), the president outlined the needs of the University. He talked specifically about the lack of adequate facilities, notably the need for a new library. His formal presentation, fresh ideas, and priorities for a new library particularly impressed Mrs. Tiffany, class of 1902, who regularly attended the meetings of the Chicago group from her home in Wheaton, Illinois.

Kathrine Macdonald Tiffany was anything but retired at the age of 76 years. Although she had outlived two husbands and devoted almost a half-century to education, she confided to a member of the Macdonald family at this time that "I have never been so busy in my life," and added, "Of course many of the things I am doing are comparatively new to me." Continued activities included church activities and editing work for a Chicago publishing house. But a heightened interest in her alma mater and a closer relationship with Chester Fritz, her only next of kin, would occupy a great deal of her time over the next twenty-four years until her death in 1978.

Mrs. Tiffany introduced herself to the new president at the conclusion of his presentation. She also requested time to talk with him personally before he left Chicago. When Starcher suggested a meeting in his hotel room at the Palmer House, she suggested they meet on the mezzanine. There they talked for more than two hours. She put what must have sounded like an endless series of questions to Starcher, taking copious notes all the while. Their first meeting resulted in several significant developments. They agreed to keep in touch and to reduce formalities by simply referring to each other thereafter as "KBT" and "GWS." They agreed completely on the need for a new library. They shared other ideas about how to build a greater University, which later both always referred to as "peaks of excellence." They established a mutual respect for each other, although Mrs. Tiffany strongly disliked Starcher's cigars, which she called "those little brown cylinders." They talked about Fritz and his life. Finally, Mrs. Tiffany subsequently mailed her nephew a 26-page, single-spaced report on the Chicago meeting.

Thus began the second and most important stage of the relationship

To Give With a Warm Hand

between Chester Fritz and the University of North Dakota. The time frame paralleled the Starcher years at the University, 1954 to 1971. It produced four peaks of excellence—including undergraduate and graduate scholarships, a library, an auditorium, and distinguished university professorships. The relationship was built around the mutual respect of three people: Kathrine Tiffany, George Starcher and Chester Fritz. They established a basic pattern whereby proposals for a greater University were submitted by Tiffany and Starcher and counter-proposals were made by Fritz. In the final analysis, the idealism of a college president and the dreams of a loyal alumna became a reality through the generosity of one former student.

In 1956, Fritz established a scholarship fund at the University intended to "help worthy students in my home state." From an irrevocable trust fund of $100,000 held in perpetuity by the Guaranty Trust Company of New York, the University was authorized to award six scholarships annually—five undergraduate stipends of $800 each, provided one of them be assigned specifically to a graduate of Lidgerwood High School, and one graduate stipend of $1,000. All were renewable.

Fritz inserted additional conditions or criteria to be used in the selection process in his letter of notification. Among qualities he specified should be sought in scholarship recipients were initiative and resourcefulness; promise of distinguished work and citizenship; potential for leadership; and indications of peer group acceptance. "It is my wish and hope that these scholarships should be not only a reward for past achievements," Fritz observed, "but a recognition of future promises."

It is not difficult to understand Fritz's motivation in providing the scholarship trust. Fritz himself knew only too well the lack of scholarships available to college students of his era and the tremendous personal sacrifices required of him to obtain a college education. His act corresponded to his own experience and represented his personal impetus. His sole concession to others was to make the scholarships initially available in 1957 rather than after his death. Good health, increased wealth, and the needs of the University helped to bring about the change.

The latter reason, the needs of the University, was scarcely an idle concern in the post-World War II decade. Both the Alumni Association and President Starcher called pointed attention to it. Starcher in particular recalled his own administrative experience at Ohio University, where there were "almost no student scholarships." Upon his arrival at UND in 1954, he found the situation barely different; he could identify only three full student scholarships.

The only significant disagreement in negotiations for the donation centered on the amount of the scholarships. Fritz wanted his scholarships to be "the best"—i.e., the largest at the University. Therefore, he proposed a larger stipend for fewer students. President Starcher, on the other hand, wanted to make the stripend less and thus be able to award more scholarships annually. They compromised on a total of six per year.

Mrs. Tiffany strongly supported her nephew's choice of scholarships. She wrote to J. Lloyd Stone in 1956:

> In fact, I am triply delighted—delighted that he had earned that much to give, delighted that he chooses to spend it for scholarships, and delighted that he gave it to UND, the university of his native state, instead of to those large, impersonal foundations.

The University awarded the first Chester Fritz scholarships in 1957. Since then more than $100,000 in scholarship aid has been distributed among eighty individuals. Too, the scholarships remain among the largest of the more than 600 privately funded financial aids presently awarded by the University. Finally, a recent analytical article dealing with former Fritz scholars confirms that the donor's hope of "a recognition of future promise" bore fruit.

The majority of recipients pursued graduate degrees and are today making substantial contributions to society. Peter Fritzell, class of 1962, now an associate professor of English at Lawrence University, said the Fritz scholarship and his UND student experience "made all the difference in my own career." Dr. James Brousseau, class of 1966, a physician specializing in internal medicine in Grand Forks, observed that he planned to attend college in another state until he received the Chester Fritz scholarship. Dr. Thomas Owen, class of 1963, professor and chairman of UND's department of chemical engineering, agreed that the mere availability of these scholarships made UND "much more attractive" an institution.

Others voice comparable sentiments. Bruce Rova, class of 1970, a lieutenant commander in the U.S. Navy, wrote that his receiving the scholarship "allowed me the opportunity to participate in campus activities...a practical background I might not otherwise have obtained because of financial pressures." Leah Manning Stetzner, class of 1970, a corporate lawyer with Burlington Northern Inc., stated that the "broad liberal education I received at UND—history, philosophy, language—has given me a distinct advantage, even in the apparently unrelated world of business." Indeed, Stetzner considers herself "especially privileged to have had this education knowing that the financial assistance, academic opportunities and experience I enjoyed are not available to everyone."

During the Starcher years, the Fritz scholars were quite visible. Both Dr. and Mrs. Starcher and Mrs. Tiffany recognized the recipients as special students and treated them with respect. These students met together on regular occasions, particularly in the Oriental Room of the Chester Fritz Library. They were encouraged to write the donor personally. Mrs. Tiffany took a direct interest in their careers and stressed Christian and American values with some of them. She viewed them in a distinguished light, expecting them also to function as leaders; she indicated to them a high sense of responsibility. Phyllis Lanes Johnson, class of 1971, a research chemist with the U.S. Department of Agriculture at the Human Nutrition Laboratory in Grand Forks, acknowledged that, "The personal interest of Mrs. Tiffany, Mr. Fritz's aunt, was also encouraging. Here was someone outside my family and my professors who had a genuine interest in my progress in school."

In December 1957, Fritz also proposed the establishment of a Chester Fritz Scholarship Fund at the University of Washington, in the amount of $25,000, the annual interest upon which was to be "divided equally into three renewable scholarships for students" there. The proposal further specified, "Only students having a record of superior scholarship, integrity of character, and showing promise of leadership" would be eligible, with preference given to University of Washington students demonstrating financial need, "seriousness of purpose, and a superior record in college work" through their first two quarters.

Fritz made other observations about the University of Washington and its scholarship program:

> I was amazed at the number of business and industrial scholarships....There was such an array that I had the impression that the university is now more like a technological school than a university. It would seem to me that the urgent need is...for scholarships in the humanities, political science, history, philosophy, literature, languages, etc....

If it is true that America's future destiny is being shaped largely in today's classrooms, then our universities should not become mere technological schools. The field of the humanities, wherein the materials are ideas and thought processes, produces as many great leaders for a country as does the study of chemistry or physics. Many of our great leaders in government have come up through the fields of the humanities and law. If the university is to become great, or near great, it would seem to me that the graduate school should be strengthened in all its main phases. However, it is not for me to tell the university what should be done.

Three years of negotiations preceded the commitment to fund the Chester Fritz Library at UND. At first, Mrs. Tiffany's long report on the Starcher presentation at the Chicago alumni meeting produced no reply. A seed, however, was planted. As Mrs. Tiffany confessed, she liked "to dream dreams for the University—and who knows, sometime one or two of them might come true."

Fritz thought seriously about the library during 1955-1956. In 1956 he ventured a proposal: "My idea was that I would give $500,000 and then someone else would match it and give $500,000." He swore both Starcher and his aunt to secrecy, threatening to withdraw the offer at any indication of publicity.

Although welcome, the proposal nonetheless caused the young Starcher administration considerable concern. At the time, the University found it difficult to raise less than $100,000 to complete the swimming pool in the Fieldhouse. To raise another half-million dollars seemed utterly hopeless. Dr. Starcher recalled that he "simply could not find the funds to match it. It was impossible."

The library became a reality mainly through the persistence of Mrs. Tiffany, the honesty of President Starcher, and the loyalty of Fritz himself. After listening carefully to the problem, and examining closely his personal finances, Fritz agreed to increase the donation: "Well, there didn't seem to be anyone around. I wasn't as affluent then as I am now, but I finally got up to a million!" In doubling the amount, however, Fritz insisted the money be applied only to the building itself. The University agreed.

With negotiations completed with Fritz, Starcher turned toward the campus. He contemplated two very enjoyable problems: with whom should he first share the good news? When should it be announced?

To Give With a Warm Hand

After much thought, Starcher decided to share the momentous news not with his fellow administrators, the alumni office, or even the faculty. He divulged it instead to the students—in particular, to the "Iron Mask," a secret, self-appointed, male-only society that had existed at the University since the 1920s. Informed of the society's existence and loyalty by President John West upon his retirement, President Starcher claimed himself as the sole administrator "who knew who they were." He told the Iron Mask of Chester Fritz and his generous gift of the library at a private gathering in the president's home that lasted well into early morning. Starcher swore the group to secrecy, to which it responded with enthusiasm and excitement. The evening remained among Starcher's most satisfying occasions during his tenure.

Publicly, the announcement of Fritz's gift came on February 15, 1958—the diamond jubilee of the University's founding. The banner headline in the *Grand Forks Herald* the next day proclaimed "U GETS MILLION FOR LIBRARY." (Below, the paper leavened the news with a story headed "Tioga Coldest in Nation with -32 Reading.") President Starcher, in making the announcement, termed the gift "one of the greatest things that has happened to the University." Journalists corroborated this statement, acclaiming it as "the largest private contribution ever made to an institution of higher education in North Dakota." George E. Sokolsky, a nationally syndicated newspaper columnist and a personal friend of Fritz's, featured the story in this manner:

> I once asked Chester Fritz what he would do with his money. He told me he would leave it all to his native state....In many ways, the Horatio Alger story never dies. Chester Fritz, the boy, could not imagine one million dollars, Chester Fritz, the man, gives such a sum to a university at which he studied for only two years. Here is a success story that is worthy of note in these days when young men seek a security guaranteed by law....
>
> Self-effacing, shy, in many ways, lonely, Chester Fritz, like the Chinese among whom he lived so long, has built himself a memorial while he still lives.

Planning for the new library kept President Starcher and Mrs. Tiffany very busy over the next two and one-half years. Both possessed a patience with detail, and nothing seemed more important than designing a truly outstanding building. Mrs. Tiffany believed that a library facility was the most important building on any campus and referred to such centers as a "liberal arts university in itself." Together, the two insisted on 12 major features for the library at UND:

1. That the building be located inside the heels of the campus' horseshoe drive, preferably at the northeast corner.
2. That the building be somewhat cubical in shape.
3. That the architecture harmonize with that of other nearby buildings.
4. That the height be at least equal to that of other academic structures on the campus.
5. That the building appear stately and possess dignity within budgetary limits.
6. That the design accommodate the installation of a console of chimes or bells.
7. That the whole of Fritz's $1 million gift be applied to the building, with equipment and books to be separately provided for.
8. That the name Chester Fritz be carved in stone and mounted above the main entrance.
9. That the building design conform closely to functional and efficient standards.
10. That the building contain, in main selected places, such simple elegance as permitted by the budget.
11. That it contain a North Dakota Room.
12. That it contain an Oriental Room.

In late December 1959, Mrs. Tiffany confided to the architect, Myron Denbrook, "Now I can report to Chester on the completed plans for that building with a clear conscience." Three months later she indicated to Denbrook that Fritz "was delighted with what he had thus far seen." Mrs. Tiffany paid particular attention to the details and attributes of the North Dakota and Oriental Rooms. President Starcher, on the other hand, stressed the importance of the tower and the University Avenue entrance. Mrs. Tiffany objected to the north-side entrance, for practical reasons: "I think too much of the snow and ice in winter will linger there," but eventually conceded that "many people have doubtless made a unanimous decision for having the main entrance on the north." Lack of funds prevented the installation of chimes or bells in the tower.

Chester Fritz returned to the United States for the dedication of the library. He came alone. His wife Vera, who remained staunchly opposed to the gift, stayed in Switzerland. Fritz flew directly to Chicago from London, where a joyful aunt greeted him at the airport. Together they drove to her Wheaton residence and telephoned President Starcher. Apprehensive about the dedication, Starcher relaxed upon hearing Mrs. Tiffany exclaim, "The young man is here!" His other anxieties also eased after listening attentively to Fritz's speech over the phone. Starcher took particular pleasure in the passage in which Fritz stated his desire to make his donations "with a warm hand."

The final leg of the return to "home pastures" proved inauspicious and somewhat incongruous for a philanthropist traveling to dedicate "his" million-dollar library. Near St. Cloud, Minnesota, in the dark before dawn, lost and almost out of gas, Fritz and his aunt searched nervously for an open service station. Finding none and unsure of their direction, Fritz halted an approaching motorist who instructed him to "go over there where you can see the light and you can wake up a man and get some gasoline."

At various towns between Sauk Centre, Minnesota, and Fargo, North Dakota, Fritz tried unsuccessfully to reach his half-sister Mrs. May Jensen. Frustrated by the continued busy signal on her farm party line, the two attempted to drive directly to the Jensen home near Chaffee, North Dakota, about 20 miles west of Fargo. They never made it. A mile away, their car sunk deeply into Red River Valley gumbo on a newly graded country road, saturated from a heavy rain. Fritz, undaunted, started walking to the nearest farmhouse and on the way also gave his loafers to the soil of the Red River Valley. North Dakota's native son was home!

The incident did not end there. The first farmer Fritz encountered refused to help, declaring, "I wouldn't dare go in there and try to pull you out." A second farmer with a Caterpillar tractor agreed and, after some time, finally succeeded in pulling Mrs. Tiffany's car back to the main highway. Fritz happily paid the farmer for his help and later sent an additional amount through Keith Jensen, his half-sister's husband. At this point, the farmer inquired about the visitor's identity. "Was this the visitor who gave North Dakota a library?" When Mr. Jensen nodded yes, the farmer exclaimed, "Damn it, I could have done it for nothing!"

Excited and behind schedule, the pair turned back toward Fargo and headed north to Grand Forks. Fate forced another detour, however, to Buxton, Fritz's birthplace. While there, he and his aunt chanced to meet state Senator Oscar Sorlie and his wife, both old family friends. The

Sorlies invited them to their home where, according to Fritz, the senator "washed my shoes" and Mrs. Sorlie prepared "some wonderful ham."

Arriving in Grand Forks in late afternoon, Fritz and his aunt drove directly to the University campus. He wanted to view the library privately and in solitude before its formal dedication. He liked the building. He recalled feeling a deep sense of satisfaction, followed by an intense pride; "Oh, I was very proud." There, quite coincidentally, he met President Starcher for the first time, as he, too, was enjoying the tranquillity of a late autumn afternoon while making one last inspection of this "Monument to Ideals" before the public dedication. A passing photographer captured their unexpected meeting with the donor's left hand symbolically raised as if pointing to the inscription—"Chester Fritz Library"—above the three doors at the main entrance.

The Starchers played host to a private dinner the evening prior to the dedication. Invited guests included the guest of honor, Chester Fritz, Mrs. Tiffany, Mr. and Mrs. Fred Orth, and Mr. and Mrs. Harold Shaft. Orth was president of the First National Bank, a member of the State Board of Higher Education, and an able spokesman for the University during the Starcher years. Shaft, a UND alumnus, was a brilliant and successful attorney who provided free legal counsel to the University for more than twenty years. Orth and Shaft were both close to the president and had been financially and professionally involved in the Fritz donation.

Dr. Starcher recalled in considerable detail his memories of the occasion. He characterized Fritz as a "simple and plain man" with an "air of distinction." Although Fritz was "an excellent conversationalist" and "very pleasant and polite," Starcher detected "a certain reserve" about him. Also, when conversation drifted toward business and international affairs, Fritz "stiffened" and "handled each question with deftness." As for the relationship between Fritz and his aunt, the younger nephew assumed the leading role; "she deferred to him in every way." But this contrasted markedly with the nature of their correspondence, wherein Mrs. Tiffany became the dominant figure. According to Starcher, Fritz depended on his aunt for "all of those little things."

Fritz holds fond memories of the evening. The Starchers made him feel entirely at home. He liked Fred Orth. He was proud when his aunt offered grace before dinner. Yet the importance of Thursday's convivial dinner remained secondary to Friday's dedication. Tomorrow would be, as Fritz so aptly described it, "My finest hour!"

The dedication of the Chester Fritz Library on October 13, 1961, marked a significant event in the 78th year of the University of North Dakota and a memorable day in the 69th year of the donor's life. Speaking to a mixed audience of dignitaries, alumni, supporters, and friends at the University, as well as a grateful president and an exuberant aunt, Fritz talked briefly, yet emotionally, about his act. The library represented "a partial payment of the benefits" he had received at the University many years earlier. It was given with the public understanding that it "should not reduce legislative appropriations for other buildings" and that the University should always keep it "well-stocked with material needed for scholarly work in every department." He viewed the library as "a working center for ideas, not a place where immature boys and girls play at studying." The most important part of the speech, a profoundly personal message, came at the midpoint of Fritz's brief remarks:

> In the autumn days of life, one becomes reflective and even pauses to take inventory, to see what, if anything, he has done to make this a better world. Most of us have started our careers on foundations built by others; and it gives one considerable satisfaction to know that he has helped build foundations from which others may climb higher, have a fuller life—perhaps even "the abundant life." And in doing this, I have preferred to give my donations while I am still living; it means more to me to give "with a *warm* hand."

According to Starcher, Fritz was surprised and overwhelmed by the extravagance of the festivities and the size of the audience. He expected neither. Both upon being introduced and during his speech, Fritz showed signs of heartfelt emotion. His voice broke and tears came in his eyes. Starcher vividly recalled a particular empathy between speaker and audience, which culminated in a deafening crescendo of applause and a standing ovation.

Fritz agreed with President Starcher's recollections. He admitted that he "got a bit emotional because here was this big applause and I had never faced an audience like this before." He also admitted to being startled by the 19 by 20 foot North Dakota mural in the library's main reading room, painted in oil by Robert A. Nelson of the University's art department. "I looked at the skeletons of the wild buffaloes, who are such a stately looking animal, and I thought to myself—am I still here?" Fritz sighed in relief at the conclusion of his short speech. "I cannot tell you how my spirits rose as the speech was over. I thought I had taken a big jump."

Eager to put the dedication behind him and return to his normal life in Switzerland, Fritz and Mrs. Tiffany departed the next morning for Chicago. He requested a private walk through the library just before leaving. As he sauntered from floor to floor, he expressed the hope that intellectually the new facility would be put to serious uses and improve the quality of education. President Starcher assured Fritz that the substantial donation that the building represented would be an example for other alumni to emulate.

A blizzard of personal letters and thank-you notes overwhelmed Fritz through the end of the year. Promoted by President Starcher and abetted by Mrs. Tiffany's many thoughtful and pointed suggestions, politicians, business leaders, alumni, faculty, and students joined the list of well-wishers and appreciative beneficiaries. The correspondence seemed endless at times, yet Fritz personally replied to each one. Mrs. Tiffany eventually placed the entire series in special albums and deposited them in the Chester Fritz Library. Ironically, an official thank-you from the state of North Dakota had to be returned for want of sufficient postage. An amused Fritz quipped that "North Dakotans seem to think that the postage they pay goes all around the world but it doesn't."

Less than a year after the dedication of the library, Mrs. Tiffany wrote her nephew about her hope for another building on campus, predicting, "It would not be a total surprise to me to read of another stately building with this inscription: Chester Fritz Auditorium."

On May 28, 1965, in a letter to President Starcher, Fritz offered $1 million toward the "construction of a distinctive auditorium" on the UND campus. An auditorium symbolized the heart of the University to Fritz, and he noted in the letter that "There is no building in which large numbers of students, faculty, and staff can listen appreciatively to the great dramas, oratorios, operas, musical concerts, artist recitals, or to lectures by outstanding contemporary thinkers."

This second contribution of $1 million, coming only seven years after the first, surprised Starcher, not the least because he personally knew that Fritz "had overspent for the library." It did not, however, surprise Mrs. Tiffany. She documented as early as 1958 the origin of the idea in response to an inquiry from J. Lloyd Stone:

> That would be almost as difficult to answer as to tell from whence comes the wind. But perhaps it was a combination of these: that Wheaton College has for some time been planning a million-dollar new auditorium for its centennial

XI

Man Man Hang

The life of Chester Fritz after 1950 is remarkable both because of his longevity and his personal growth. Even as he approached his 90th birthday, Fritz remained in good health, keenly aware of world events, and in control of his personal and financial affairs. Physically and mentally, Fritz never retired, as his deportment, humor, and the crispness of his varied correspondence plainly reveals. Business associates and friends who have known him best in late years all characterized him as a gallant, generous person who personified a wise senior statesman—a man of considerable conversational charm, long-term financial experience, and penetrating cultural sagacity.

Fritz himself did not regard his life after 1950 as having been nearly as significant as his career in China. He acknowledged, however, that segments of the past thirty years are not only historically important but also sufficiently interesting for inclusion in this book. Accordingly, he talked freely of his search for a new home and lifestyle after 1950, his second marriage in 1954, and his fascinating success as a private investor.

Ever Westward to the Far East: THE STORY OF CHESTER FRITZ

Further, he explained his long residence in Switzerland, the sale of his chalet there in 1977, his current domicile in Monte Carlo, his precious metals investments of 1977, his latest philanthropies, and the process of aging.

Conversely, Fritz was little inclined to discuss details of his will or to assign a dollar value to his personal fortune. These subjects, as well as aspects of the recent past, might be best filed under one of Fritz's most frequently employed Cantonese aphorisms: "Man Man Hang," which translates literally as "walk slowly" or "take care."

Fritz knew a restive life between 1951 and 1958. He found it difficult to find a permanent home and an acceptable lifestyle to replace his life in China. Initially he selected New York as a home and purchased a 15th-floor apartment in the Hampshire House overlooking Central Park. The location was convenient to his financial interests, while the park offered a taste of Thoreau amidst an ocean of skyscrapers and a shore of asphalt. Even so, something was lacking. He was not satisfied with life in New York or with the United States as a permanent home. Geographically, he preferred mountains; his philosophical preference was for a culture with a positive attitude toward older people. In China society honored age, while in America society worshiped youth.

Fritz traveled widely during 1952-1953. He first visited England, where he arrived in time for the coronation of Queen Elizabeth II, whose procession he viewed from Sir Victor Sassoon's flat at the Ritz Hotel. Next, he tried island-hopping through the warm Caribbean Sea with a close Chinese friend, Flora Sun. Fritz admitted he considered marrying her, but in the end doubted that it would have worked. Finally, in 1953, he moved to Rome with plans to retire. Again, he shortly changed his mind: "It didn't work out that way. There is always tomorrow."

Fritz then packed his bags for an extended sojourn to the Belgian Congo (now Zaire) "to see the country." He never left. He met the lady who was to become his second wife.

Vera Kachalina was born within walking distance of St. Basil's Cathedral in Moscow on July 11, 1906. She was the daughter of a well-to-do Russian couple who owned a dacha, a country place outside the city, where the family typically spent the summer season. Her father was a large landowner and a member of the Russian stock exchange. Her mother was known as an elegant lady and a great skater. Vera can still recall her excitement at the first snowfall and its reward of a ride in a sleigh with troika hitch. According to Fritz, the peculiarity of this form of

Oil portrait of Chester Fritz by Boris Chaliapin, unveiled in August 1974.

locomotion is that "The center horse trots while the two horses on either side gallop along with the trotter."

Life changed tragically for the Kachalina family with the advent of the Russian Revolution in 1917. Vera's parents refused to leave Moscow and eventually were killed during the revolutionary violence. Reportedly, Vera's mother adamantly insisted, "I was born here and I am going to die here!" The upheaval ended Vera's four years of training at the famous Bolshoi Dancing School and cast her into the realm of the rootless. She left Russia in 1922 on the Trans-Siberian railway for Harbin, Manchuria, where a large Russian emigre community had gathered during the hostilities. Relatives there kindly took her in.

In Harbin, Vera met and married Alexander Baylin, a Russian whose parents owned and operated a large flour mill in Siberia. The young couple subsequently moved to Peking where they lived for the next 22 years. Baylin was engaged in the export trade. Vera was a popular and attractive young lady, much in demand at social functions. The couple had one daughter, Monique. After World War II, the Baylins separated and eventually divorced.

Thus, although Fritz and the Baylins lived many years in China, they never met there. According to Fritz,

> I never met Vera in China but we were introduced to each other in Rome in 1953. She had then left China with her daughter, whom she was putting through college. I was introduced to her by a mutual friend—Mr. Luciano Riggio, who, incidentally, was a very good polo player.
>
> Vera and I were married at the Fraumunster, the historic cathedral of Zurich, Switzerland. We celebrated our silver wedding anniversary on March 25, 1979 as this is the date of my birthday. We were actually married on 21 March 1954.

After their marriage, the Fritzes made Rome their home for the next four years. They enjoyed the historic attractions of the city and its varied hues and moods. Rome seemed, Fritz said, like "a great museum...life was so fascinating there at first."

> We had a penthouse atop a large apartment building, the view from which was superb. A big, wide terrace went around two sides of the apartment building and we could look down the Tiber River and see St. Peter's in the distance. In the summertime we could dine on the wide terrace.

Yet, Italy could also be tiresome. By 1957, Fritz concluded that while it was "a wonderful country to visit, I didn't want to live there any longer." The dearth of dependable servants particularly irritated the Fritzes and contributed to their decision to depart Rome.

> Italian servants are peculiar people. If there was a soccer match between Naples and Rome or Rome and some other big city—your servants were just gone! And every Saturday the washing machine broke down and it was always 1,000 lire to get it fixed. That was part of the weekly program!

In 1958, having sold most of their furnishings except for their Chinese pieces and mementos, the Fritzes moved to Switzerland. There is "nothing more peaceful for the nerves, soul, and body" than Switzerland, Fritz declared. They lived in several locations briefly but gradually came to prefer Gstaad, a small, exclusive community high in the Bernese Oberland. In 1959, having decided upon permanent residence in the country, the Fritzes built an imposing chalet of their own design in Gstaad, which they named Chalet Vera. Vera conceived the interior plan and living arrangements which, when completed, were widely acclaimed.

Financially, the years following 1950 were far more profitable for Fritz than those preceding. Except for his South American holdings, half of which belonged to Culbertson, Fritz operated as a private investor and speculator. He combined years of experience in foreign exchange transactions, precious metals trading, and stock and security markets with impressive discipline and nerve. He applied one paramount principle to his every venture: "In China if you didn't haggle and bargain for the item under consideration you didn't survive. That experience has influenced my life and it has helped me in many circumstances, although perhaps sometimes I overdo it."

Fritz's daily regimen consists of reading the Wall Street Journal and the latest editions of the seven financial advisory services to which he subscribes. His investment philosophy is deceptively simple but demonstrably sound:

> The ideal market to be in is one in which the fundamentals of supply and demand are recognized and operate. But when you have hysterical and psychological factors like someone trying to corner the market, then you are on unsound footing.
>
> When I am satisfied with the market I generally operate on the basis when the cannons are roaring you buy and when

the violins are playing you sell. A good stock market investment is a question of obtaining good information and acting upon it. You have to get all the facts before you get carried away on psychological factors.

Fritz quadrupled the $1.8 million he had banked in China within the four years 1951-1955. He invested 15 percent in precious metals as a precaution against inflation. He claims to have done "very well in IBM." And he confided that once he even invested in bonds.

Mr. Tsuchiya, manager of the Mitsui Bank in Shanghai before the war, suggested the investment. "If I had any American dollars," Tsuchiya advised Fritz, "I would buy old-issue Japanese government bonds." Previously (and presently), Fritz paid little attention to bonds "because they pay a low rate of interest and the potential profit or capital gain is small," but Tsuchiya's "advice was enough for me."

These Japanese government bonds were issued long before the war and would be soon discussed in the then-current peace negotiations conducted by John Foster Dulles, the American secretary of state. Mr. Dulles was inclined, I felt, to give very generous terms to the Japanese, who at that time were anxious to show the world what a good credit risk they were and would make a very profitable settlement of the outstanding U.S. dollar bonds which had been originally in the U.S. I felt that inasmuch as there was a limited amount of these bonds still standing with the American public, it would not cost the Japanese very much to redeem and pay the accrued interest covering a period of ten years.

These Japanese bonds were quoted on the New York Stock Exchange in the low forties (par value of $100). They were retired at par and they also paid ten years of accrued interest. I made a lot of money on these bonds!

In addition to buying a generous stock of bonds for myself, I also bought bonds for Mr. Tsuchiya and I opened an account with our office in Montevideo under a nom de plume for him. When these bonds were re-sold, I sent the profit to Mr. Li Ming who was a good friend of Tsuchiya's. This money was then sent on to Tsuchiya's son who was at Harvard University, as the father was having a difficult time obtaining U.S. dollars to finance his son's education.

In the 1950s Fritz also stoutly rejected professional counsel to place his assets in a living trust. Replying to one such recommendation, he wrote:

> I am not convinced that it is wise to liquidate now sufficient securities and place the proceeds in a trust providing for a portfolio. As I look back twenty-five years and observe the price movements in bonds and stocks, I am very happy with my results as compared to bonds. With the consistent depreciation in the purchasing power of the dollar I am uninterested in bonds and prefer long-term growth stocks.
>
> It occurs to me that if I have the ability to suggest and the knowledge required for intelligent suggestions, then why would I need a Trust Fund Management? I have been in the security business for many years and I believe the results as measured by my estate would not indicate that I need at this late date management of my affairs.
>
> I am concerned in reducing my estate and distributing my income and capital now as I choose and not as the people in Washington or elsewhere may decide. Furthermore, I wish to take advantage of these tax deductions and thereby lessen the burden of the full impact of my donations.

Within a decade it became dramatically apparent that Fritz's personal management of his own portfolio had proven much the wiser course. In 1964, after notifying Marshall, Granger and Company in New York of his intention to donate a second $1 million toward the construction of the auditorium at the University of North Dakota, the firm sent Fritz a report of his financial worth in a rather unusual letter:

> After starting each day reading the world's news, which primarily consists of stories of disaster, selfishness and impending doom, it is indeed refreshing to have one of our days begin, as it did yesterday, with your letter of February 4th. Your generosity to and consideration for mankind sets an example which makes this a better world in which to live. We would have fewer problems if more men would follow your lead.
>
> You particularly must be gratified that this new pledge will have been made possible through improved stock market conditions. Our files contain several inches of correspondence about the last gift which revolves around the horrible fate awaiting a donor who fails to protect (in trust) the capital

required to complete a gift. You seem to be in the enviable position of having eaten your cake (tax savings) and having it too (a new gift as well as the old).

Again we wish to thank you for brightening our lives. It would be gratifying if more of our tax problems revolved around such generosity.

As the years passed, speculation circulated in Fritz's home state, especially at the University of North Dakota, as to "the other reasons" why Fritz insisted on living in Switzerland. A favorite theme dealt with the avoidance of paying income taxes. One professor suggested to his students that Fritz "snuck into the United States" for the library dedication in 1961. Another told a class that Fritz had obtained "a special legal dispensation" from the government to attend the dedication.

Although Fritz consistently sought to maximize his tax benefits and allowances, primarily with a view to helping others, he vehemently denied maintaining European residence for the purpose of avoiding American taxes.

I pay American taxes just as if I lived in America. The United States is the only country in the world, with the possible exception of the Philippines, which requires their citizens to pay taxes on all sources of income regardless of where they live. So I pay full American taxes and I also pay taxes in the country in which I live.

The sale of Chalet Vera in 1977 must rank as one of the most lucrative business transactions that Fritz arranged in his later years. The long, drawn-out negotiations occupied a considerable amount of his time during the latter half of 1976 and the first half of 1977. Several potential buyers tested Fritz's business skills and patience. In the final analysis, however, experience, discipline, and a habit of haggling paid tremendous dividends. The purchase price of 4.5 million Swiss francs, ($2.7 million) without furnishings, was the highest price ever paid for a chalet in Switzerland according to Fritz.

Many factors contributed to the decision to sell the chalet. At 85, Fritz observed that the winters in Bernese Oberland were "too rugged for us." The Fritzes owned two other properties in Monte Carlo and Lausanne and already were spending considerable time at them. Fritz said, "I sold the chalet because I was keeping three homes and I was tired of maintaining them. I spent my time writing checks, whereas I wanted to hear the birds sing and to smell the flowers along the way." A second major factor was the real estate market. Although Vera desired the chalet should not be sold, Fritz disagreed. The cannons were roaring. "This is it! We are getting out!" The final factor came as a result of good estate re-evaluation. As Fritz explained, "If I leave the chalet and I die and it goes to my estate, they're going to take 24 percent of the chalet." The high inheritance tax to be paid to the Canton Berne was simply unacceptable to Fritz. Once Fritz had digested these considerations, he made a firm decision to sell at an acceptable price, in cash, with no delays.

The circular for the sale of Chalet Vera was impressive:

> Deluxe chalet, first time on the market, with commanding position, altitude 1150 m, facing south with unobstructed view on all four sides. Designed and constructed by V. Somazzi, Berne, one of the leading architects in Switzerland.
>
> Residence with 12 rooms, 5 bathrooms. First class building materials, with copper drains. Central heating and hot water system Hoval-oil burner.

Advertisement of the chalet, situated on 5,270 square meters of land and bounded by a tall pine hedge caught the Gstaad community by surprise. The news spread quickly to potential buyers who fit the social profile of the area.

Constructed on three floors, the chalet included a garden floor with two guest rooms and a servants' wing with three bedrooms and a separate entrance. The first floor contained a spacious living room and a beautiful dining room, both paneled in solid walnut walls and ceilings, with large windows. The first floor also featured an Italian marble fireplace, a library in solid oak and a large solarium terrace open on one side with Japanese-style sliding doors onto a balcony which ran the full length of the chalet, a fully equipped electric kitchen, and a separate servants' dining room. The second floor, reached by a circular carpeted stairway, had a large hallway and two master bedrooms with pine paneling opening onto a large balcony. Each bedroom had a mirrored tile dressing room and Italian ceramic mosaic bathroom from floor to ceiling. The chalet also had a spacious attic and a large two-car garage. It was, as Fritz so aptly described it, "a chalet of quality."

The selling price of the chalet was negotiable. Fritz as an experienced trader knew, however, that once established, the seller could never go up in price—only down. As a ruse Fritz initially stated 8 million Swiss francs would be an acceptable price for his chalet, but it was not a serious asking price. The price established came to be 5 million Swiss francs. The terms, as Fritz privately explained to his friends in the community, were that "The first man who puts the money on the table gets the chalet."

Chester Fritz through his legal representatives received several inquiries regarding Chalet Vera. The potential buyers represented a microcosm of the elite international business community. All were successful entrepreneurs, and each would be a worthy adversary in negotiating the sale.

Mr. Leifheit, a German industrialist, emerged as the first serious bidder. He recently had sold his factories to ITT and was in search of a permanent retirement home. By phone, Leifheit offered Fritz the asking price for the chalet. Fritz accepted immediately but because a property sale in Switzerland is not legal unless in writing, he instructed his lawyer to prepare the necessary papers. In the meantime, Mrs. Lefiheit told her husband that the chalet was "too big," and since they already owned four other homes she was not interested. As Fritz interpreted, "She changed her mind. This is a privilege of ladies."

Adnan Kashoggi, a flamboyant entrepreneur-merchant from Saudi Arabia, became the second potential buyer. While Kashoggi was flying around the world in his private Boeing 727, aptly named "The Flying Palace," he sent his half-brother to Fritz with instructions to make a firm offer at the list price provided the seller would agree to a six-month rental. When Fritz inquired about the size of the Kashoggi family, the half-brother responded, "two wives, three concubines and four sons (ages 4-14)." Fritz said, "No deal, Chalet Vera is a home and not a hotel."

Two other parties expressed tentative interest but soon dropped out. The finance minister of Iran sent his personal secretary to make an offer. The secretary told Fritz's representative that "The chalet is 80 percent sold," but no further negotiations took place. A Belgian banker, one Mr. Lambert of Brussels, also expressed interest but nothing transpired.

Basil Peter Goulandris became the eventual buyer of Chalet Vera. A Greek by birth, Goulandris owned worldwide shipping interests, had considerable capital, and possessed a Permit C which qualified him as a Swiss citizen except that he could not vote. Goulandris, known to associates and competitors as the "Golden Greek," was an astute businessman. The negotiations took nearly four months and, according to Fritz, followed "many strange turns."

Goulandris initially offered 4.5 million Swiss francs. Fritz accepted his oral offer but before the papers could be prepared Goulandris withdrew

Ever Westward to the Far East: THE STORY OF CHESTER FRITZ

his offer in favor of a second bid of 4 million Swiss francs. Fritz responded—"not acceptable." After some delay, Goulandris raised his offer to 4.1 million Swiss francs. Again, "not acceptable." Goulandris countered with additional bids of 4.2 million and 4.25 million, but Fritz held fast.

Goulandris played his trump card. Mr. Von Grunigan, one of the pillars of the Gstaad community, approached Fritz: "Chester, you are asking too much for your chalet." Fritz replied, "Fred, you have seen it. It is a chalet of quality. Most chalets have plaster walls. Here the walls are of wood—walls and ceilings!"

The haggling and delays excited Fritz. He confided to his lawyer: "This is a jousting tournament. I want a showdown. I want a decision." Fritz played his trump card. He sent word to a Mrs. Bill, a daily, who worked in various private homes in Gstaad: "We would be honored if you would be with us this summer as we are planning to come back to Gstaad." Goulandris got the message.

The showdown was at hand. "The meeting was very cold on a very cold day," Fritz recalled. Sitting alone in his Monte Carlo study, the call came from Berne: "Goulandris says he will pay 4.5 million. What do you want to do?" Fritz vividly recalled the moment:

> There it is right out! An old investment proverb flashed through my mind: A bull can make money. A bear can make money. But a hog cannot make any money. I accept the offer under the following conditions: 500,000 down and 4 million within 14 days.

The lawyer called back. Goulandris wanted to spread his payments over three years. "Not acceptable. I may not be here then." Another call—Goulandris said, "I'm not going to argue anymore. Tell him, I accept it on his terms!" Fritz had won:

> It was a great relief for me to know that this transaction was now completed in Swiss francs. The money after four months' negotiation was finally paid into my bank account on my birthday. This should not be viewed as a mere coincidence. Every night I read the Bible. I felt confident that He would guide me and complete the transaction. And so I have deep gratitude for the manner in which the transaction was consummated. I am convinced that prayer was a very important help in these transactions.

The news of the sale swept through the streets of Gstaad, and many residents refused to believe the amount. Some said, "Chester Fritz never got 4.5 million. He got less than 4 million." According to Fritz, there is an old Arab proverb: "Don't believe what you hear, only what you see." Louis Franck, a close personal friend, remarked that during the entire negotiations, Goulandris never saw Fritz. At that point, Fritz interrupted, "I never saw him either." The match was over.

Fritz paid 800,000 Swiss francs to the Canton of Berne as a capital gains tax for the sale of his chalet. The Fritzes had enjoyed eighteen happy years in Switzerland, and Fritz said in paying the tax, "I am not going to squawk." Fritz also applied the Swiss tax against his U.S. federal income tax. After paying the tax, Fritz confided to Harold Hochschild, "I now feel that I am a real benefactor to Canton Berne in that we have provided a substantial payment to them, as by coming to Gstaad we did not build a Swiss cow barn but an outstanding chalet." Hochschild agreed and suggested the Swiss people should "build a monument to you." Fritz responded, "I hope they don't. If they do they will send me the bill!"

The figure of 4.5 million Swiss francs or the U.S. dollar equivalent in 1977 of $2.7 million represented a huge profit for Fritz. When asked how much it cost to build the chalet, Fritz responded, "That is not a fair question! When I built it, I did not build it to speculate. I built it for a home. It cost about 1 million Swiss francs to build plus the cost of the land. So I had a big profit."

Invariably the question of what happened next seemed appropriate.

Two gifts emerged directly as a result of the sale. The first, a $50,000 donation to the Adirondack Museum in upstate New York in honor of Harold Hochschild; the second, a diamond for Vera, a flawless 11-carat stone costing $346,000. The remainder was invested in South African gold mine shares.

> I immediately bought American dollars which I placed on loan in a big bank in Amsterdam and with the Socite General. And simultaneously, I bought Swiss francs six months forward and every six months I rolled it over. So I am on and continue to be on a Swiss franc basis. The American dollar has fallen from its high estate. Today the Swiss franc is around 61 cents, even a little higher, wherein it was maintained around 23 cents until the American dollar weakened.

Fritz notified the administrator of his estate, the First National Bank in

Grand Forks, of the transactions, stating, "The sale of this property for cash at this time will simplify the probating of my estate and thus avoid long delays and possible legal complications."

Gold and silver have proven outstanding investments for Fritz since 1977. With his long experience in precious metals, he occupied a singular position from which to survey the rapidly changing environment of metals markets and to capitalize on it. After careful analysis of inflationary trends, rising oil prices, and international tensions, Fritz took large positions in silver and gold futures, doubling his stake twice between 1979 and 1980.

And, even more shrewdly, he claimed his profits in silver before prices peaked at about $48 an ounce. When Fritz "heard that the Hunt brothers were operating" in the silver markets, "I said, 'This is where I get off'...because the market could no longer be judged on fundamentals and it was now a psychological market." Later, he stopped buying gold directly, but not without taking handsome profits.

Fritz had this to say of his attitude toward gold and the policy of the American government in the 1970s:

> I have always bought gold to 15 percent of the value of my assets as a kind of insurance policy against inflation. Gold has risen in price from July 1933 from $35 an ounce to a high of $850 an ounce.
>
> America was anti-gold. We don't want the price of gold to go up. Washington is still anti-gold. But look at it! Every time they sell gold the price goes up. Gold is defeating Washington. The United States is the only government which has been selling gold. We are selling our most liquid asset. We are selling the family jewels!
>
> As long as you have deficits you will have inflation. As long as you have inflation people will continue to buy gold as a store of value to protect themselves against increasing growing inflation.

But his proudest investment since 1977 has been in South Africa. "I took a very bullish view of South African gold mining shares which, in my opinion, were very depressed in price." Against strong advice from brokers who urged him not to buy, Fritz acquired 200,000 shares over a period of two years with the proceeds from the chalet sale. "I felt otherwise on the subject," because he believed the brokers' minds had been too much influenced "by the civil war going on in Rhodesia where the rebel organization was well organized." In Fritz's estimate, however, South Africa was hardly "another Rhodesia and I saw major differences between the two countries and decided to invest heavily" in South African mining.

So, at age 85, Fritz had picked another fabulous combination. Most of the South African stocks quadrupled in price, with the highest-quality stocks paying attractive dividends of 20 percent. For example, Fritz bought 10,000 shares of Blyvoorruitzicht at $3 to $4 per share. By 1980 the stock had attained a value of $30. He purchased 4,000 shares of Vaal Reefs at an average price of $20 per share, which sold for $80 three years later. In addition, Vaal Reefs and West Drienfontein paid annual dividends of 20 percent.

In 1979, Fritz extended his "warm hand" to the University of Washington. On April 14, President John Hogness announced a gift of $1 million to the School of International Studies from Chester Fritz, class of 1914. Fritz explained in his letter both the motive and purpose of his gift:

> I make this donation in appreciation of the hospitality and benefits I received in Seattle and from the University of Washington. It is my wish that most of this donation, but not necessarily all, should go to help develop the China program.
> I would prefer to emphasize benefits in the way of undergraduate and graduate scholarships and visiting lectureships.

The public announcement followed brief but deliberate negotiations between the donor and Dr. George Beckmann, provost of the university, who first learned of Fritz's intentions in January. Fritz indicated that he was considering a donation of $1 million in stocks to be divided in two lots for tax reasons. The first lot would be forthcoming "in the near future" and the balance early in 1980. He also made clear his desire to activate the donation as soon as possible, while "I am still around."

The University of Washington responded within eleven days. Provost Beckmann applauded the "timeliness and wisdom of the gift," in particular, because of the recent establishment of diplomatic relations between the United States and the People's Republic of China. He noted that current events made it clear "that this country is on the verge of an immense new interest in China" and that the Fritz contribution "will not be lost on the entire community." Beckmann seized the occasion to propose the creation of a "Chester Fritz Endowment for Chinese Studies" at the university for five principal purposes:

1. Distribution of 50 percent of the fund for graduate and

undergraduate tuition scholarships and fellowships for faculty research in Chinese Studies.
2. Appointment of a visiting faculty in furtherance of Chinese Studies.
3. Establishment of a Chester Fritz Publications Fund to support books and other works relating to the Chinese Studies program.
4. Acquisition of special collections for the China library.
5. Distribution of 5 percent for administrative expenses connected to the maintenance and expansion of Chinese studies.

In agreeing to the endowment proposal, Fritz concurred in a pattern adopted twenty-five years earlier at the University of North Dakota with the Chester Fritz scholarships. In that donation, too, Fritz insisted that the endowment operate only from the interest earned on the sale of stocks, not from the principal, which was to be held in perpetuity.

Fritz agreed to the University of Washington's proposal in February and approved the subsequent public announcement of the gift. In March, Beckmann urged the donor to present himself personally for a special day to be observed in his honor. At 87, Fritz declined because of "my advanced age," but added, "I shall be with you in spirit."

Ensuing events prevented a smooth transition. Fritz became justifiably irritated by the delay in the transfer of his stocks from the First National Bank in Grand Forks to the University of Washington. In April he wrote, "It is not my purpose to seek out the person responsible for this strange journey that the shares have been forced to undergo." Beckmann apologized, conceding that the transfer had indeed "taken longer than we had anticipated," and acknowledged that the university's policy was "too restrictive in cases such as this involving large amounts of securities registered on national stock exchanges."

Nevertheless, Fritz added a codicil to his will in 1979 declaring that 50 percent of his residual estate be awarded to the University of Washington. In a gesture of its gratitude, the university in June 1981 published a leather-bound edition of Fritz's 1917 diary of his tour through western China.

Several considerations prompted Fritz's generosity to the University of Washington, not the least of which was his desire "to help our relations with China because that was where I had filled my rice bowl." The university, for its part, fostered his goodwill in the late 1970s, encouraging Fritz's benevolent mood. He admitted that "They showed a lot of interest in my diary," and "I learned there was a long list of readers and they planned to publish it. This gave me deep satisfaction." Conversely, Fritz had been "a little bit disappointed" that no one at the University of North Dakota seemed "interested in it and I hadn't heard of anybody reading it."

Actually, relations between Fritz and the University of North Dakota had eroded noticeably after 1971. They continued at a low ebb for most of the decade and centered increasingly upon the past rather than the future. Understandably, the triangular relationship of Fritz-Kathrine Tiffany-George Starcher, which stood at the heart of Fritz's earlier stewardship, eroded, especially after Tiffany and Starcher retired. For his part, Fritz concluded that he had contributed quite adequately to the institution. And even had the University been aware of Fritz's continued financial good fortune, it behaved in a complacent and satisfied manner, and doubted that any more proposals would have been well received.

All this is suggested in the episode of the Fritz portrait. In the early 1970s, the University decided upon a further gesture of gratitude, and in the spring of 1974 publicly announced that an oil portrait of the benefactor would be unveiled during the first intermission of the world premiere of an opera based on Ole Rölvaag's novel of the prairie frontier, "Giants in the Earth." The unveiling would take place, naturally, in the Chester Fritz Auditorium, the second and newest building bearing Fritz's name at the campus, so-named at former President Starcher's stout insistence. Taken together, the operatic premiere and the portrait unveiling provided a grand finale to the administration and leadership of George Starcher.

Starcher, who conceived the idea of a formal life portrait, won Tiffany's endorsement. Boris Chaliapin, an artist of wide reputation, best known for the 400 covers he did for *Time* magazine, agreed to the work for a fee of $4,000. Tiffany wrote her nephew that only a nominal commitment of time would be necessary and that he would scarcely notice the interruption in his routine at Gstaad. It turned out otherwise.

Chaliapin arrived at Chalet Vera on September 3, 1973, and stayed for two weeks. Soon the subject grew impatient with his guest and the time consumed in sittings. Fritz complained to his aunt that Chaliapin

> arranged for sittings in the forenoon and afternoon. This went on for some days, but I became so exhausted that I felt compelled to ask him to cancel the forenoon sessions. Sitting inactive for some hours made my eyes extremely tired....

For the first few days, when I was having morning and afternoon sittings, we asked him to have lunch with us, as he mentioned that he would like to have a snack instead of going down to the village at lunch time. His daily activity here at the Chalet altered our routine and made Vera very disturbed because other duties became more complicated.

At one point, Fritz questioned the artist about the project. "Do you mean these other men (Roosevelt, Nixon, etc.) sat for a week at a time like I am?" "Oh, no," replied Chaliapin, "I painted them from photographs."

"You know, this is a request of the University and $4,000 is a bit high for your fee," Fritz countered, applying pressure. Eventually, following some predictable haggling, Chaliapin agreed to drop the price by $500. Fritz's answer, when asked why, went straight to the point: "I paid for it, you know. There was interest money left over from the auditorium balance and the University simply debited the cost of the portrait."

The principals gave the finished product mixed reviews. Vera felt it made her husband appear much "too grim and serious." Fritz, perhaps expecting something more flattering, thought it "made me look old." Neither, however, objected to the pose or colors.

The unveiling took place, as planned, at a gala ceremony in the auditorium on April 4, 1974, to the accompaniment of a specially prepared brochure. Starcher's successor as president of UND, Thomas Clifford, alluded to the text of the brochure in his remarks at the ceremony:

> The shirt worn by Mr. Fritz in the portrait is pink, and it is believed the reason for that choice of color dates back to a horsemanship competition in the Far East in which he participated in his younger years. A pink shirt was the much-coveted award to the winner. Mr. Fritz won the shirt, an achievement which was very pleasing to him, and that accomplishment of the younger Mr. Fritz seems now to be immortalized in the portrait.

The factual inaccuracy of the brochure dumfounded Fritz. He had not been awarded a pink shirt upon his victory in the paper hunt of 1927; he had won a red coat! The University had inadvertently immortalized Fritz "in error." "It was the red coat!" exclaimed Fritz. "The University has immortalized it as the pink shirt!" Fritz demanded an apology, refusing to let the incident rest. More than two years later, in December 1976, he wrote his aunt that "apparently no one wants to admit a gross mistake." He called Starcher about it, who said he "would look into the matter and correct the report, but I never heard from him either or anybody else in this regard." Ultimately, the University did reprint the brochure, having revised it to read the "shirt worn by Fritz is red." Yet, the damage had been done; little could be done to correct the portrait itself, easily the most permanent element in the entire affair.

A second irritation developed on the subject of other alumni donations. Fritz maintained that University officials consistently advised that "his donation" would spark other alumni contributions. "Over the years I heard comments from different people at the University, identifying individual alumni who were going to make large donations." Fritz, after having kept a running score of these expectations, declared it "a great disappointment to see the small amount actually given."

Two claims in particular proved disconcerting. These involved Herbert Treichler, class of 1908 and a leading mining engineer, about whom it was advertised that "he was one of the richest men in the United States and that he was going to give a large donation." Fritz, after a brief pause, remarked, "I think he gave $25,000 in his will."

Fritz reserved his strongest criticism for Thomas Campbell, class of 1903. Nicknamed "Mr. Wheat," Campbell reputedly held title to being the largest wheat farmer in the world during World War I.

> University officials said, "Oh, he is going to give a lot of money!" But it was a washout. He stubbed his toe. But what really annoyed me was reading about the financial support Campbell was receiving from the federal government in farm subsidies—huge amounts! It was taxpayer's money and he gave only a small amount to the University of North Dakota.

Disappointment, to be sure, but not without a sincere understanding of it all. "It is much easier to talk about giving your money away," Fritz observed, smiling broadly, "than actually doing it. It doesn't hurt so much!"

Relations between Fritz and the University have improved since 1979. The North Dakota Legislature's appropriation of $4.5 million for an addition to the Chester Fritz Library impressed him. President Clifford, in his remarks at the groundbreaking on September 3, 1980, reiterated Fritz's wish of nineteen years earlier that the library represent "a long reach into the future" and asserted that the addition, subscribed by the people of the state, fulfilled Fritz's dream of a "library of distinction."

Ever Westward to the Far East: THE STORY OF CHESTER FRITZ

No less significant is Clifford's willing authorization to provide for the publication of this book. The original proposal stemmed from an article by Dan Rylance, University archivist, entitled "Chester Fritz Maintains His Roots" in the April 1979 issue of the UND *Alumni Review,* subsequently reprinted in *North Dakota Horizons* magazine for Winter 1980 as "Chester Fritz: North Dakota's Great Friend." Fritz welcomed both versions warmly. In July 1979 Clifford endorsed the projected biography as part of the University's centennial observance and activities, and as a genuine "thank you" to its subject. Fritz, in turn, responded to the proposal in a letter to Rylance on August 2 of that year:

> I was impressed with your proposed approach and your carefully laid plans of an outline for a proposed book. This is indeed an ambitious effort, or, as the British would say, "a stout effort"....
>
> I agree that an oral history interview would be most practical. As I review the past there come crowding into my mind pleasant memories of other days and of other places....
>
> Now that you have the green light from my side I look forward to hearing further from you in this regard.

In addition, the University pleasantly surprised Fritz on the occasion of his 89th birthday on March 25, 1981. President Clifford mailed him a published edition of his 1917 "Journal to West China." Rylance and James F. Vivian of the University's history department prepared and edited the diary for publication in two formats: a regular issue of the *North Dakota Quarterly* for Spring 1981, under the title "The Journal of Chester Fritz: Travels through Western China in 1917," and as a book, *The Journal of Chester Fritz* (University of North Dakota Press, 1981). Fritz responded to the unexpected event with characteristic warmth and pride.

For a man born to nothing, self-sufficient since age 12, who accumulated a large fortune over a long, varied life, the ultimate disposition of his assets is very important. Estate planning and will revision have held perennially high priority on the Fritz financial agenda since 1951. For this and other reasons, Fritz knew well that "most people do not investigate these matters until it is too late."

Toward the end of the decade Fritz concluded that his home state of North Dakota afforded the safest, simplest environment for probating his will. "I wanted my will to be probated in North Dakota" because under the state's statutes, he insisted, "I could give as I wish, to the beneficiaries I selected, and without the burden of these extra taxes." To this end, he appointed the First National Bank in Grand Forks to act as his executor and trustee, with Harold Shaft, a local attorney, as his legal advisor.

Fritz moved quickly and thoroughly to preclude any possibility of his will falling under the jurisdiction of New York law. "I was determined to avoid the probate courts of New York," he explained. "I avoided, as I would the plague, those probate judges. I instructed my advisors to remove my name from all financial houses in New York." With the passing of years, Fritz also changed his residence from Italy to Switzerland to Monte Carlo, in large part because of tax and succession laws and the amendments sometimes attached to them.

His aunt, Kathrine Tiffany, likewise took an interest in the subject on his behalf, offering information and encouragement to her nephew in order to protect his estate for more "worthy purposes." She read Swiss law with a sharp eye and surprised both American and Swiss lawyers with her keen understanding of treaty relationships between the two governments. Less helpfully, she conjured other plans that Fritz simply could not accept, like retiring to North Dakota and making it his permanent and final domicile. She urged him in a 1959 letter to consider the relative "peace of mind" he would find in his home state, where he could personally witness the University "grow in greatness."

Kindly, but firmly, Fritz rejected these suggestions as wholly unrealistic, reminding her that although "I have never voted in the United States, I am still entitled to have my will probated" there. He did purchase, however, a small tract of land in Cass County.

> I bought land in Cass County and built a home which I gave free of use to Mr. and Mrs. Keith Jensen. Mrs. Jensen is my half-sister, who took care of my father during his later years. I had thought at one time of establishing my domicile in North Dakota, [in] Cass County, and this offered certain benefits in the way of laws of succession and inheritance taxes, but this was not a success. I continued to let them use the house and the land and that will be bequeathed to them in my will.

While living in Switzerland in 1969, Fritz wrote Shaft of the consequences for his estate should he die there:

> As you know, Switzerland is not a republic but a confederation of cantons where the laws, and especially tax laws, vary widely. As Swiss law would apply to succession, it would

have an important effect as regards compulsory legal portions of various classes of heirs. If the heirs concerned do not receive these minimum proportions under my will, they could be set aside by a Swiss court as far as necessary to meet their claims, a minimum total of 7/16 of the estate (surviving spouse 1/4, half brothers and sisters together 3/16).

Plainly put, he simply could not afford to die in Switzerland. The fact that nearly 50 percent of his estate should fall by law to his relatives, no matter how distant or removed, Fritz considered unacceptable. "To meet these problems," he told Shaft, "I am considering the advisability of changing my domicile to another country."

Monte Carlo, Monaco, became his new home in 1972 after much research and consultation with trusted counselors. He purchased the fifth floor of a new condominium, "Le Sardanapale," on Avenue Princesse Grace overlooking the Mediterranean Sea. Comprehensive interior remodeling followed, as did the purchase of another floor for servants' quarters. Today Vera's bedroom looks out upon the blue seafront, while her husband's scans the rich greenery and flowerbeds to the side of the famous Monte Carlo casino. From here Fritz can observe the long faces of some departing patrons; "I gamble, too, but not at those odds." For the past several years the Fritzes have enjoyed the winter season in Monte Carlo (November 15-May 15) and then journey to Lausanne for the summer, where they own an apartment on Lake Geneva.

Real estate prices in Monte Carlo have soared since 1972. The Monaco principality is now as popular as a year-round attraction and winter resort as it used to be as a famous and exclusive summer sunning beach. The condominium itself has been dwarfed by the new Loews and Mirabeau hotels to either side. Fritz has not appraised his property recently, but concedes knowingly that it is a "very valuable piece of real estate."

Fritz mirrored a sense of satisfied relief in having completed his careful search for the most advantageous probate conditions under a minimum of foreign interference and legal complications.

> Here I am subject to only the assets I have in Monte Carlo....Here is what I am driving at—I want my will to be probated in North Dakota. There I can give as I wish and not be burdened with heavy taxes to the beneficiaries I have

selected. So that is the way I have lined it up, after a lot of worry and traveling around trying to get adjusted.

Fritz remained a stern taskmaster to those entrusted with effecting the provisions of his will. He periodically requests and receives actual practice runs of its administration. He grades the participants accordingly and sometimes demonstrates irritation with unprofessional performance. He commented occasionally that, of course, he can never know definitely how well they will perform after he is gone, but persists in demanding practice and near-perfection in the meantime.

Fritz is convinced that the inevitability of death involves unique responsibilities for a person of wealth. His beneficiaries likely will never fully comprehend how unusually devoted he is to their interests. He has worked hard and long to ensure that his demise will not cheat those who will be the final recipients of his good works.

Although averse to divulging details of his will, he admitted that Vera, his wife, and the two universities he attended will be the principal recipients. As for the two institutions, he said, "My residuary estate shall be divided equally between the University of North Dakota and the University of Washington. The amount concerned might eventually be a large sum depending upon the wheel of fortune and the value of shares in the United States, Canada, and South Africa."

Nor would Fritz estimate the size of his fortune. When asked, he invariably replied, "That is not a fair question." Even so, he summarized the total of his gifts in the context of a general statement about his financial well-being:

> Since my departure from China I have made substantial donations, in excess of $4 million. The earnings I have made after I left China are far in excess of my earnings up to the time of my departure. My accumulation of wealth was made in the New York stock market but primarily in the gold and silver markets.

God endowed Fritz with a sound, healthy body; its occupant has safeguarded the gift throughout his life. Depending on age and circumstances, Fritz always adhered to some form of physical exercise. Ten-minute sessions of sit-ups started his every morning for nearly 80 years. In his prime in China between the wars, he was an accomplished horseman, riding one or another of his polo ponies during the early dawn. After the war, again in China, he swam "every day all the year round" in the waters of Repulse Bay, Hong Kong. And he claimed that

Ever Westward to the Far East: THE STORY OF CHESTER FRITZ

even in the winter, "The water was not as cold as the air." In recent years vigorous ninety-minute walks just before lunch have been the rule.

In 1972 Fritz talked frankly to his aunt (then 92 herself) of his experience with aging, when he was undergoing a recurring bout of vertigo. "Old age can be a real ordeal, and one must accept it," he said.

> Time and erosion are taking their toll. During the past few months my general health has deteriorated. The length of my daily walks has shortened and I feel weaker. I eat one meal per day, a midday lunch with meat, only grilled, at that time. I eat mostly Italian pasta dishes, viz., rice, spaghetti, noodles, necci romana, grilled chicken, etc.

Fritz believes that for him each added day is made easier by the presence of God and the following prayer:

> Look Back...And Praise Him.
> Look Up...And Trust Him.
> Look Around...And Serve Him.
> Look Onward...And Expect Him.

Two contemporary associates of Fritz since 1951 provided keen insights into his character and personality. Dr. D. J. Morris of Berne, Fritz's legal representative since 1965, offered this perceptive view of his client:

> I judge him to be a very shrewd businessman and a tough negotiator, but a man of complete integrity in his business dealings. Among his personal qualities I particularly admire and appreciate his zest for life, his sense of humour and his intellectual curiosity. He is also a man of great personal charm, whose good nature cannot be disguised by an occasionally gruff exterior!

Mary Economou, senior partner of Business Aides Associates in Monte Carlo, took time for this insightful profile of her present boss:

> I met and started to work for Mr. Fritz in 1977, through the recommendation of his then part-time secretary in Monte Carlo who could not keep up with the amount of work he generated. Her comment was that although a prolific writer and a hard worker, Mr. Fritz was a charming man. This proved to be quite true because in a very short time he became not only a good client but a man everyone in the office admires and loves.
>
> It is also correct that he is a hard worker who can dictate

close to four hours per day at what one can describe as a very "brisk" pace. What is amazing is his memory, which can only be likened to that of the proverbial elephant. He remembers names and addresses of most of his friends and the circumstances leading to his meeting them, and can quote you word for word what he dictated seven years ago, or worse, what you said seven days ago and have already forgotten. He also remembers, with gratitude it must be said, every good turn done him.

Mr. Fritz is an honest, straightforward, and generous man, who is proud of his beginnings in North Dakota, of his schooling there, and of what he has accomplished in his lifetime. He is a source of information in many varied aspects of business, travel, history, and art. Apart from his knowledge of China and the East, a knowledge that is extensive and impressive, he knows and is conversant with most subjects you care to bring up. Yet his lack of affectation and ostentation is one of the many points that endear him to all. He talks and treats all persons in the same easy manner, from titled personalities to street cleaners. Furthermore, his common sense and his sense of humor are so developed that he can laugh at himself and his foibles.

Another point that has never ceased to amaze me is his generosity and civic-mindedness. And I speak of the type of generosity that goes unrecognized and without the fanfare that a million dollar donation to a Univesity may create. I refer to the more modest but very frequent and repetitive gifts given to all sorts of associations and charitable institutions, which go unnoticed and unheralded. He finds it very hard, I found, to refuse to share the results of his good fortune with others less fortunate than himself. Since I have known him, he has never refused any request for a gift to a charitable institution.

Mr. Fritz has a deep belief in his Maker. And I cannot help but believe that his Maker does care and look after him.

One should not, though, get the impression or form a picture of a man "too good to be true." He is real, human, and as such has his little frailties. But the "wholesomeness" of the man and his achievements reduce his failings to insignificance and one retains only admiration, affection and a wish to emulate him. I consider myself fortunate and proud to know him. He is an exceptional man...the likes of whom we shall not see again.

Indeed to all who have known him through his long and distinguished career, Chester Fritz is truly an exceptional man. Fritz, for his part, would generously extend to all who have known him a simple farewell: "Take care" or "walk slowly" or as the Chinese say

MAN MAN HANG

Epilogue

Since 1951 life for Chester Fritz has been enviably independent, exceptionally secure, and proudly rewarding. The eighteen years he spent in Switzerland compared favorably to his dozen best years in Shanghai before World War II, and represented a successful effort to find an equally compatible ambience. His second marriage, to a cosmopolitan and cultured woman, has complemented his career and stabilized his emotions through more than a quarter-century of loyal companionship. His demonstrated ability to augment his worldly riches without the complications of capital partners and conflicting obligations distinguishes his later career. And his willing generosity amounting to more than $4 million, besides attesting to his creed of philanthrophy, has given him honest joy, deserved pride, and sincere satisfaction, even as he lived to witness the results.

The dominant strains of Fritz's personality and career are not difficult to perceive or isolate. There are few complexities in his makeup, only several strong traits. The disappointments and anxieties of his formative years might have scarred a lesser person, but Fritz surmounted them, partly with the guidance of remarkably devoted foster parents, both of whom instilled in him a needed sense of value, purpose, direction, and discipline. If he never completely conquered the shyness born of his youth and consequent penchant for privacy, time and experience revealed an amazing fund of resourcefulness and deep reserve of confidence. Unlike all too many people who gravitate through life either unable or unwilling to rank their goals, Fritz early fixed on a definition of self-interest and clung to it. His career thereafter mirrors his success in adapting circumstances and conditions to his objectives. Fritz freely admits that he is not the master of his own fate; yet he has done better than most.

Lacking family and familiar friends, Fritz necessarily acquired a rare ability to meet, converse with, and obtain the trust of able and knowledgeable people regardless of race, place, and culture. No matter where in the world he traveled, he exhibited a remarkable sense of judgment, humanity, and adaptability. His assertiveness and habit of hard bargaining, which some have found abrasive, have carried him far, and at no cost to his integrity or conscience. Probably this explains why his most trusted friends also generally have been his closest business associates.

Fritz elected to be generous in the best tradition of American philanthropy, an attitude too much taken for granted. He would deny that the fact that he had no children of his own, due partly to circumstance and partly to personal choice, has facilitated the impulse. As with most sincere benefactors, Fritz's sense of civic duty applies more to humanity at large rather than to particular individuals with the exception of such family as he possesses. Wealth may have allowed Fritz a material consumption and enjoyment of which most can only dream, but it has not challenged his belief in individual merit, his unassuming respect of others, and his suspicion of patronizing pretensions.

As Fritz began his 90th year, he remembered well that, "It has been a long journey from Buxton, North Dakota, to Monte Carlo, Monaco." That journey, although accomplished "usually alone in foreign countries and in oriental bazaars where the laws of survival operate and where the going can be rough at times," had nonethless been "always fascinating." Although Fritz acknowledged he was walking his last mile slowly, the journey had not yet ended.

Dan Rylance

Appendix

Chester Fritz's Remarks at Dedication of the Chester Fritz Library,
Delivered at the University of North Dakota, October 13, 1961

President Starcher, Governor Guy, faculty, students, fellow alumni, and other friends of the University:

Your enthusiastic welcome has been heart-warming—in fact, it has been almost overwhelming! It is an interesting experience to come back to the home pasture, and especially after long absences. I have been so busy with my own work elsewhere that this is only my second visit to this University since I left here as a student over fifty years ago; though you may be assured that this University has often been in my thoughts.

In my activities I have not been accustomed to speaking to audiences of this size; so now I am going to turn to what I have written, that I may not be tempted to go beyond my allotted time and that my few remarks may at least have the virtue of brevity.

When I left this campus as a student in June of 1910, little did I dream that I would be returning for an occasion like this. And of course then I could not have any idea of the deep satisfaction that this dedication ceremony is giving me today. It is a peculiar kind of pleasure, the kind of pleasure that comes from knowing that a long-term debt is finally about to be paid off. For the giving of the library building is, to me, a partial repayment to the State of North Dakota for the training I received in its public school system.

I shall not dwell now on the high importance of an adequate library for a university dedicated to quality scholastic standards; that is a theme you have doubtless heard many times.

But now that we have the building, I am trusting that from time to time, alumni and other friends of this University will augment with private funds the regular legislative appropriations to the University for the growth of the library, so that this library will always be kept well-stocked with the type of books, magazines, and other materials needed for scholarly work in every department of the University. For it is my hope that this will become a library of distinction, a library that will be a working center for ideas—not a place where immature boys and girls may play at studying, or where they may idly sit and "observe the passing scene." But I hope it will be a center where purposeful men and women do serious work, in preparing themselves for the larger serious work of the future. The Good Book says we are placed on this planet for "good works." This includes preparation; and the future belongs to those who prepare for it.

In this divided world, it is of the utmost importance that we prepare to meet our national and international responsibilities. By calmly studying present facts, and by evaluating the lessons of the past, we can then meet with greater confidence, more wisdom, and more courage the increasingly intricate problems of the future. The rewards come to those who think clearly, and who act with courage.

In the autumn days of life, one becomes reflective and even pauses to take inventory, to see what, if anything, he has done to make this a better world. Most of us have started our careers on foundations built by others; and it gives one considerable satisfaction to know that he has helped build foundations from which others may climb higher, have a fuller life—perhaps even "the abundant life." And in doing this, I have preferred to give my contributions while I am still living; it means more to me to give "with a *warm* hand."

This library represents a long reach into the future; and it is my fervent hope that it will bring appreciable benefits to many students, and faculty, and other people throughout my native State. And in giving this building, it has been my thought that this gift should not reduce legislative appropriations for other buildings that this growing University needs.

Now, while I still have the floor, I wish to share these additional

Appendix

thoughts with you: I wish to express publicly my sincere thanks and gratitude to the many people who have helped bring this building to its now near-completion. This has been a cooperative undertaking. The gift of money alone did not set this stately building full-grown on the University campus. The following people, and doubtless many more, too, are deserving of your thanks as well as mine. First, there is President George W. Starcher, who has worked foresightedly and understandingly on every phase of the project, from its initial stage up to the present hour; also, the State Board of Higher Education, who graciously accepted the offer and gave assurance of the building's future usefulness to the University; the various newsmen, who sent out the story in such form as to make this building an asset to the entire State; the University Business Manager E. W. Olson, who received and regularly checked out the funds; the architects and the contractors, who worked so diligently and so intelligently to make this a truly functional as well as a beautiful building; the 1961 Legislature, who voted the $200,000 appropriation for the book-stacks, tables, chairs, and other necessary library equipment; Head Librarian Donald J. Pearce, who has done much planning for the everyday flow of library work, and so efficiently organized the tremendous transfer of hundreds of thousands of books and innumerable other library materials to their permanent places in this building—despite the discouraging frustrations from not receiving the new equipment on promised schedules; and there is also Dr. Foster Y. St. Clair, who composed the thought-provoking inscription to be over the entrance to the inner library, *"By the Light of Knowledge, Men Read the Laws of Life";* and Professors Robert A. Nelson and Stanley O. Johnson, who designed and created those appropriate large pieces of art work, both within the building; and also the enthusiastic group of faculty women, headed by Mrs. George W. Starcher, who selected and arranged the Oriental furnishings in the unique and distinctive Oriental Room—a room provided for your occasional pleasure. Again, our thanks to all of you, for your excellent work on this cooperative project.

Finally, the numerous expressions of appreciation that have been coming to me, ever since this building was first announced, have been so deeply gratifying that this afternoon "my cup is full," yes, running over. I thank you.

Bibliographical Essay

The principal source of information for this book was Chester Fritz himself. This included his own historical material housed in the Orin G. Libby Manuscript Collection in the Chester Fritz Library at the University of North Dakota. His memories were also recorded during two sessions in December of 1979 and April of 1981; this interview material was supplemented by fifty cassette tapes of reminiscences Fritz recorded and sent to the library by mail. And finally, his pen generated a series of weekly letters containing additional information, answers to difficult questions, and many corrections.

The second source of information was oral and written interviews with essential people associated with Chester Fritz. Charles Culbertson, Fritz's long-term capital partner, provided an extensive oral interview about Shanghai and China, the history of their firm, polo and paper hunts, and the character and personality of Chester Fritz. Harold Hochschild, Fritz's former employer at the American Metal Company, explained in great detail American investment opportunities in China following World War I, the history of his firm, and its relationship with Chester Fritz. He also discussed the later accomplishments of his friend. Kent Lutey shared by mail his thoughts about social life in Shanghai, the personalities and attributes of Joseph Swan, Charles Culbertson, and Chester Fritz. He also shared by mail his library of books and albums on

Bibliographical Essay

paper hunts and the game of polo. George W. Starcher gave an extensive interview on Kathrine Tiffany and the relationship of the University of North Dakota to Chester Fritz. Ralph Stillman, the guiding genius of the success of Fritz's firm in Latin America, commented significantly on that operation as well as on the Manila branch and on Culbertson and Fritz personally. Heinz Rothschild commented by letter on all aspects of the Latin America operation. Dr. D. J. Morris and Mary Economou wrote highly personal and meaningful expressions of their association with Chester Fritz in his later years.

James Vivian, professor of history at the University of North Dakota, researched relevant federal records in the National Archives, microfilm rolls of the *North China Daily News*, and numerous secondary works.

The majority of photographs were reproduced from a wide assortment of personal albums which are part of the Chester Fritz Manuscript Collection at the University of North Dakota. These excellent photographs were supplemented by others obtained from the University of Washington, the Traill County Museum in Hillsboro, North Dakota, from individuals whose names appear in the book, and from Chester Fritz.

INDEX

Alger, Horatio, 6, 25, 91, 203
Allen, Stanley, 29, 31, 32, 33
American Metal Company, 72, 76, 79-82, 83-85, 93, 95, 96-100, 102, 106, 120, 165, 242
Anderson, Maxwell, 20, 21

Beckmann, George, 225-26
Billings, Montana, 19
Boise, Charles, 196
Boyd, Harry, 27
Brousseau, Dr. James, 200
Buxton, North Dakota, 1, 2, 3, 205, 238

Campbell, Thomas, 229
Carroll, Paul, 36-37
Chaffee, North Dakota, 7, 11, 16, 19, 205
Chaliapin, Boris, 227-28
Chiang Kai-shek, 87, 88, 147, 162, 180
China Inland Missions, 48-49, 57, 58, 62, 66
Clifford, Thomas J., x, 209, 228, 229-30
Covarrubias, Miguel, 142
Culbertson, Charles D., 101, 102, 103, 104-06, 108, 120, 131-32, 134, 136, 144, 147, 148, 154, 159, 160-61, 171, 172, 175, 179-81, 185, 190-91, 242, 243

Denbrook, Myron, 204, 210
Dingle, Edwin J., 43, 44, 48, 52
Douglas, Malcolm, 27-28, 29-30, 32, 37
Dulles, John Foster, 217
Dunbar Flour Company, 78
Dunbar, Lambert, 78

Economou, Mary, 234-36, 243
Essig, Emil, 150, 160

Fargo, North Dakota, 3, 4, 5, 6, 12, 205
Federal Incorporated, USA (Swan, Culbertson and Fritz subsidiary), 168
Fisher Flouring Mills, 29-31, 72, 79
Fisher, O. D., 30-31
Fisher, O. W., 30, 32
Flanner, Janet, 141
Fordney-McCumber Tariff, 73
Franck, Harry, 28-29
Fritz, Anne Belanger (mother), 2, 3, 5, 6-7
Fritz, Bernardine Szold (first wife), 138-45, 147, 148, 155-57
Fritz, Charles F. (father), 1, 3-5, 6, 7, 15, 16-17, 19
Fritz, Charles T. (grandfather), 1-2
Fritz, Chester W.:
 ancestry, childhood, and early life, 1-17

as student at University of North Dakota, 17-22
"Sock and Buskin Club" theater activities, 20-21
leaves North Dakota, 22
moves to Seattle, attends University of Washington, 23-29
early business experiences, 19, 24-25, 26
with Fisher Flouring Mills:
 in Seattle, 29-32
 in Hong Kong, 32-40
tours western China, 40, 41-70
with Dunbar Flour Company, 78
business activities with Swan, Culbertson and Fritz, 101-23
 partnership formed, 98-100
 Fritz joins firm, 106
 role in South American operations, 185, 191-92
recreational and sporting activities of, 124-37
 paper hunt riding, 125-32
 polo competition, 132-36
 travels in Japan, 136-37
marriage to Bernardine Szold (first wife), 138-56
divorce and subsequent relationship, 156-57
travels in Mexico and Central America, 145-46
World War II experiences and internment of, 147-55
 decides in prewar years to remain in China, 121-23, 147
 returns to China following 1940 visit to United States, 147
 Japanese conquest of Shanghai, 147-51
 internment and repatriation, 151-55
 returns to China following end of hostilities, 159-60
leaves China, 181-82
in international metals markets, 40, 71-100, 110-11, 116-21, 158-82, 224-25, 233
personal life and business activities after leaving China, 213-36
marriage to Vera Kachalina Baylin (second wife), 214-16
investment philosophy of, 216-17
character of, 237-38
writings, ix, x, 37-39, 41-42
interviews, x-xii

244

on Chinese society and customs, 92-93, 109, 110
charitable donations, vi
  to University of North Dakota, ix, 193-212, 226, 233, 239-41
    relationship with after 1971, 227-30
    "portrait episode," 227-29
  to University of Washington, 201-02, 225-27, 233
  philosophy of giving, 207, 239-41
Fritz, Vera Kachalina Baylin (second wife), 204-05, 214-16, 220, 228, 232, 233
Fritzell, Peter, 200

Geiger, Louis, 196-97
Goulandris, Basil P., 221-22
Grand Forks, North Dakota, 2, 16, 17, 205, 206
Grand Forks Herald (newspaper), 14, 21, 203
Guaranty Trust Company, 102, 183-84, 199

Hancock, John, 195
Harding, Warren G., 73
Haskell, Margaret, 20
Hochschild, Harold, iii, v-vi, 69, 76, 80-84, 94-95, 96, 97-99, 106, 142, 172, 223, 242
Hogness, John, 225
Holt, Blondie, 18
Hyslop, W. Kenneth, 194

Iron Mask (University of North Dakota student secret society), 203

Jensen, May (half-sister), 205, 231
Johnson, Edo, 211
Johnson, Phyllis Lanes, 201
Johnson, Stanley O., 241
Jones, Bobby, 190

Kane, Thomas, 193
Kashoggi, Adnan, 221
King, Frank, 14
Klotz, Sergius, 145-46
Koch, Frederick, 20

Langer, William, 196
Lidgerwood, North Dakota, 6, 7, 8, 10, 12, 13, 14, 15, 17, 18, 199, 211
Lutey, Kent, 102, 124-25, 133, 134, 152-53, 185, 242
Lynch, Hoyt, 13, 31-32

Macdonald, Alexander, 15, 17
Macdonald, Kathrine B. *See Tiffany, Kathrine Belanger Macdonald*
Macdonald, Neil C. (uncle), 7, 8-9, 10, 11-12, 13, 15, 16, 32-33, 194, 209-10, 211
MacDougal, Bruce, 25-26
Marmor, Milton, 164, 165
McVey, Frank, 20
Mei Ling-soong (Madame Chiang Kai-shek), 87, 180
Merrifield, Webster, 14, 17
Miaotze (tribe), 50-52
Mishler, Robert, 87
Morris, Dr. D. J., 234, 243
Movius, Herbert, 18
Mysberg, Frederick, 161
  arrest and trial of, 169-71

Nelson, Robert A., 207, 241
Nonpartisan League, 9
North Dakota, University of, 9, 10, 13, 14, 15, 16, 243
  during Fritz's years as student, 17-22
  Fritz's contributions to, 193-212, 226, 233
  and Alumni Association, 195, 196, 197, 199
  Fritz's relationship with after 1971, 227-30
  "portrait episode," 227-29

Olson, E. W., 241
Orth, Fred, 206
Owen, Dr. Thomas, 200

Page, Howard, 45
Parizek, William, 15, 18
Pearce, Donald J., 241
Perón, Juan D., 188-190
Pittman Act of 1918, 118
Pittman, Sen. Key, 118-120
Polo, Marco, 41
Premchand, Sir Kikabhai, 174, 178-79
Premchand Roychand & Sons, 172-76, 178

Richardson, Charles E., 29-30, 31, 35, 43, 70, 71, 72, 73, 74, 75, 76, 78-79, 80, 81, 82, 83-84
Robinson, Edward G., 145, 146
Robinson, Elwyn B., 209-10
Rölvaag, Ole, 227
Rothschild, B. Heinz, 185-86, 189-90, 191-92, 243
Rova, Bruce, 201
Rylance, Dan, ix-xii, 230

St. Clair, Dr. Foster Y., 241
Sassoon, Sir Victor, 89-90, 102, 107, 142, 145, 214
Shaft, Harold, 206, 231
Shanghai, 85-93, 148-49, 160
Silver Purchase Act, 119-20
Smith, Bruce, 66
Snow, Edgar, 90
Sokolsky, George E., 203, 212

Index

Sorlie, Oscar, 205-06
Starcher, George W., 197-200, 201, 202-205, 206, 207-09, 210, 212, 227-29, 239, 241, 243
Starcher, Mrs. George W., 241
Stetzner, Leah Manning, 201
Stillman, Ralph, 104, 105, 106, 116, 117, 181, 183-92, 243
Stilwell, Joseph W., 86, 87
Stone, J. Lloyd, 195, 196, 197, 200, 208, 210
Sun, Flora, 214
Sun Yat-sen, 84
Swan, Culbertson and Fritz, 101-23
  partnership formed, 98-100
  branch offices, 116-17
  wartime operations and effects of World War II on, 121-23, 147-55
  South American operations, 104, 183-92
  ceases operations in Asia, 158-59, 179-80
Swan, Joseph E. C., 101-04, 147, 154, 155, 184, 186, 242

Tiffany, Kathrine Belanger Macdonald (aunt), x, 2, 6-8, 9-12, 15, 16, 22, 32-33, 41-42, 76, 139, 143, 147, 156, 159, 194, 198-207, 208-09, 210-11, 227, 231, 234, 243
Timberlake, Rep. Charles B., 73, 75, 76
Traill County (North Dakota) Museum, 243
Treichler, Herbert, 229
Tsuchiya, Mr. (Mitsui Bank manager), 217
Twamley, Edna, 194-95

University of North Dakota. *See North Dakota, University of*

Vancouver, British Columbia, 25
Vivian, James F., 230, 243

Washington, University of, 25, 31, 37, 243
  during Fritz's years as student, 26-28
  Fritz's contributions to, 201-02, 225-27, 233
West, John C., 195, 196, 197, 203
Wolff, Walter, 159-60, 180

Young, Roland, 14

This book, published during the observance of the 100th anniversary of the University of North Dakota, is one of several Centennial activities commemorating the men and women who have made this institution what it is today.